# SOLDIER, SAILOR, BEGGARMAN, THIEF

# Soldier, Sailor, Beggarman, Thief

*Crime and the British Armed Services since 1914*

CLIVE EMSLEY

OXFORD
UNIVERSITY PRESS

# OXFORD

UNIVERSITY PRESS

Great Clarendon Street, Oxford, OX2 6DP,
United Kingdom

Oxford University Press is a department of the University of Oxford.
It furthers the University's objective of excellence in research, scholarship,
and education by publishing worldwide. Oxford is a registered trade mark of
Oxford University Press in the UK and in certain other countries

© Clive Emsley 2013

The moral rights of the author have been asserted

First Edition published in 2013

Impression: 1

British Library Cataloguing in Publication Data

Data available

ISBN 978-0-19-965371-3

Printed in Great Britain by
MPG Books Group, Bodmin and King's Lynn

For Jenny

# Foreword and Acknowledgements

Most of my research during my academic career was focussed on the history of crime and policing. At a succession of conferences and seminars, colleagues working on different periods and in different countries raised the issue of crime in wartime and specifically how it appeared to decline at the outset of a war and increase at the end. We even held occasional meetings that addressed the issue directly, though no serious monograph appeared on the subject, at least with reference to the British experience. The topic therefore seemed like a good one to keep me thinking and researching when I retired. My first acknowledgement therefore must go to the Leverhulme Trust, to which I am immensely grateful for the award of an Emeritus Fellowship that enabled me to do the research for this book.

The Open University's system of producing teaching material through course teams has always expected colleagues to comment, freely and frankly, on each other's work. This might, at times, be painful, but it is also immensely beneficial. Colleagues, now good friends, have continued to do this on other work. I have been lucky in working with a series of young (or at least younger) scholars who share my interests; my thanks to Peter King, Paul Lawrence, Gerry Oram, Chris A. Williams, and John Carter Wood for their suggestions and advice on aspects of this research. Chris and John kindly read much of a manuscript draft and offered invaluable advice and corrections. Any errors that remain are entirely mine. I also want to remember the late David Englander who, metaphorically, introduced me to Isaac Bogarde; as a boy in Brick Lane, David used to persuade 'Darky' to buy him ice-creams. David's ever-cheerful East End attitude urged me to probe deeper into the dodgy-doings of squaddies and others. Neil Kinselley kindly arranged for me to meet and question a group of Redcap veterans like himself. Help and advice has also come my way, most generously, from Piet Chielens, Qunitin Colville, Dominiek Dendooven, Stefan Dickers, Bruce Houlder, Robi O'Cleirigh, Mark Roodhouse, Anat Stern, David Taylor, James Treadwell, Jim Whitfield, Isobel Williams, and Antoon Vrints.

My thanks also to the staffs of various archives that have helped me, notably those at the Imperial War Museum, the Brotherton Library Special Collections, and the Archive of the Royal Military Police. I am grateful also to the copyright holders who have allowed me to quote from various private papers and memoirs. Every effort has been made to trace and to contact copyright holders; in a few cases this was not possible and the author and relevant archives would welcome correspondence in such instances.

Finally, and as ever, my largest debt of gratitude is to my wife and hence the dedication.

# Contents

# List of Figures

# List of Tables

# List of Abbreviations

| | |
|---|---|
| APM | Assistant Provost Marshal |
| ATS | Auxiliary Territorial Service |
| BAOR | British Army of the Rhine |
| CO | Commanding Officer |
| CRMP | Corps of Royal Military Police |
| IWM | Imperial War Museum |
| JAF | Judge Advocate of the Fleet |
| JAG | Judge Advocate General |
| MPHC | Metropolitan Police Historical Collection |
| NAAFI | Navy, Army, and Air Force Institutes |
| NCO | Non-Commissioned Officer |
| RASC | Royal Army Service Corps |
| RSM | Regimental Sergeant Major |
| SIB | Special Investigation Branch (Military Police) |
| STU | Special Training Unit |
| WRAC | Women's Royal Army Corps |
| WRNS | Women's Royal Naval Service |

# Introduction

In 1947 the Home Office published a survey of the Criminal Statistics for England and Wales between 1939 and 1945. On the first page it declared:

> In times of peace when the number of persons serving in the Armed Forces is comparatively small, the number of ordinary crimes, such as thefts, frauds, etc., dealt with by courts martial is also small. During the years covered by this volume, when the number of persons serving with the Forces was very large, the number of offences against the ordinary criminal law dealt with by courts martial, such as thefts and frauds for example, must have been considerable.[1]

The implication of this is that the section of the Home Office responsible for the annual presentation of Judicial Statistics had little or no idea of the number of ordinary criminal offences dealt with by military and naval tribunals during the war. Moreover, it appears that no separate records were kept in the Home Office of the number of service personnel who had committed offences under the ordinary criminal law and who had been tried in civilian courts.

In 1944, three years before this official statement of ignorance about military crime, Laurence Olivier made his film version of Shakespeare's *Henry V*. It was a production strong on patriotism and the heroism of the king and his small army—the 'happy few', the 'band of brothers', simply 'warriors for the working day', fighting heroically as their ancestors had done, 'like so many Alexanders', in the 'vasty fields of France'. The film was partly financed by the government and was intended as a morale booster. It was dedicated to the commandos and parachute troops of the British Army but, even without the dedication, the contemporary echoes were obvious.

Productions of Shakespeare tend to emphasize certain elements of the text. The patriotism and the heroism are present in *Henry V*, but so too are the grim side of war and the grim side of soldiers. Olivier excised some of this from his film, such as the incident when, during the battle of Agincourt, and following an attack on his baggage train, Shakespeare's Henry, like the real king, orders his men to kill their prisoners. But Olivier kept the scene when, as dawn breaks on the day of the battle, Shakespeare gives the stage to three common soldiers, Bates, Court, and Williams, reflecting grimly that 'there are few die well that die in battle'. Visited by the disguised king, they debate the treatment that might be afforded a captured king compared with that afforded a common soldier, and whether death in battle wipes

---

[1] *Criminal Statistics, 1939–1945*, Cmd. 7227, 4.

away sin, especially if the cause is a wrong one. King Henry acknowledges that there will be some criminal offenders among an army and, while he does not mention it, he knew some of these men when, as Prince Hal, he consorted with Sir John Falstaff and his cronies in London's Eastcheap. Bardolph, one of Falstaff's gang, is hanged for robbing a church in *Henry V*. And after Agincourt, another member of the gang, the braggart Pistol, is beaten up by a superior officer, Captain Fluellen. Pistol, having learned also of his wife's death, vows to desert, to return to England and follow a life of crime (*Henry V*, Act V, Scene 1).

> Old I do wax; and from my weary limbs
> Honour is cudgell'd. Well, bawd I'll turn,
> And something lean to cutpurse of quick hand.
> To England will I steal, and there I'll steal;
> And patches will I get unto these cudgell'd scars,
> And swear I got them in the Gallia wars.

It might be difficult to make these unpleasant themes the central focus of a production of *Henry V*; while actors, directors, and literary critics might consider sub-texts and background texts, the play consists only of Shakespeare's words. It is possible, though a largely fruitless exercise, to argue about whether the real Henry was a war criminal for ordering the killing of prisoners. It is possible to speculate about what Pistol did next, but there is no evidence beyond Shakespeare's text. Historians, in contrast, can delve into archives and hope to throw light on the activities before, during, and after wars of men like Bardolph and Pistol. The problem is that, particularly in countries on the winning side in a war, or where the military are held in high regard, focussing on the criminal behaviour of soldiers can be seen as tarnishing the memory and courage of tough, ordinary soldiers like Bates, Court, and Williams. Shakespeare might be said to get away with it since his King Henry's distance from Bardolph and Pistol in the play emphasizes how far he has travelled since his riotous youth. The military historian who touches on criminal behaviour by soldiers at war cannot easily turn his offenders into comic rogues such as Falstaff and his gang, but he often seeks to separate ordinary soldiers from such behaviour and, by implication, to excuse it, in a way that the evidence does not necessarily warrant. Sean Longden looked at the seamy side of behaviour by men of Field Marshal Montgomery's 21st Army Group, which landed on D-Day in June 1944 and fought across north-west Europe until the German surrender was signed on Lüneburg Heath eleven months later. He noted that all kinds of men were involved in illicit activities but, following the statements of military provosts, he was also tempted to emphasize the role of 'criminal elements that had been called up for service'.[2] Longden also stressed the men's needs for survival. The recollections of old soldiers can be the same. Petty theft or looting can thus be excused as 'scrounging' and not theft at all, with a common offender often portrayed as a Jack the Lad looking out for and providing for his mates. Humour also takes away the sting. General Brian Horrocks, one of Montgomery's corps commanders,

---

[2] Longden, *To the Victors the Spoils* (2004), 198–9.

enjoyed telling the story of the highlander who robbed a captured German field cashier on Walcheren Island. The cashier complained bitterly, but insisted that the soldier could be identified as he had signed a receipt. Unfortunately, the grubby piece of paper that the German held as a receipt read simply: 'This bastard had 11,000 guilders. He hasn't got it now.'[3] But in addition to the humour and the justifications, there can also be a mixture of embarrassment and shock in attempts to defend what is often quite indefensible.

During the First World War, Jim 'Yank' Reynolds drove a horse-drawn wagon with a Guards Brigade on the Western Front. He described being

> broken in to the gentle art of scrounging, or winning things. The Frenchies' gardens and poultry runs were my school. I [...] helped in various jobs from getting the vegetables to go with the chickens, to getting the chickens or eggs to go with the veg.

Reynolds went out with another member of his unit who had decided to make a profit by harvesting the gold teeth of dead Germans. But, after seeing his comrade set about a dead German's jaw with an entrenching tool in order to collect a tooth, Reynolds decided that such profiteering was not for him. The extraction of gold teeth for profit appears not to have been something confined to Reynolds's comrade in the Great War.[4]

William Hindle arrived on the Western Front in May 1915; he was one of Kitchener's volunteers and, like his comrades, had been issued with a pamphlet warning against looting and anything that might dishonour the name of the Army. Within a week, however, a member of his unit broke into the cottage occupied by an elderly Frenchman whose son was away at the front. The old man was badly beaten and his home ransacked. Hindle's entire unit was given 'a severe lecture'. The culprit was identified and court-martialled; and in his memoir Hindle expressed sorrow that such a man should ever have belonged to his regiment.[5] Gunner Frank Hollingsworth's battery was also given a severe lecture by its Commanding Officer (CO) after they had looted a village during the withdrawal in the face of the Ludendorff Offensive. Hollingsworth admitted to searching for something that would replace his louse-ridden shirt and underwear; and the whole battery had helped themselves to beer and wine from a local *estaminet*. Captain 'Buster' Brown 'laid down the law that looting must cease, although he qualified his remarks by hinting that he was prepared to turn a blind eye to small items, such as collecting hens' eggs and killing a chicken or two.'[6]

Within a few days of arriving on the Western Front in 1918, Fusilier Albert Bagley was caught up in the same offensive. He found himself moving through a village that had been relatively untouched in the previous four years of fighting, but which was now the centre of a battle. He and his fellow soldiers began breaking into

---

[3] Lindsay, *So Few Got Through* (1946), 179.

[4] IWM (D) 99/13/1, J. H. Reynolds (no folio numbers). Ken Lukowiak described meeting a 'senior soldier' during a lull in the battle for Goose Green during the Falklands War. The older para had two pairs of dental pliers 'to acquire gold'. Lukowiak, *A Soldier's Song* (1999), 39.

[5] IWM (D) 01/36/1, W. V. Hindle (no folio numbers).

[6] IWM (D) 82/21/1, F. Hollingsworth, 16–17.

shops for food and for souvenirs. Bagley and a comrade climbed into a shoe shop through a broken window.

> my pal [ . . . ] started looking about going through various drawers, out of which he pulled a small parcel wrapped in white paper and tied with red string. He brought it to the window to examine the contents, heedlessly standing on a pair of ladies' fine shoes. I expected to see some patent medicine judging by the outward appearance, so you can imagine my surprise when he opened it and it contained three wristlet watches, all very small and of quaint design. On close examination one was gold, one silver and the other nickel plated. He readily gave me the silver one and I merely put it in my tunic pocket and forgot all about it.

Outside the shop other men were exchanging their booty. One soldier who had acquired six safety razor sets exchanged individual sets for a watch, a pocketknife, a leather pocket wallet and a revolver. Bagley went on to offer a justification for this behaviour.

> Of course, you may be disgusted, but let me put this before you [ . . . ]
>
> Regarding the eatables, you must remember that [ . . . ] we had had no food whatever for two days and two nights, and we had been on the move practically all that time on an empty stomach, so perhaps you will agree we were justified in taking the various eatables. Now as to the other articles which we took, it can be said in defence, that, supposing the men had refrained from taking any of these things they would only be destroyed by shellfire, and also they had no real owners, so it could hardly be called 'stealing', and further, if the Germans had got back into the village they wouldn't think twice of taking anything they fancied, which they had already done whilst in possession of the village. So reader, perhaps now, you may look upon our acts as not those of common thieves.
>
> If we had left everything untouched for the reason that it was theft etc. it would have made no difference, as it wasn't as if anyone was the loser of these articles, for during the next day or two the whole place was shelled to atoms by both sides, and was in possession of the Germans more than once.[7]

There were similar recollections from the Second World War. As his tank unit fought its way towards Lisieux in August 1944, Trooper W. Hewison confided to his journal:

> We normal law-biding citizens of the kingdom are as soldiers have always been. When an army sweats blood and guts to win a town [ . . . ] it presumes that that town is their prize—quite forgivable really. And also because the civvies generally have flown, and houses are open and there's no one to stop you—you loot. And as you rifle the house, murmuring 'What a shame!' frequently at the shell-holes in the walls, and the general damage of the place, sympathising with the unfortunate owner, at the same time pocketing his best silver, and a couple of watches maybe. It is a result of the quashing of that small animal instinct in man which promotes him to pillage and destruction— hence when all opposition to these instincts are removed, he has a hey-day. It is very

---

[7] IWM (D) 02/04/1, A. E. Bagley, 8–9.

unfortunate, but there it is. If we, who have lost men and sweated pints [ . . . ] *don't* pick up a thing or two there, the base-wallahs will. A poor excuse I know.[8]

Peter White, who became a successful portrait painter after the Second World War, had a Jack the Lad in his infantry platoon as it fought its way into Germany in 1945. Private Jones, a big man whose favoured weapon was a Bren gun and who carried the ammunition of two men, had been a paratrooper before joining White in the King's Own Scottish Borderers. He continued to wear his paratrooper's smock with the flap that clipped between a man's legs hanging loose like a tail. He also wore a monkey-skin cap, which he had stitched himself, with his camouflage face veil hanging at the back, and this made him look 'like Robinson Crusoe with a Foreign Legion neck flap'. On his feet Jones wore a Belgian miner's clogs, 'part wooden, part leather, topped with anklets made from the felt linings of mortar bomb cases'; these, he insisted, were 'warmer than those provided by his majesty'. Jones, it seems, could be guaranteed to find preserved foodstuffs, pigs to butcher, eggs to fry, poultry to roast, and milk to drink, as well as pillows, straw, and wooden farm doors to roof and cosy slit trenches. But Jones also acquired other things: 'added to his unorthodox apparel, monkey-fur cap and so on, his fingers sparkled with rings and shiny stones, and his windproof paratrooper jacket glittered with gold watch chains ending in bulging pockets.' Jones was killed by shrapnel in the concluding days of the war when White's unit came under heavy shellfire.

> Had he finished the war at this rate of hoarding he would have retired a wealthy man [ . . . ] The loss of Jones, the 'one man army' as he was dubbed, was a very depressing blow on the Platoon, indeed the Company.[9]

At about the same time as Jones's death, at least one other platoon commander was shocked to see men systematically robbing civilians.[10] This was the way that German troops were thought to behave, not British soldiers. Perhaps the men's actions were driven by the righteous fury among many allied soldiers after they had entered, or had heard of comrades entering concentration camps and death camps. Yet even this cannot be used to justify the robbery of civilians, even supposedly enemy civilians. Similarly, legally and morally, it is no defence to argue that because something is lying around and might be destroyed by shellfire, then the taking of it is justifiable. Being hungry might serve as an extenuating circumstance in a court of law when it came to sentencing an offender for the theft of food, but it would not negate the possibility of a criminal charge. From the perspective of the victim of a thieving soldier, theft was still theft and damage was still damage, and the victims, whose voices often go unheard, were not always enemy civilians.[11]

---

[8] IWM (D) 79/32/1, W. Hewison, 22–3.

[9] White, *With the Jocks* (2001), 181, 189–90, 238, 250–1, 298, 301, and 303.

[10] Unfortunately I have been refused permission to quote from this memoir. Personal communication, 12 January 2012.

[11] Tangentially it is important to note that military personnel are not always the perpetrators of looting. See, for example, Gardiner, *The Blitz* (2010), 324–30.

Anne de Vigneral lived with her husband, her two children, and her father in Colombières-sur-Seuilles, a few kilometres inland from Sword Beach where British and Canadian troops came ashore on D-Day. At first she and her neighbours were thrilled: '*C'est INDESCRIPTIBLE, les uns pleurent, les autres rient.*' But within a day or so their enthusiasm for their liberators was diminishing as British and Canadian troops looted and smashed through their property and that of their neighbours. The liberators, she recalled, showed no compunction about rampaging through the bedrooms of her home while she and her family were eating. The soldiers took what they fancied, including Madame de Vigneral's watch and sewing machine, and her father's wedding and signet rings; anything for which they had no use was left strewn across the floor.[12] There are offences that no one can properly defend, even when the perpetrator is the platoon's Jack the Lad. The British Army pursued those who had pillaged Madame de Vigneral's property. A few weeks after the thefts she was entertained to lunch by two British officers and afterwards taken to an office in Bayeux where she was able to identify and recover her property.

Surprisingly, in spite of the growing interest in the history of crime and what seems like a permanent interest in military history, neither historians of crime nor those who have looked at the military, and at the popular areas of the 'new military history' and 'war and society' that emerged shortly before the growth of research in the history of crime, have turned their attention specifically to crime among the armed forces. Much of this is probably the result of the compartmentalization of history. Social historians of crime do not often move in the same academic circles, or attend the same conferences and seminars as military historians. Moreover, there can be hostility to anyone that addresses criminal offences by service personnel, even in a serious academic fashion. In his 'warts and all' social history of British soldiers, Richard Holmes noted 'there are those who prefer their pictures to have blemishes air-brushed.'[13] When a highly regarded American criminologist set out to publish a study of rape committed by American soldiers during the Second World War, he found difficulty in getting a publisher. He was also abused for addressing such a topic. Robert Lilly's *Taken by Force* was first published in 2003 in French and then, in 2004, in Italian, before appearing in its original English-language form in 2007. One of the more venomous critics on the Internet still felt it possible to dismiss the book on the grounds that Lilly was not a bona fide historian but 'a fucking sociologist'.[14] The Australian historian Peter Stanley sought to deflect any such hostility in the introduction to his account of the seamy side of the Australian Imperial Force during the First World War. Recognizing that hundreds of books had been written about the 'good' and that his work addressed things 'that many may wish unsaid', he rightly urged that a perspective on military offending would contribute to understanding 'more about the men [ . . . ] the

---

[12] IWM (D) 78/35/1, A. de Vigneral, ff. 3–4, 8, and 17.
[13] Holmes, *Soldiers* (2011), xxix–xxx; and see note 10 above. Holmes also notes that there are some also who prefer to concentrate on 'an image of unrelieved savagery' or who want to portray the army as a brutalized tool of the ruling class.
[14] Lilly, *Taken by Force* (2007), xxii.

society they came from, and the war that changed or ended the lives of so many.'[15] The justification for what follows in this book is the same. The armed forces of a country reflect the society from which they come, both the good and the bad; failure to admit that there can be criminal offending among members of the armed forces is a failure to appreciate the complex make-up of those forces and the pressures and temptations that face them. As is shown in what follows, it is quite wrong to dismiss criminal offending within the Army, the Navy, or the Air Force simply as the work of 'criminals' who just happened to find their way into, or to be conscripted into the armed forces. Equally, while not every soldier, sailor, or airman who left the Army, Navy, or Air Force was traumatized or corrupted into pursuing violent or criminal behaviour, or to becoming a down-and-out, sleeping rough and begging on return to civvy street, there were one or two that appear to have been seriously affected in this fashion.

There have been studies of wartime crime in Britain, or rather in England and Wales, particularly for the period of the Second World War. These have focussed on the home front, but they have scarcely considered the extent to which war might have affected the broader pattern of crime and, while they have touched on offending by members of the armed forces, this generally has been subsumed within the broader canvas.[16] Historians researching crime before the 19th century have no official statistics from which to start any analysis but they have often noted how, for contemporaries at least, the outbreak of war appeared to herald a decline in the incidence of crime. The implication of this is that naval and military recruitment had removed many young men, always the most crimogenic part of the population, from the country. Research into the less formal criminal justice structure of 18th-century England has also shown that many offenders were taken directly to recruiting officers by their victims or persuaded to enlist by magistrates without either a trial or a conviction. In either case no criminal indictment, and often no formal court record remained for any historian to add to any statistics of crime that he or she might have sought to construct. Moreover, contemporaries noted how the outbreak of a war often coincided with a decline in the number of criminal offenders brought before the courts; such crime rates as have been constructed for Hanoverian England suggest that, in peacetime, indictment rates were more than one third greater than those of wartime.[17] A similar wartime decline in crime was reflected in press reports of the much more bureaucratic criminal justice system of the early 20th century. Two months after the outbreak of war in 1914, for example, in his address to the Grand Jury at Quarter Sessions, the recorder for Portsmouth was reported as commenting that 'the outbreak of war, in Portsmouth as in other places, had seen the inhabitants

---

[15] Stanley, *Bad Characters* (2010), 10.

[16] Smithies, *Crime in Wartime* (1982); Thomas, *An Underworld at War* (2003). The exception to this is Spencer, *Crime and the Services* (1954).

[17] King, *Crime, Justice, and Discretion* (2000), 153–9; King 'War As a Judicial Resource' (2002); Emsley, *Crime and Society . . . 1750–1900* (2010a), 34–5.

generally putting away that which was bad in times of national stress.'[18] At the beginning of 1915, the Grand Jury of Middlesex was told that crime in the county had fallen by 90 per cent; and later in the year the mayor of Berwick was given white gloves for the third time that year, signifying a session without indictable crime.[19] Early in 1916, the semi-official *Justice of the Peace* expressed its belief that the drop in crime was the result of a large number of criminals, 'or the class from which our criminals come', joining the Army. 'This class', it went on, 'often makes excellent soldiers.'[20] Some magistrates urged offenders to enlist in place of punishment or simply to avoid trouble in the future. A young thief in Portsmouth was told that enlistment 'will be a golden chance to live a clean and useful life. Go and play the man and fight for your country; and you will hear no more of this.' Similarly, a dockyard worker fined for assaulting his common-law wife was 'strongly' advised 'to go and fight the Germans.'[21]

But, while the press and others celebrated the apparent fall in crime at the outbreak of war and saw war as a way for offenders to redeem themselves, not everyone shared such opinions. Early in 1915, for example, Dr James Devon, prison commissioner for Scotland, protested to the Annual General Meeting of the Glasgow Discharged Prisoner's Aid Society that the decline in the numbers imprisoned since the beginning of the war was, in reality, the result of new legislation that gave people more time to pay fines. Devon also considered that it was a libel on the Army to say that it was composed

> of men who were in the habit of going to prison. The confirmed criminal was as little use in the Army as out of it, and was a source of possible danger. People who trained for a trade or profession developed certain characteristics accordingly, and the man who had served an apprenticeship to crime developed characteristics making him useless for lawful purposes.[22]

Dr Devon was following early 20th-century assumptions about professional criminals; but he appears also to have been letting his patriotic heart rule what his head must have learned from his role as a prison commissioner. Professional criminals figure prominently in media accounts of crime, but while there are some who seek to gain their livelihood from lawbreaking and who can be violent and dangerous, there are rather more who lurch from one petty offence to another, passing years in prison as one brief sentence follows another. These latter individuals constitute an irritant rather than a serious threat. Equally, the thief and the beggar, the gangster and the down-and-out might once have been good soldiers or sailors.

Unlike many of its predecessors, the Second World War does not seem to have commenced with contemporaries or the press commenting much upon a decline in

---

[18] *Evening News and Southern Daily Mail*, 8 October 1914, 3; for similar comments to the Hampshire Assizes see 5 November, 4; and for a slightly different view expressed to the Hampshire Quarter Sessions see 20 October, 6.

[19] *The Times*, 8 February 1915, 3 and 22 October, 5.

[20] *The Justice of the Peace*, 18 March 1918, 134.

[21] *Evening News and Southern Daily Mail*, 3 September 1914, 3 and 23 September, 3.

[22] *The Scotsman*, 31 March 1915, 12.

crime. One exception was Captain F. J. Peel, the chief constable of Essex, who, in the summer of 1941, pointed to shifts in the pattern of crime within his jurisdiction.

> For the first time in several years the number of offences shows a decrease [ . . . ] in the parts of the county nearest London and is probably due to the fact that a large number of youthful offenders, who previously operated from the East End [ . . . ] are now serving in H.M. Forces. The reduction is to some extent offset by an increase in other districts where a considerable number of houses [ . . . ] have been broken into [ . . . ] by military personnel.[23]

Like Dr Devon, Captain Peel seems to have had his eyes set on professional offenders rather than youths and young men slipping into offending as almost a rite of passage in their lives. At the beginning of the war such young men appeared in courts, where magistrates and judges listened to character evidence and used their discretion to determine their sentence. Their discretion was often similar to that deployed by their predecessors in the courts of Hanoverian Britain. At the Bedfordshire Quarter Sessions in March 1940, for example, a 19-year-old offender expressed his wish to join the Army; both the police and the principal of a local training school for young offenders spoke up for him and stressed that he was an orphan with no one to provide him with the necessary care and attention. The magistrates agreed to put him on probation until he could enlist. Two months later, at the County Assizes, a young soldier who pleaded guilty to breaking and entering asked to be allowed to continue serving with his regiment. The judge bound him over for twelve months, saying that 'the Army was the right place at present for young men of his age.'[24] Two years later a young Scots Guardsman appeared at Marlborough Street Police Court protesting that he had resorted to crime because he wanted to get into a unit that was doing some fighting. He had, he said, spent two years hanging around doing nothing; his officers agreed that he had potential as a soldier. The magistrate remanded him on bail for six months on the grounds that if the young man did not make good, then he would have him back for sentencing. A few weeks later another young man, found guilty at the Buckinghamshire Quarter Sessions of breaking and entering, was said by the police to have registered for military service, but not to have attended a medical examination as he had failed to notify the authorities of a change of address. The chairman of the bench said that they would all prefer to see him in the armed forces rather than prison; the young man was bound over to appear for sentence at the next sessions unless, in the meantime, he began military service.[25] But the discretion of a judge or a magistrate was generally dependent on the circumstances of a case and not every offender got a second chance. In the summer of 1943, for example, the deputy recorder of Salford heard a succession of burglary and housebreaking cases involving an 18-year-old sailor. The sailor, who had deserted at the beginning of the year and who pleaded

---

[23] Quoted in Smithies, *Crime in Wartime* (1982), 47.
[24] *Bedfordshire Times and Standard*, 29 March 1940, 12, and 24 May, 9.
[25] *News of the World*, 15 February 1942, 2 and 5 April, 2.

guilty to three charges of burglary and housebreaking, asked for another twenty-five offences to be taken into account; he also requested that he be given the chance to return to the Navy. The recorder gave him short shrift and sent him to Borstal, adding that the armed forces 'were not a refuge for people who had committed a large number of criminal offences.'[26]

Across many centuries in Britain the ends of wars have brought fears, reflected in the comments of Shakespeare's Pistol quoted above, that returning soldiers, trained to kill, and brutalized by battlefield experiences, would announce their return with a violent crime wave. Such fears have been noted in studies of both violence and the cult of the robber in all forms of English writing since the Middle Ages.[27] They have also been highlighted by historians looking at crime in the 18th century, when years of war were more numerous than years of peace.[28] These concerns about the behaviour of demobilized soldiers were not unique to the British Isles and have been noted by a number of historians ranging over different periods and different geographical regions. In France, the precursor of the *Gendarmerie Nationale*, the *Maréchaussée*—the men of the marshals of France—was created in the early 16th century to protect the king's subjects from the king's soldiers. Banditry and brigandage in Europe were often perceived to be the result of demobilization; they were also blamed on stragglers and deserters. In Napoleonic Europe the ranks of bandits were often filled with men avoiding the conscription introduced during the French Revolution and brought to a new degree of efficiency under Napoleon. Street violence in at least one major American city in the summer of 1865 was put down to men returning brutalized from the Civil War. Twenty years later a senior figure in the Prussian Ministry of the Interior made a statistical study of interpersonal violence in France and Germany and concluded that the increase in such violence might have been, at least in part, the result of the brutalizing impact of the Franco-Prussian War.[29] These fears were apparent again in the aftermath of the First World War. In Germany they appear to have been aggravated by the trauma of defeat and revolution, moreover the concept of the brutalized veteran inured to violence, and fully prepared to use it for his own ends, provided a rational explanation for the growth of the violent politics of the interwar years. After all, on the eve of the First World War, most Europeans considered themselves to be superior to other peoples and believed that their continent was the most civilized. The trauma of the war could thus be used to explain the violence and mass murder experienced by the following generation and which appeared to have halted and even thrown into reverse the advance of Enlightenment progress.[30] This, in turn, points to other important, longer-term issues about violence, masculinity, and the armed services.

---

[26] *Manchester Guardian*, 29 June 1943, 3.

[27] Cockburn, 'Patterns of Violence' (1991), 85–9; Spraggs, *Outlaws and Highwaymen* (2001), 106–7, 113–14, 171, and 193.

[28] King, *Crime, Justice, and Discretion* (2000), 159–61; Beattie, *Crime and the Courts* (1986), 262.

[29] See, inter alia, Emsley, *Gendarmes and the State* (1999), ch. 1; Emsley, *Crime, Police, and Penal Policy* (2007), especially 46–9 and 96–9; Adler, 'The Making of a Moral Panic' (1996); Starke, *Verbrechen und Verbrecher* (1884), 64 and 152.

[30] Emsley, 'A Legacy of Conflict?' (2010b); Elder, *Murder Scenes* (2010), 23–7 and 125.

From at least the 18th century, respectable society in Europe had begun to shift its ideas of masculinity. The behaviour of the ideal man increasingly depended on his probity, respectability, and good works, rather than on his strong arm and his preparedness to resort to violence. Violence began to be perceived as a problem and it was something that, increasingly, the state set out to stigmatize in its laws and to punish. These issues have been particularly well studied for the English context, with the focus principally on the 19th century.[31] The armed services remained to one side of this shift for the obvious reason that, ultimately, violence was central to their trade. This did not mean simply that the services became the haven for those who clung to an old image of masculinity that privileged the man who was aggressive, violent, and who drank hard. The issue of masculinity within the armed forces is a complex one. The so-called 'teeth arms', such as the infantry, for example, are inclined to prioritize the more traditional forms of masculinity, in contrast to the 'support arms' such as engineers, transport, and logistics personnel. Nevertheless, during the 19th century such distinctions were rarely made by the public, and garrison towns and naval bases acquired unenviable reputations for the drunken revels of soldiers and sailors, both groups being known to confront and to fight the local civilian police. Such towns were also noted for prostitution, the classic offence, in Victorian eyes, of the female element of the criminal classes.

The British Army had a poor reputation among much of the British public during the 19th century. While other major European powers had followed the practices developed in Revolutionary and Napoleonic France of conscripting young men annually into the armed forces for a short period, the British maintained a volunteer army. The Duke of Wellington is often quoted for famously stigmatizing his soldiers as 'the scum of the earth enlisted for drink', and for a comment to the effect that he did not know whether they frightened the enemy but 'by God, they frighten me.' The quotations are juicy, but are also generally cited out of context; nevertheless, for many years after Waterloo the stigma stuck.[32] The Army was seen as a refuge for the destitute, the feckless, and the criminal. In 1876, for example, an anonymous contributor to the *United Services Magazine* regretted that both the Army and the Navy depended 'for their very existence, mainly on the lowest stratum of the population, the denizens of the slum and out-of-the-way corners of our great towns.' Most of the Army's recruits in the years before 1914 were young, unskilled, poorly educated, and often illiterate.[33] Their officers, drawn from the gentry, the professional and propertied classes, and also—in increasing numbers—from the sons of Army officers, saw many of their men as coming from what was termed the 'criminal classes'; and so too, did many civilians. Rudyard Kipling captured the perception famously in 'Tommy'.

---

[31] Wiener, *Men of Blood* (2004); Wood, *Violence and Crime* (2004); Emsley, *Hard Men* (2005).

[32] For the origins of these quotations see Elizabeth Knowles (ed.), *The Oxford History of Quotations*, Oxford Reference Online, accessed 9 March 2011, at <http://www.oxfordreference.com/views/ENTRY. html?subview=Main&entry=t115.e3385>.

[33] French, *Military Identities* (2005), 31–5. The quotation is from Anon, 'Remarks on the Present Condition of the Army', *United Services Magazine*, 1876, 209–13.

I went into a public 'ouse to get a pint o' beer,
The publican 'e up an' sez, 'We serve no red-coats here.'
The girls be'ind the bar they laughed an' giggled fit to die,
I outs into the street again an' to myself sez I:
O it's Tommy this, an' Tommy that, an' 'Tommy go away';
But it's 'Thank you, Mister Atkins,' when the band begins to play –
The band begins to play, my boys, the band begins to play,
O it's 'Thank you, Mister Atkins,' when the band begins to play.

I went into a theatre as sober as could be,
They gave a drunk civilian room, but 'adn't none for me;
They sent me to the gallery or round the music-'alls,
But when it comes to fightin', Lord! They'll shove me in the stalls!
For it's Tommy this, an' Tommy that, an' 'Tommy wait outside';
But it's 'Special train for Atkins' when the trooper's on the tide –
    The troopship's on the tide, my boys, the troopship's on the tide,
    O it's 'Special train for Atkins' when the troopship's on the tide.

The anonymous author of the article in the *United Services Magazine* included naval recruits in his lament about the failure of 'the better portion of the working classes and the lower middle classes' to join the armed services. In general, however, critical attitudes among the public were not as apparent towards members of the Royal Navy as they were towards soldiers. Yet Jack Tar on leave, on shore, and on the drink could be as boisterous, as troublesome, and potentially as dangerous as Tommy Atkins.

Even as Kipling was writing his *Barrack Room Ballads*, however, this generally critical perception of the soldier was beginning to mellow, or at least to become more complex, and for a variety of reasons. The public had been moved by the reports of the sufferings of the soldiers during the Crimean War, and literary and artistic representations became more sympathetic, even romantic. Soldiers as well as sailors began to be the central characters of adventure stories for boys. Military reforms, particularly the introduction of short service, meant that soldiers were discharged while still young, fit, and able to work, rather than moving directly from the Army to the Poor Law casual wards. The ferocious discipline and absolute, often abusive power of Navy captains was challenged by lower deck organizations and publicized by the crusading newspaper, *The Bluejacket*, and the monthly *The Fleet*, founded, respectively, in 1898 and 1905 by Lionel Yexley, a former petty officer. Symptomatic of these changes was the creation of charities such as the Soldiers' and Sailors' Family Association and the Soldiers' and Sailors' Help Society, established respectively in 1885 and 1899. Even so, on the eve of the First World War, old soldiers were still the largest single contingent in the casual wards.[34] Moreover, while offending of various sorts appeared to be decreasing in the Army, there were still large numbers of men brought before courts martial every year. The Army had around 400,000 men in 1914 and the Royal Navy around 143,000. If

[34] Gregory, *The Silence of Memory* (1994), 93–5; Carew, *The Lower Deck* (1981).

courts martial can be taken as a measure of relatively serious offending, it is of significance that, in the decade before the war, the Army court martial figures dropped from around 8,000 to around 5,000 a year. The figures for the Navy (which included the Royal Marines) never reached a tenth of either figure but had also dropped to less than 200 just before the war, though it should not be assumed from this that naval discipline was, or became, any less harsh during the period.[35]

There was no way in which Britain could successfully have fought the two world wars of the 20th century by sticking to the idea of relatively small professional armed services recruited from volunteers. Many young men answered Lord Kitchener's call in 1914 and enlisted for King and Country. But the New Army forged from these volunteers was decimated on the Somme, and in 1916 Britain followed the lead of her principal ally, France, and principal opponent, Imperial Germany, and introduced conscription. Professional, volunteer services were restored during the interwar period, but the advent of the Second World War saw the re-establishment of conscription. Britain thus fought the two world wars with mass armies and navies, and maintained mass armed services for roughly a quarter of the 20th century—from 1916 to 1919, and again from 1940 to 1961. The offences committed by the enormous numbers of men brought into the armed services during these years form the principal focus of this book; and, within this, it is the Army that is the centre of attention. This is partly because of the sheer size of the Army, but also because it appears to have had more criminal offenders than the other services. In 1943, for example, an enquiry into detention barracks in the British Isles found some 5,200 men incarcerated for various offences; of these about 70 per cent were soldiers and the remainder were divided roughly equally between sailors and airmen.[36] Finally, for no clear reason, the surviving Army sources appear much more extensive. Records for RAF courts martial in The National Archives are extremely meagre, while the Admiralty records do not contain anything like, for example, the detailed letter books of the Army's Judge Advocate General.[37]

This book, of necessity, touches upon offences that were unique to the armed services, but its main focus is on crimes that could be committed by civilians as well as service personnel. Crime is neither absolute nor unchanging. It is generally behaviour that defies a society's norms and that society chooses to punish in some way; in modern societies crime is defined by legislation outlining the offence and prescribing the penal sanction. Homicide, theft, and various forms of assault are, and have been, generally perceived as the principal kinds of crime; and the majority of indictable offences brought before the civilian criminal courts in Britain during the period of this book were different forms of property appropriation. But other behaviours, homosexual activity and attempted suicide for example, were labelled as criminal for much of the period. Moreover, both property crime and

---

[35] Figures constructed from *General Annual Report of the British Army, 1911*, Cd. 6065, and idem, *1920*, Cmd. 1610; *Return of the Number of Courts Martial held . . . on Seamen of the Royal Navy, 1912*, Cd. 7167.

[36] *Report of the Prime Minister's Committee of Enquiry into Detention Barracks 1943*, Cmd. 6484, 6.

[37] The only documents for RAF courts martial appear to be thirty-six petitions for the years 1924 to 1950 held in AIR 30/211 to AIR 30/247.

interpersonal violence cover a vast array of activities of varying seriousness. As a consequence, much of what follows considers individual cases in order to illustrate the range and complexity of criminal behaviour as well as the range of victims and offenders and the complexity of motives.

The book does not offer a simple argument about displacement, suggesting that, in time of war, criminal offending was merely shifted by mass recruitment from the civilian to the military sphere. The 19th-century fathers of criminal statistics, André-Michel Guerry and Adolphe Quetelet, made the assumption that the same number of crimes would be committed each year in broadly the same pattern and distribution.[38] A similar assumption appears to lurk behind the Home Office quotation with which this chapter began. This book does not start with such an assumption and it does not attempt to argue that recruitment into the armed forces simply shifted crime from the jurisdiction of the civilian criminal justice system to that of the military. The boundaries between civilian and military personnel, court jurisdictions, and their respective institutions of enforcement and punishment were often permeable. Indeed, some of the preceding paragraphs have already given examples of young servicemen prosecuted before civilian rather than service courts. Moreover, while looting was essentially theft by another name, it would be folly to assume that the incidence of wartime looting by soldiers simply replaced some of the theft that would have been committed by the same young men in peacetime. Some crime might have been displaced. Some might have been prevented by the strict discipline and supervision of Army barracks and camps; equally, some seems to have been the result of the boredom and inactivity that could surround barrack or camp life. Other offences appear to have been fostered by the community of service life and by the opportunities provided by that life; and there were offences, such as desertion, that were specific to the armed forces. Moreover, as a result of the deployment of large numbers of civilians into the armed services during the two world wars, military jurisprudence and its system of punishment became significantly influenced by the practices of their civilian equivalents and by the perceptions of crime and justice held by those individuals recruited only for the duration of the wars.

The book is divided into three parts. The first deals with the criminal justice system of the armed forces in the first half of the 20th century. It draws broad comparisons and contrasts between military and civilian law, describes the range of courts and service police organizations. It also highlights various changes that occurred in the system as a result of the wars and the recruitment of the mass armies and navies. The patriotic volunteers of 1914 and 1915, and the men who were conscripted for wartime service appear to have expected a criminal justice system much more like that of the civilian world than the one that they found; and so too did their families and friends at home. The two world wars appear to have contributed significantly to a greater transparency and an increasing civilianization of the criminal justice systems within the armed services. The second part of the

---

[38] Emsley, *Crime, Police, and Penal Policy* (2007), 120–1.

book begins with a discussion of what can be gleaned from wartime offending by using the criminal statistics, both those of the Home Office and those prepared by the armed forces. It then addresses different forms of criminal offending committed by service personnel principally during the two wars. It suggests that service life offered considerable opportunities for different varieties of offending. On occasions this offending was related directly to experiences and opportunities found within the armed forces. Much criminal activity was essentially the same as that committed in the civilian world and, on occasions, it assumed the major proportions of what is now labelled as organized crime. Even with such offences, most service offenders left their criminal behaviour behind when they quit the armed forces—arguably in the way that many young offenders give up their deviant behaviour after a relatively few incidents. But this part of the book stresses also how for some years individuals suffered psychological trauma as a result of war. Such trauma might have led to some forms of criminal offending and it was employed as a mitigating circumstance in courts. The third part of the book sketches service offending in the period after the Second World War, together with the changing structures of criminal justice in the armed services as conscript forces gave way once more to forces recruited only from volunteers and as the military justice system continued its process of civilianization. This part concludes with a brief exploration of some of the early 21st-century concerns about the numbers of former service personnel in Britain's burgeoning prisons.

# 1

## 'The Object of Military Law Is to Maintain Discipline'

### Different Laws for Different People

On the eve of the First World War Christopher Henry Heddon was in his early thirties; he was a solicitor working in a practice that had offices in Harrogate and Ripon. He probably never thought that he would ever serve as a soldier in the British Army, and the British Army probably never expected to have men like Heddon volunteering for service. In 1915, however, Heddon answered Kitchener's call; for the next four years he was a driver in the Army Service Corps, never rising above the rank of private. Probably Heddon was not a particularly good soldier, but in 1918 he became involved in a series of incidents that resulted in a court case which raised issues about the differences between civilian and military law.

During the summer of 1918 Heddon's wife became seriously ill. Heddon, who had just been posted to a barracks in York, tried to visit her regularly at weekends. It is unclear whether his requests for leave, his decision to take weekend leave without permission, or some other incident led to the clash between Heddon and his officers. He considered that a junior lieutenant was acting in a fashion unbecoming an officer and a gentleman, and he wrote a letter of complaint to his CO, Major G. C. Evans. The major had a meeting with Heddon in which he allegedly told him: 'I always knew you were a rogue. Now I know you are a damned fool.' There was dispute over whether the major used the adjective 'damned', but Heddon took the outburst to be a criticism of him as a solicitor. There followed interviews with Evans's superiors, and an alleged threat from a colonel to have Heddon transferred to the infantry and sent to France post-haste. Evans eventually sentenced Heddon to fourteen days' confined to barracks for his 'frivolous' complaint about the lieutenant. Heddon objected that he had not been given the opportunity to present his case and demanded a court martial where, he believed, his side of the case could be heard. The court martial was convened and, in preparation for it, Heddon was arrested and held in Fulford Prison, York for eighteen days. It was at this point that Heddon launched a civil action against Major Evans for false imprisonment, malicious prosecution, and slander. The court martial was adjourned pending the result of Heddon's civil action. During the pause in events Heddon was demobilized on 24 January 1919, and his wife died the following month of a combination of diphtheria and influenza.

Heddon's civil action finally reached court at the end of April 1919. Five days of evidence were reported in detail by the newspapers, but it was not until the beginning of June that Mr Justice McCardie gave his verdict. McCardie concluded that different behaviour by one or more of Heddon's officers could have prevented the whole 'unhappy history'. He recognized Heddon's hardship but he did not think that Major Evans had exceeded his authority; he therefore found for the defendant but, since Heddon had said he would make no appeal, he did not award costs. And McCardie raised some important points about military law and its relationship to the ordinary law that applied to civilians. He stressed that it could not be possible for military men alone to be the interpreters of military law. 'So to hold would exclude the Court from one of its important functions. The judges were the interpreters of the law.' In passing McCardie noted a significant change that had developed in the Army during the war. Major Evans's defence, he explained, had been

> in substance that the Courts could not inquire into the exercise of military discipline. That submission appeared to be based on what might be called the doctrine of compact. Whatever basis existed for compact in the case of a voluntary army, he could see no satisfactory basis in respect of those who were in the Army only by virtue of the compulsory provision of the Military Service Act.[1]

The interwar period saw the restoration of the principle of British armed services being recruited from volunteers alone. Conscription was reintroduced in the late spring of 1939 and continued until the early 1960s. Throughout the period of the mass armed forces, recruited by conscription, the coexistence of military and civilian law provided the potential for confusion and friction.

## PARALLEL HISTORY: CIVILIAN LAW AND MILITARY LAW

As explained in the introduction, by 1914 the British professional soldier was losing some of the old stigma that had been directed against him. The volunteers who came forward to answer Kitchener's call in 1914 were mainly young men from respectable backgrounds; they went to war willingly, though it is probable that they became less willing, and certainly much more apprehensive, as they came face-to-face with the reality of industrialized warfare. It would be wrong and perhaps unfair to label as unwilling the men conscripted after the Military Service Act of 1916 and, later, during the Second World War; though it probably would be fair to say that they were not always enthusiastic but well aware that they were not easily going to get out of it.

Once in the services, the new soldier, sailor or airman, whether volunteer or conscript, became part of a new community. The military, and many military historians, have made much of the regiment, the ship, or the squadron as a family.

---

[1] The case was reported extensively in the press on 30 April, 1, 2, 3, 15, and 16 May 1919. The discussion of the case is based primarily on the reports given in *The Times* and the *Manchester Guardian*. The quotation from McCardie's verdict is taken from *The Times*, 5 June 1919, 5.

These institutions did provide some elements of family, but some of the closest-knit military communities were probably to be found at the much smaller level of the infantry platoon and its three or four sections of around ten men, of the artillery battery and its gun crews of around half a dozen men, and so on. Infantry companies of around a hundred men correspond closely with the anthropologists' assessment of the size of the well-balanced hunter-gatherer community. These small military groups develop their own occupational values and beliefs, which include looking out for and supporting each other. Research by two United States Intelligence Officers, who had trained as academic sociologists, concluded that the German Army held together and fought on in the closing months of the Second World War, not because of Nazi ideology, but because of the strong bonds that developed between groups of soldiers.[2]

Military communities are subject to the laws of the states that they serve, but they also have their own norms, their own laws, and their own courts. Legal systems can be written from scratch, but this has not happened in Britain. English criminal law has never been simply codified. British military law developed similarly. During the 18th century the celebrated commentator on the English law, Sir William Blackstone, considered military law was not real law but 'something to be indulged'. It had no settled principles and its decisions were arbitrary. During the 19th century, constitutional questions over whether the sovereign or parliament had the ultimate control of the Army reverberated in questions about military law. Members of Parliament increasingly espoused the ideas of legalism that would have given civil rights to servicemen; the military commanders, in contrast, thought in terms of obedience and enforcing discipline, and the idea that soldiers had rights that might challenge a superior's authority was intolerable. This situation remained unresolved at the beginning of war in 1914.[3]

Crime is defined by the criminal law; essentially it is behaviour for which the perpetrator is subject to some form of sanction in a court of criminal jurisdiction. Generally criminal behaviour breaks the accepted norms of a society. Norms can change, as in the case of homosexual behaviour, for example, and their edges also can be extremely fuzzy, so that sometimes offences defined in law as crime can be excused and even approved by some communities within the broader society.[4] But, and this was stressed in the *Manual of Military Law* published on the eve of the First World War, there were certain things in civilian life such as 'desertion and disobedience to orders' that could not be tolerated in a hierarchical, disciplined community like the Army, especially in wartime. The 1943 *Committee of Enquiry into Detention Barracks*, which was chaired by an eminent judge and holder of the Military Cross, explained further:

---

[2] Hockey, *Squaddies* (1986), especially chapter 9; Junger, *War* (2010), 239–46; Shils and Janowitz, 'Cohesion and Disintegration' (1948).

[3] Rubin, 'Parliament, Prerogative and Military Law' (1997); Oram, 'Armee, Staadt, Bürger und Wehrpflict' (2011).

[4] These issues are discussed further in Emsley, *Crime and Society . . . 1750–1900* (2010a), 2–10; and Emsley, *Crime and Society in Twentieth-Century England* (2011), 2–5.

All legislation to be effective must be backed by what jurists call a sanction, that is to say, power to inflict a penalty of some sort on the disobedient. Such sanctions, in the case of civilians, except in extreme cases, take the form of fine or imprisonment. Good citizens would behave without sanctions, but bad ones would not and there are and always will be a small minority who break the law in spite of the penalties but who nevertheless must be restrained for the protection of society. A member of the Fighting Forces undertakes additional liabilities—the deprivation of a considerable part of his personal liberty, the obligation of obedience to lawful commands and the whole catalogue of duties summarised in the word 'discipline.' Without discipline the Fighting Services would perish. In wartime the country would perish with them.

The *Manual of Military Law* put it bluntly: 'the object of military law is to maintain discipline.'[5]

In many ways the military's norms and laws are similar to those of the civilian's world, but in some ways they are very different. Under the 'Bloody Code' of Hanoverian England, the punishment for a felony was, in theory, death. The term 'in theory' is necessary since it would have been impossible to execute everyone convicted of a felony. In consequence, the courts employed discretion over who was sent to Tyburn Tree or its equivalents outside London, and secondary punishments, most notably transportation, were developed as an alternative to execution. Disquiet about the centrality of capital punishment in the criminal justice system grew during the 18th century, and so too did disquiet about forms of corporal punishment—particularly branding, and the slitting of the nose or the ears. By the close of the century, while flogging was maintained, other corporal punishments were no longer used. At the same time, the idea of depriving an offender of liberty by a period of imprisonment during which he, and less commonly she, might be reformed, was becoming popular with penal reformers. By the 1830s capital punishment was restricted to murder and treason; flogging was given a new lease of life during the 1860s to deal with street robbery, but increasingly all kinds of punishment were removed from public view. The last public execution in England was carried out in 1868.

While the debates continued about who had the ultimate authority over British military law and justice, the military's criminal justice practice tracked that of its civilian counterpart. The formal criminal work of magistrates' courts had been increasing since the 18th century but expanded particularly with a series of Acts of Parliament in the 1840s and 1850s. The summary jurisdiction of commanding officers, which was the lowest of the formal settings for military justice and hence the nearest military equivalent to the magistrates' court, was increased in 1865 and again in 1910. The rise in summary jurisdiction accompanied a decline in the statistics of offending in the Army, just as the statistics of offending in the civilian population levelled out and, in some instances, declined. The 1910 extension of the powers of a commanding officer to deal with petty offences was noted also to have contributed to a decline in the number of courts martial. During the second half of

---

[5] *Manual of Military Law*, 1914 edn, 6; *Report of the Prime Minister's Committee of Enquiry into Detention Barracks*, Cmd. 6484, 3–4.

the 19th century the Army also tracked civilian penal policy in other ways; most notably more use was made of fines and imprisonment rather than inflicting physical punishment on the offender's body. The branding, or more properly the tattooing of 'bad characters' and of deserters, was abolished in 1871. The number of strokes that could be inflicted in a military flogging had been reduced to fifty by the beginning of the Crimean War, and was halved to twenty-five in 1879. But the Zulu War of 1879 saw an enormous increase in the use of the lash and in 1881 a disquieted Parliament abolished the punishment.[6]

While Jack Tar generally received a better press than Tommy Atkins, he was not subject to a service law that was greatly different. Indeed, the number of small, summary punishments inflicted on sailors by their officers appears to have been significantly greater than the number imposed on soldiers and, though they generally came under naval discipline, marines. The 19th-century Royal Navy was as rigidly class-bound as the Army, and the Admiralty clung to its legal exceptionalism. While Parliament abolished flogging in the Army, the punishment was only suspended in the Navy, and the Admiralty retained the right to sanction its use without parliamentary approval. As late as 1939 flogging was still listed as a punishment in *King's Regulations* and all ships, supposedly as a deterrent, continued to carry the traditional cat that was used to administer a flogging.[7]

## THE DEATH PENALTY

Victorian Britain prided itself on its progress and humanitarianism, yet its determination to hold on to capital and corporal punishment set it apart from many liberal European states and many of the individual states of the United States. Similarly, the Military Code, promulgated in 1881, and under which British servicemen went to war in 1914, was closer to that of the old empires of East Europe than to that of the liberal, constitutional republics of France and the United States.[8] In the Army there remained twenty-seven capital offences (see Table 1.1): twelve of these offences were applicable at any time; the remainder were only applicable on active service. Most of the capital offences related specifically to military activities but, among those punishable by death if committed when on active service was the offence of housebreaking, a crime that had ceased to be capital in the criminal law of England during the 1820s.

The death penalty, particularly for desertion, during the First World War has been the area of British military justice most exhaustively studied. There is a broadly accepted figure of 3,077 death sentences passed on men of the British and Imperial Armies during the war. Most of these sentences, 2,004 of them, were

---

[6] These issues are discussed at length by, among others, Skelley, *The Victorian Army* (1977), chapter 3. For the impact of the 1910 reform see *The General Annual Report on the British Army for the year ending 30 September 1911*, Cd. 6065, Part VI, Table 1, note (b).

[7] Carew, *The Lower Deck* (1981), 31; Sears, 'Discipline in the Royal Navy' (1991).

[8] Oram, *Military Executions* (2003), 30–1.

**Table 1.1** Offences Punishable by Death under the Army Act 1881

| Offences punishable by death at any time |
| --- |
| Abandoning post |
| Shamefully casting away arms in the presence of the enemy |
| Corresponding with the enemy |
| Assisting the enemy |
| Serving with enemy forces while a prisoner of war |
| Cowardice before the enemy |
| Causing a mutiny |
| Inciting others to mutiny |
| Joining a mutiny |
| Failing to inform CO of mutiny |
| Striking or threatening to strike a senior officer |
| Disobedience |
| **Offences punishable by death only on active service** |
| Commission of an act that imperils HM Forces |
| Leaving CO to go in search of plunder |
| Leaving a guard, picquet, patrol, or post |
| Forcing of a safeguard |
| Striking a soldier acting as a sentinel |
| Impeding a provost marshal |
| Violence towards a person bringing provisions |
| Housebreaking |
| Causing false alarms |
| Treacherously revealing the parole or watchword |
| Misappropriation of provisions |
| Sleeping or drunk whilst a sentinel |
| Leaving a post whilst a sentinel |
| Desertion |
| Inciting others to desert |

for desertion. Three hundred and forty-three of the sentences were carried out.[9] The caveat that these are broadly accepted figures has to be added since, occasionally, cases turn up that do not appear in the official statistics. In his wartime memoir, *Goodbye to All That*, for example, Robert Graves describes two soldiers in his regiment being executed for having shot their company sergeant major. Further details have been unearthed that correct some parts of Graves's account, but the fact remains that the executions were carried out and that no official record exists of the men's court martial.[10] Similarly, among the private papers of Corporal H. E. Shelton, held in the Imperial War Museum, are summaries of the evidence brought against Shelton for mutiny during the 1919 expedition to Russia. The papers also contain a copy of the guilty verdict and the death sentence pronounced by the court. Shelton was not executed; there was a suspension of the death

---

[9] Oram, *Death Sentences* (1998a).
[10] Graves, *Goodbye to All That* (1960), 93–4; Putkowski and Sykes, *Shot at Dawn* (1992), 33–4.

sentence shortly after the Armistice of November 1918. By August 1919 he appears to have been demobilized and was back in London. Details of Shelton's offence and court martial appear nowhere in the official War Office records.[11] These, and other gaps, are probably not the result of any conspiracy, but stem rather from the difficulty inherent in collecting and recording statistics from a range of theatres. The records of cases tried on the Western Front usually took about two weeks to arrive in London after the trial and confirmation of the sentence; but from the front in, for example, Mesopotamia, it could be months before any details arrived. In addition, in the general confusion and pressure in a military headquarters it seems that the records of some cases were lost; others appear to have gone missing in transit or were simply sent to the wrong office, a problem that was to reoccur during the Second World War and later.[12]

In 1914, in both civilian and military law, death sentences and executions were designed to deter as well as to punish. In the civilian world the motivation and the justification were that the punishment would deter others from committing murder. In the military world the motivation and justification were wider; the death sentence could be passed for murder, but it existed also to enforce discipline and obedience and hence it covered a much wider range of offences. The executions on the Western Front in May 1916 of Private J. Fox of the Highland Light Infantry and Driver John Hasemore of the Royal Artillery are particularly illustrative of this. Fox was shot for striking a superior, Hasemore for threatening behaviour. Their punishments were exceptional; most of the death sentences passed by courts martial for disobedience, insubordination, and striking or threatening a superior during the war were commuted to penal servitude or a prison sentence with hard labour. But all of these punishments underline the extent to which the motivations behind deterrence could differ between civilian and military law. In Fox's case his behaviour was aggravated by abuse; he had not only sworn at, but twice kicked the officer who had reprimanded him for a dirty rifle and dirty boots. Hasemore was incorrigible and had been disobedient on a succession of occasions. He had refused to submit to Field Punishment Number 1, which involved being tied to a fixed point, often with arms and legs painfully outstretched; also he had refused to carry horse equipment, refused to march properly, and had used insubordinate and threatening language to his superiors.[13]

---

[11] IWM (D) 06/94/1, H. E. Shelton. No white, British soldier appears to have been executed following a court martial after the Armistice, though others were, specifically Black and Asian troops from the Empire, Chinese labourers working for the Army, prisoners of war, civilians in areas under martial law and several men from the Slavo-British Legion serving in Russia. See Oram, *Death Sentences* (1998a), 64–8.

[12] WO 81/177 f. 314, to Brig. H. Scott-Barrett, 26 August 1944, expressing concern that the proceedings of a General Court Martial, which had resulted in the dismissal of a captain in the Royal Marines and which had been confirmed by General Montgomery as the commander of the 21st Army Group appeared not to have been seen and approved by the brigadier himself and seemed 'to have wandered to the Admiralty, who wanted to have nothing to do with them [ . . . ] and finally to the Royal Marines, who by request sent them to me, and I have sent them back telling them to get on with the promulgation as soon as possible.' For a later example see below p. 183.

[13] Putkowski and Sykes, *Shot at Dawn* (1992), 78–80.

During the First World War the death sentences passed by courts martial increased immediately before major offensives and continued at a high level until the end of the action. The implications are that the tensions before a major battle might have increased the frequency of desertion and that senior officers were determined to take tough measures to ensure that men stayed at their posts and did their military duty. There appears also to have been a difference in the number of executions carried out according to the different kinds of military division involved. Men in the divisions of the old Regular Army seem to have been more vulnerable than those of the Territorial Army or of the New Army recruited in 1914. It was as if the senior officers of the Regular divisions, even when the losses in their regiments were replaced by new volunteers and conscripts, still clung to the old notion of the rank and file being the 'scum of the earth enlisted for drink' who needed a tough, firm hand to keep them in order. Yet even some Regular officers who considered their men to be, at least in part, rogues and blackguards, still had a strong affection for them and intensely disliked the use of the death penalty for desertion. Lt. Col. J. W. Allen told his wife how he had written a report on one of his men with the express intent of 'getting him off the death sentence. I don't believe in shooting these men as many really cannot help it and may improve.' But there were times, it seems, when justice took second place to a belief that discipline had to be enforced and when divisional commanders could be put under pressure by the high command to pursue a harsh policy.[14] Field Marshal Haig, for example, believed the Australians to be particularly poorly disciplined and, much to his annoyance, the Australian Defence Act forbad the execution of any Australian soldiers. Haig endeavoured, unsuccessfully, to get authority to execute Australians. Early in 1918, on learning that there was a greater proportion of Australian troops in prison compared with any other group under his command, he expressed his frustration in a manner that demonstrated his belief in the deterrent value of the death penalty:

> nearly one Australian in every hundred is in prison. This is greatly due to the fact that the Australian refuses to allow the death penalty to be awarded to any Australian. Before we introduced the 'suspended sentence' in February 1915, the British had 5.1 men per thousand in prison. By June that year the numbers fell to 1.2 and in August to .7 per thousand. Really the absence of crime in the Army is quite wonderful.[15]

Haig's understanding of 'crime' here appears to have been limited to desertion and cowardice; and while the Australians had an unenviable reputation for crime and unruliness, it seems that they were not more likely to commit the capital offences of desertion and cowardice for which most British and other imperial troops were sentenced to death and shot.[16]

---

[14] Oram, *Military Executions* (2003), especially chap. 4; Brotherton, Liddle Collection, (GS) J. W. Allen, letter 110, 6 June 1915; and see also (GS) A. J. Richardson, December 1916, 96.
[15] Quoted in Oram, *Worthless Men* (1998b), 115.
[16] Stanley, *Bad Characters* (2010), 172–6 and 212.

Overall roughly one in ten of the death sentences issued by courts martial during the First World War were carried out. Yet excluding those for military crimes in a period of tension before an offensive, the relation between other capital offences and the number of executions was reminiscent of developments in civilian policy. The officer corps in general believed, like Haig, that the threat of capital punishment kept men in line and ensured that they did their duty. In other words, that it deterred men from running away in the same way that, in the civilian world, the death penalty was believed to deter people from committing murder. Unfortunately it is impossible to measure deterrence. Moreover, whatever their unruliness and whatever the high command's inability to shoot any of them, the fighting qualities of Australian soldiers were rarely in question, and this puts a significant question mark over the deterrence argument.

Aside from the questions of cowardice and desertion, however, and whatever Military Law authorized, the offences that led to other military executions during the war largely resembled those that led to civilian executions. In the civilian law, by the beginning of the 20th century, capital punishment was only permissible for murder and high treason. The death sentence in the Army was, as noted above, suspended in November 1918. Before the suspension, about two dozen soldiers from the British and Imperial armies had been sentenced to death by court martial for murder; rather more than half of these sentences were carried out. Between September 1914 and January 1920, another two dozen soldiers were sentenced to death for serious offences, excluding murder, against civilians. Two of these had their sentences quashed; all of the others had the sentence commuted, usually to a prison sentence of hard labour or penal servitude.[17] Subsequently two soldiers from the Regular Army occupying the Rhineland during the ten years following the war were sentenced to death by courts martial for rape. In one instance the accused also killed a lance corporal from his regiment whom he had found with his woman victim. According to the official historian, the German victims were 'of the prostitute class', but because, under German law, unpremeditated murder was not a capital offence, both men were reprieved and sentenced to prison terms; one to fifteen years and the other to penal servitude for life.[18] It appears that the Army of Occupation was sensitive to the image that it presented to the German population and did not wish to demonstrate any similarity to what was understood as the harsh Prussian militarism that was denigrated in Britain and that, according to many politicians and contemporary commentators, had been the cause of the war.

---

[17] There is some discrepancy in the figures, especially in those for men sentenced for murder, hence my use of 'about two dozen'. The overwhelming majority of reported executions for murder come from the Western Front, where the British had their biggest concentration of troops; but it is also possible that the details of some cases were lost in transit. These figures also omit civilians and men recruited for labour corps (there were large numbers of Chinese labourers on the Western Front, some of whom were executed for murder) and locally recruited muleteer units in, for example, the Balkans.

[18] Edmonds, *Occupation of the Rhineland* (1987); see also Jeffery, '"Hut ab", "Promenade with Kamerade for Schockolade"' (2005), 467–8.

On the home front, and especially in the decades following the war, the concern grew that some of the men sentenced and shot for desertion or cowardice were suffering from shell shock. A War Office enquiry into shell shock, published in 1922, gave impetus to calls for the abolition of the right of courts martial to pass the sentence of death. Significantly too, the Labour MPs who led the campaign for abolition were men who had served during the war. Senior Army officers strongly opposed such calls but, from the middle of the 1920s, Parliament began restricting the range of capital offences available to courts martial. Finally, in 1930, Parliament abolished the power of military courts to pass capital sentences except for crimes of treason, mutiny, and murder.[19]

Occasionally during the Second World War some senior officers urged a restoration of the capital sanction, especially in theatres where they believed that morale was under strain and that the men required an extra prompt to deter them from leaving the front line. A corps commander in Normandy in 1944, for example, explained that

> There were genuine cases of shell shock but the great majority were merely frightened, and wanted an excuse to get out of it. The shelling was horrible, and most frightening, but if people were allowed to leave the battlefield every time they were frightened the army would have disintegrated in no time.

His solution: 'Horrible as it is I am in favour of the death penalty in certain cases.' The Army Council and the War Cabinet stood firm against such requests, though probably more from concern about the potential political repercussions.[20] In at least one instance, however, a senior officer issued instructions that authorized both corporal and capital punishment directly counter to military law and regulations.

When Orde Wingate led his Chindit columns behind Japanese lines, a special punishment code was circulated by word of mouth, with the false addition that it had been legitimated by a secret order from the commander-in-chief in India. This code directed that serious offences, such as stealing rations or sleeping on sentry duty, might be punished with a flogging; more serious, or repeat offences might be punished by banishment from the column with a rifle and five rounds of ammunition; any man guilty of cowardice was to be shot. There is no evidence that any officer shot an offender; two men were turned loose, one of whom made it back to safety. In an echo of Field Punishment No. 1 from the First World War, a man who pilfered rations was tied to a tree in the sun during a midday halt. Perhaps as many as ten or a dozen men were flogged and, in the summer of 1946, a distinguished Chindit commander, Major Philip Graves-Morris DSO MC, faced a court martial for ordering such a sentence on two of the men in his column two years earlier. The case focussed on only one of these men, who had received twelve strokes 'across the shoulders with a stick, a little thinner than a schoolmaster's cane.' The man had

---

[19] Report of the War Office Committee of Enquiry into 'Shell-Shock', Cmd. 1734; McHugh, 'The Labour Party and the Campaign to Abolish the Military Death Penalty' (1999).

[20] French, 'Discipline and the Death Penalty' (1998), 538; and see also, Peaty, 'The Desertion Crisis in Italy' (2002), 78–9.

been found asleep while on sentry duty and had been sentenced to twenty-eight days' field punishment. The problem was, Graves-Morris maintained, that there was no means of carrying out field punishment during the campaign and that the offence was so serious that something had to be done. His defence counsel, G. Russell Vick KC, suggested further that 'field punishment was no use as the campaign was worse than field punishment.' Graves-Morris, the defence explained, had spelt out the problem to the offender, had suggested the beating and had asked the man to think about it. The man had agreed to the punishment by signing a statement to this effect. Evidence was put before the court that such punishments had been a common practice for serious cases during the campaign, but the Judge Advocate declared that had an officer disobeyed Wingate's instructions 'he could not be charged with disobeying orders.' In the event the court agreed to Graves-Morris's plea of condonation, and their recommendation was confirmed by the General Officer Commanding London District.[21] Understandably former Chindit commanders were angry that one of their number had been prosecuted in this way. Major General 'Joe' Lentaigne saw the whole thing as whipped up by the brother-in-law of the beaten sentry, who happened to be a shop steward. Lentaigne had also sought to get the publicity 'muzzled' and was upset by the War Office's unfortunate turn of phrase that Graves-Morris was to be court-martialled 'for certain incidents involving two soldiers in the Burma campaign. It read like sodomy to all who know nothing about it.'[22]

## THE AIMS AND REALITIES OF MILITARY LAW

Military life had many more regulations regarding behaviour and deportment and the British military also had a catch-all for miscellaneous military offences under Section 40 of the 1881 Army Act. This authorized the punishment of a military offender guilty of 'any act, conduct, disorder, or neglect, to the prejudice of good order and military discipline.' It could be used to deal with serious matters such as the prevention of rumours likely to affect morale. In the early months of the First World War, for example, a soldier in the Bedfordshire Regiment was charged under Section 40 for saying

> that British soldiers were being shot by their officers out at the front for trivial offences and that a drummer boy of the Norfolk Regiment had been shot for not keeping up with the regiment because he stumbled and fell.[23]

Sample charges prepared for the Military Police (MPs) in the summer of 1944 are illustrative of the elasticity of Section 40. Men could be charged with:

---

[21] *Manchester Guardian*, 6 July 1946, 6 and 25 July, 2; *The Times*, 6 July 1946, 2 and 25 July, 2; and see in general, Bidwell, *The Chindit War* (1979), 136–7 and 246–7.

[22] IWM (D) 91/9/1, Major W. V. H. Martin, letter from Lentaigne, 1 August 1946.

[23] WO 84/9 fol. 422.

Slovenly conduct, i.e. having the collar and top four buttons of his battledress unfastened and his hands in his pockets [ . . . ]
Irregular conduct, i.e. failing to salute a commissioned officer whose badges of rank were apparent.[24]

Sometimes military regulations were said to have been enforced with little regard for the circumstances. Private T. A. Silver of the East Surreys complained that he was given seven days' field punishment in the winter of 1914–15—'which meant I had to do more dangerous and dirty jobs [ . . . ] [including] putting out barbed wire and cleaning latrines'—for going on sick parade in a muddy uniform. Silver's medical problem was frostbite which, a few weeks later, led to him being sent home and spending almost three months in hospital. He claimed only to have gone on sick parade with mud on his uniform since the parade was held immediately after a night march back from the trenches.[25]

There were complaints that regulations were enforced with senseless ferocity by non-commissioned officers (NCOs), by officers, and by the military's own police institutions. Towards the end of 1916 there was a campaign, spearheaded in the press by the radical journalist, and former army sergeant, Robert Blatchford, against the use of Field Punishment No. 1. Blatchford and others stressed that Britain now had a citizen Army, and patriotic citizens in the king's service should never be treated with such brutal 'Hun-like' methods.[26] Yet tough drills and punishments remained, in the eyes of many, the best way to transform citizens into soldiers. In September 1941, Major A. S. Williams MC was brought before a court martial for allowing his NCOs to treat a company of soldiers with brutality. In the event the major and his NCOs were acquitted. The summing up of Major R. S. Bacon, Deputy Judge Advocate, suggests that the Army believed tough treatment to be necessary for conscripts. According to Major Bacon, Williams's company was

a nightmare by comparison with a body of Regular trained soldiers. It would be manifestly absurd to apply the same criterion in a unit such as this as in a Brigade of Guards. It would be straining fantasy to the limit to imagine that this company was bearing any sort of resemblance to a body of trained soldiers.[27]

Military law could also be used to enforce the differences of rank and to ensure that such differences were maintained. Robert Graves recalled how, in France towards the end of 1915, a battalion commander ordered the ferocious Field Punishment No. 1 for a private who, in conversation, had addressed a lance corporal by his Christian name. The lance corporal himself lost his stripe for not reprimanding the man.[28] Nor were officers exempt from such regulations. They were expected to behave like gentlemen and to maintain the appropriate divide between themselves and their men. Many Regular Army officers, particularly during the First World

---

[24] WO 171/3370, 76 Provost Company, 1944.
[25] IWM (D) 74/108/1, T. A. Silver (no folio numbers).
[26] WO 32/5460.
[27] *The Times*, 18, 19, 20, and 22 September 1941 (quotation 22 September, 2); *Manchester Guardian*, 19 and 20 September 1941.
[28] Graves, *Goodbye to All That* (1960), 150.

War, feared that the massive expansion of the Army meant that large numbers of unsuitable men were receiving commissions. Early in 1916 an argument between junior officers at Aldershot, during which an accusation of 'liar' was made and a blow was struck, resulted in a court martial. The defending officer explained to the court that this would have been a 'tin-pot' affair in the civilian world, and went on to emphasize that the accused had been promoted from the ranks of the Territorial Army:

> There were [now] in the commissioned ranks people who were drawn from a class not usually associated with such conditions in His Majesty's service, and when they got people in that class put into commissions they must expect things they would not ordinarily expect. In dealing with men of the New Army, officers commanding did not, in awarding punishment, proceed on the same lines as they would have done with men serving in the Regular Army. When they had a man who gave a week's notice to his Commanding Officer—a thing that occurred recently—they would appreciate the fact that a person able to do a thing like that did not stand quite in the same mental attitude towards his superiors as one who was used to the Army before.[29]

But it was not just newly commissioned officers who failed to behave appropriately as officers and gentlemen and who, as a consequence, found themselves before a court martial. In October 1939, for example, a captain of the Seaforth Highlanders' Infantry Training Centre at Fort St George was brought before a court martial charged with drunkenness and disturbing his men in their barrack rooms at 3.00 a.m. Perhaps more seriously, however, he was accused of behaviour in a local pub that was contrary to that of an officer and a gentleman; allegedly he called a lance corporal 'a dirty little fucking bastard [and] behaved in a familiar manner with the said soldier by placing his hands on his shoulders feigning to fight him and offered to fight the best man in the place.'[30]

Section 40 was not much concerned with offences that would come under the jurisdiction of a civilian court. Section 41 of the Army Act was different. It recognized the primacy of civilian courts in dealing with serious crimes committed by soldiers, and particularly when those crimes were committed in the United Kingdom.

> A person subject to military law shall not be tried by court martial for treason, murder, manslaughter, treason-felony, or rape committed in the United Kingdom, and shall not be tried by court martial for treason, murder, manslaughter, treason-felony, or rape committed in any place within Her Majesty's dominions, other than the United Kingdom and Gibraltar, unless such person at the time he committed the offence was on active service, or such place is more than one hundred miles as measured in a straight line from any city or town to which the offender can be tried for such an offence by a competent civil court.

---

[29] *Aldershot News*, 28 January 1916, 7.
[30] WO 84/53, 63–64; for a similar example of an officer in a Searchlight Regiment offering to fight any man that he found asleep on his post, see 12–15; and for a junior officer in the Royal Tank Corps court-martialled for drinking and overfamiliarity with his men before the war, see *Daily Mirror*, 27 December 1935, 1.

The act was drafted when many soldiers were likely to be in far-away lands with non-European populations; but Section 41 could also be employed at times for military convenience. In India towards the end of the 19th century, British soldiers accused of assaulting or killing people from the indigenous population sometimes appeared before civilian courts and sometimes before courts martial. A conviction in a civilian court for such an offence could promote anger among soldiers and other Europeans. In 1890, for example, Private Thomas O'Hara was convicted of shooting a civilian while out with some comrades on a drunken spree. Protests followed; fault was found with the behaviour of the judge, the verdict was quashed, and O'Hara and his companions were retried by a court martial on the lesser charge of being absent without leave. When Lord Curzon became viceroy in 1899, he was alarmed by the way in which Europeans tended to be acquitted by juries for crimes of violence against Indians. He was also disquieted by military cover-ups and by the way in which justice often seemed to be undermined by military *esprit de corps*. He initiated a clampdown on such behaviour and, while there were the inevitable protests that this weakened British authority over the Indians, the number of recorded assaults by Europeans on Indians declined sharply in the first five years of the new century.[31] At the same time, when men were charged with capital offences before courts martial during the South African War, the offences were often redefined with reference to the respective races of perpetrator and victim and the context of the war. Four men were executed on capital charges, including the celebrated case of two Australian officers—Harry 'Breaker' Morant and Peter Hancock—found guilty of shooting Boer prisoners. But where black Africans were the victims it was generally a different story; and, more surprisingly, so it was in the astonishing instance of a British officer who shot a white British war correspondent in the head following a drunken argument during the siege of Mafeking. The officer was initially sentenced to death; this was reduced to life imprisonment; but he was then released to assist in the defence of the town against the Boers.[32]

A major problem arose during the Dublin Easter Rising of 1916 when Captain J. C. Bowen-Colthurst completely lost his head, shot an innocent young man, and then had a further three equally innocent civilians arrested and shot. Among Bowen-Colthurst's victims was a notable Dublin eccentric Francis Sheehy-Skeffington, a campaigner for socialism, votes for women, and vegetarianism, and against alcohol and the war. The Army had no love for Sheehy-Skeffington, and little love for Major Sir Francis Vine, who was determined to see a fellow officer, Bowen-Colthurst, brought to book; but it considered Bowen-Colthurst expendable. Above all, it wanted the affair handled quietly. The Deputy Judge Advocate General decided that Bowen-Colthurst should be charged with murder and manslaughter; but, even though Bowen-Colthurst was on active service, the Deputy

---

[31] Wiener, *An Empire on Trial* (2009), 128–9, 160–3, 173, and 175.
[32] Miller, 'Duty or Crime?' (2010).

JAG also considered that, since the offences had been committed in Great Britain, the trial would have to be held before a civilian court. The Irish law officers agreed, though they also noted the likelihood of wide coverage of any such trial, and the potential for trouble and disorder. A meeting between the Lord Chief Justice, the Solicitor General, the Director of Public Prosecutions, the Irish Attorney General, and the Deputy Inspector General of the Royal Irish Constabulary came up with a solution. Within four days of the meeting, a new regulation was prepared under the wartime Defence of the Realm Act, and this enabled Bowen-Colthurst to be tried by court martial. He was convicted of murder and confined to a hospital for the criminally insane; when, eventually, he was released, he emigrated to Canada.[33]

The discussions about the form of Bowen-Colthurst's trial illustrate the more general question of where trials involving service personnel might occur, and under whose jurisdiction. The committee charged with enquiring into courts martial in 1919 understood that offences of a civil nature 'were usually dealt with by the Civil Courts, except where the complainant and witnesses were almost all officers or soldiers.' The committee recommended that this practice continue.[34] But often, as in the civilian courts, an individual could face multiple charges, some of which related to service discipline and some of which were criminal offences under civilian law. In such instances, and following long-established legal principles, it was deemed fair that the accused should have to face only one trial and, since the disciplinary offences could not be heard in a civilian court, it was logical that this trial should be before a court martial. Thus, for example, in August 1941 Lieutenant William Murray Edwards faced a court martial on six charges relating to his being drunk and assaulting a German prisoner. Five charges came under the Army Act: one for drunkenness; three for 'conduct prejudicial of good order and military discipline'; and a fifth charge of 'behaving in a scandalous manner unbecoming the character of an officer and a gentleman.' Only the assault charge was noted as coming under Section 41 as a criminal offence in civilian law.[35] The surviving, fragmentary details of a few cases sent to the Judge Advocate General are not always clear as to why a decision was made about under which jurisdiction a case should be tried. In October 1939, for example, both a lance corporal of the infantry and a gunner were prosecuted before courts martial under Section 41 for what were criminal offences under civilian law: the former for the theft of a ten-shilling note from a girl; the latter for the theft of hair oil and toothpaste. The following month a private of the Gordon Highlanders was prosecuted similarly under Section 41 for the theft of a silk scarf, a tortoiseshell ring, and a tankard; in this instance it was clearly specified in the correspondence of the Judge Advocate General that the trial was taking place before a military court as, at the time of the offence, the accused was in Canterbury on 'active service'.[36]

---

[33] Foy and Barton, *The Easter Rising* (1999), 189–92.
[34] *Report of the Committee Constituted by the Army Council to Enquire into the Law and Rules of Procedure Regulating Military Courts Martial*, Cmd. 428, 5.
[35] WO 71/1061.
[36] WO 84/53 16–17, 25–6, and 262–3.

## CIVILIAN JURISDICTION AND MILITARY
## JURISDICTION: PROBLEMS AND RESOLUTIONS

Towards the end of 1941 the Central Conference of Chief Constables in England and Wales considered a draft Home Office Circular 'Criminal Offences committed by Soldiers and Airmen'. In a preliminary discussion among chief constables from the north of the country (No. 3 District) George Vaughan, of the West Riding, suggested that there ought to be more consistency in deciding who should deal with offences other than those that were purely military. Major J. M. Garrow, his counterpart in Derbyshire, noted that commanding officers preferred to deal with minor offences themselves.

> He said the ordinary procedure with deserters who had, in addition, committed some civil offence, was to hand them over to a military escort and they were later dealt with by the Military for desertion only. He suggested that the Military should be empowered to take minor indictable offences into consideration when dealing with a desertion charge.

In the end the Central Conference agreed that when a military tribunal was to hear a criminal law case and when there were civilian witnesses, for the convenience of those witnesses if for no other reason, the court should sit near to the place where the offence was committed. In addition, the police requested that they be informed of the results of any such trial when it involved injury to a civilian or damage to civilian property.[37] A related problem was highlighted at roughly the same time by Chief Inspector D. E. Cleat of the Colchester Police. He protested that his men were being tied up for six or seven hours when cases were handed over to the military, while the same cases could have been dealt with by magistrates in ten minutes.[38]

Yet in spite of the problems of jurisdiction, on occasions the ability to hand offenders over to the military could be useful to the police. On the eve of the First World War a naval surgeon was court-martialled for being drunk on duty at the Royal Naval College, Greenwich. He had been apprehended by a Metropolitan Police constable on duty at the college who explained that 'it was not the custom to report an officer holding the King's commission for being drunk. If he was incapable or disorderly it was another matter. The police were placed in an extremely difficult position.'[39] But civilian and military police could also work usefully together. Dorothy Wheatley, a member of the ATS Police, recalled working occasionally with police detectives while posted to Hull. 'We could', she explained, 'get them into places under military rather than civilian law.'[40] At the end of the Second World War the Ghost Squad, the undercover unit of the

[37] OUPA, ACPO Bag (32) 88, Central Conference of Chief Constables, 1939–1960, 11 December 1941, f. 3.
[38] *Police Review*, 24 December 1941, 778.
[39] *The Times*, 24 July 1914, 10.
[40] IWM (D) MISC 236 (3354), Accounts of Service with the ATS Provost.

Metropolitan Police, was able to engage in a deception with the Military Police to protect an informant. 'Hymie the Gambler' had been recruited by the squad to facilitate a police sting; he had agreed to infiltrate a gang that was forging clothing coupons. The police had to arrest Hymie along with the other offenders, but they were able to extricate him from the proceedings by organizing an elaborate charade during which, in front of the rest of the gang, Hymie was handed over to the Military Police as a deserter.[41]

Some service personnel attempted to use military necessity as a way to circumvent the ordinary, civilian law. In January 1915, for example, an orderly attached to the Royal Fusiliers appeared before magistrates in Epsom for driving a motor car at excessive speed. His defence was that his commanding officer had ordered him to proceed 'as quickly as possible' and, had he failed so to do, he would have been liable to a court martial. Under the new Defence of the Realm Act, it was claimed, a serviceman in the execution of his duty could not be obstructed by anyone, not even a police officer. The magistrates were unconvinced and fined the orderly £2 'subject to any point of law the defendant's advocate might see fit to raise.' Ralph Neville, one of the bench, quipped of the case to courtroom laughter: 'It is getting rather like living in Germany.'[42] Some months later, when a sapper was brought before the magistrates in Bedford for riding a bike at night without red rear lights, an officer stepped up to defend him. According to the officer, the sapper 'had to take a message, and his duty was to obey his officer. If anyone should be fined it was the officer who gave the order.' The bench were unimpressed and, as the chairman pointed out, 'as they could not fine the officer, they must fine the man.' A few weeks later Army personnel tried another tack before the same bench; the bikes were government property and while new ones had been requested, they had not yet arrived. This argument also fell on deaf ears.[43] At the end of the First World War a similar problem arose at the Aldershot Police Court where an Army driver was prosecuted for driving a lorry without identification plates. The War Office contended that the lorry had all of the appropriate registration for a vehicle in use by the Army on the Western Front and that it had circulated an order to the effect that the regulation permitting this was still in force. The chairman of the bench pointed out that it was the magistrates' duty to enforce the law of the land, not War Office regulations; a fine was imposed of ten shillings and sixpence and the magistrates allowed the case to go to appeal.[44] Similar problems arose during the Second World War. In July 1941, for example, two military dispatch riders, carrying messages from the prime minister, were stopped for speeding near Bromley Common by two Metropolitan Police motorcycle officers. There appears to have been some exaggeration about the length of delay on the part of the dispatch riders, and the police themselves might not have been entirely blameless in the affair. The

---

[41] Roodhouse, 'The "Ghost Squad"' (2003), 184–5.
[42] *The Times*, 12 January 1915, 5.
[43] *Bedfordshire Times and Independent*, 8 October 1915, 8, and 29 October, 9.
[44] *Aldershot News*, 9 July 1920, 8.

upshot was that a system of time-limited chits was devised to enable dispatch riders working for Downing Street to proceed 'at the utmost speed.'[45]

Tension between civilian law and military regulations could lead to friction as well as jokes in the courtroom. In the summer of 1918 a number of men from the 2nd Battalion of the East Yorkshire Regiment were deployed in that county on work of national importance in shipyards and munitions factories. Much of this work was heavy and involved long hours. The men involved believed that they had been promised excusal from drill as a result; but their battalion commander begged to differ and issued summonses fining them for failure to fulfil the requisite number of drills. The Competent Military Authority for the area reported 'considerable friction' at Hull Police Court where the magistrates appear to have shown sympathy for the men against their officers though, in the event, they had to order the payment of the fines.[46] At the Bedfordshire Assizes in May 1940, three soldiers failed to appear to answer criminal charges. An officer attending the court sought to explain that he had heard from another officer that the men had been summoned to appear the following week. The judge was unimpressed with the excuse and declared that 'he personally was the direct representative of the King in the County and he objected to the casual way in which someone—he did not know who—was treating him.' He went on to state that he now expected a proper explanation from the military authorities, and to demand that two of the defendants appear before him at the Northamptonshire Assizes in the following week and that the third appear later at the Leicestershire Assizes. The Army complied.[47]

## THE PROBLEM OF THE 'CRIMINAL'

In the closing decades of the 19th century there were heated debates within the emerging discipline of Criminology—or Criminal Anthropology as it was often called—about the extent to which a criminal was moulded by heredity, nurture, or environment. The British were not prominent in these intellectual debates, but there was a popular assumption that the overwhelming majority of criminals came from what was termed the residuum, the lowest sections of the urban working class. Indeed, any glance at the police court columns of the Victorian and Edwardian press would have shown that the largest number of people brought before the courts were from the poor working class—though their crimes were invariably petty if, sometimes, violent. It was this class that produced the largest number of recruits, especially for the Army, and why soldiers still appeared to many to be 'the scum of the earth enlisted for drink'. It is always comforting to consider criminals as the 'other', a social group different and distinct from ordinary, law-abiding citizens.

Professional Army and Navy officers and provosts were inclined to blame 'criminals' for crimes committed by servicemen. Equally they were tempted to

---

equate many deserters with criminals; as one provost bluntly observed in August 1944: 'the majority of long-term deserters have civilian criminal records and are skilful and dangerous types.'[48] On the other hand this assertion was contradicted in the Army's own report on discipline during the Second World War, which stated that 89 per cent of deserters had no known record of civil crime or juvenile delinquency.[49] Reasons had to be found to decide which of the men sentenced to death for desertion during the First World War were to be executed; it was impossible to execute all 3,000 of them. During the second half of the 19th century the bureaucrats at the Home Office had developed a series of preconceptions that were converted into practice when considering who, among those sentenced to death, might benefit from the prerogative of mercy; but none of this was formulated and written down as 'rules'. The Army had no time to develop such a protocol; nor had a commander in previous conflicts ever been required to consider how to exercise mercy with such large numbers sentenced to death. There is evidence to suggest that many of the men selected for execution following a conviction for desertion or for a similar offence, were those who were regarded in the eugenicist's sense as inferior or worthless, or who were found to have committed criminal offences before they joined the Army.[50]

An analysis of the criminal careers of convicts in Dartmoor Prison at the time of the notorious riot in January 1932 underlines the difficulty of drawing clear distinctions between those offenders who had been in the armed services and those who had not. There were at the time of the riot 442 convicts in the prison, most of whom were considered to be among the country's most serious offenders. The criminal records of 427 men survive, revealing that forty-four of them, not one of whom had fewer than seven convictions, had at some point been convicted by a court martial. Twenty-six of these had been convicted during the First World War, and eight immediately afterwards; their offences ranged across theatres and involved everything from assault to larceny. Most of the forty-four men had committed their first criminal offence before joining the services but for nine, or one-fifth, their court-martial conviction was their first criminal conviction.[51]

There was recognition that an offender, released from prison on licence and with the requirement that he report regularly to the local police, might choose to enlist. There were some in the Army, and probably rather more in the civilian world who thought that an offender might find reformation in the services. In 1916 the Home Secretary instructed the Commissioner of the Metropolitan Police that 'no steps should be taken to enforce the obligation [to report to the police] as long as the man remains in His Majesty's services.' A circular to provincial chief constables suggested that they follow suit. When, in the post-Dunkirk summer of 1940, a man convicted of housebreaking was released on licence from Dartmoor and informed

---

[48] WO 204/6713, Plan for Special Drive against Absentees and Deserters.
[49] WO 277/7, 48–51.
[50] Oram, *Worthless Men* (1998b); for the developments in the Home Office see, Chadwick, *Bureaucratic Mercy* (1992).
[51] Brown, 'Crime, Criminal Mobility and Serial Offenders' (2011).

the Bideford Police that he had enlisted in the Pioneer Corps, the Devon Police asked if the same instructions applied in the new war. The Home Office concluded that, since such a large proportion of the forces were currently stationed in the British Isles, it was important that the police be kept informed of the whereabouts of men on licence; however, given the problem of where men on licence might be stationed, they were allowed to report by letter. There were only twelve such men in London at the time.[52]

Concern about habitual offenders making their way into the ranks led, in the autumn of 1942, to the creation of unskilled labour companies. It was thought that employing such companies on projects that assisted the civilian community would prove to be beneficial all round; it was subsequently estimated that about a third of the men passing through the companies were 'reformed' and restored to their fighting units. There remained concern about young delinquents finding their way into, and being allowed to continue serving in the Army.[53]

In 1940 several battalions of young soldiers, that is youths aged under 19 years, were recruited to guard installations such as aerodromes. Unfortunately the officers put in charge of them were often poorly selected for the task, the soldiers' training was poor, and their job was boring. As a result, a number of the youths slipped into various forms of offending. In May 1940, for example, two teenage soldiers were tried at the Northamptonshire Assizes for breaking and entering a railway store.

> Both were stated to have had good characters, but the police and a representative of the Army regarded [the elder, 19-year-old Private] Marshall as the ringleader and the military did not want him back because of his bad influence.

Private Marshall was sent to Borstal for 'not more than three years'; Private Charles, his 18-year-old accomplice, was bound over for twelve months and returned to his unit.[54] A year later an almost identical case, involving three teenage soldiers stealing from the Women's Voluntary Service canteen in Biggleswade, and for rifling the coin boxes in the town's public lavatory, had a similar outcome. Magistrates at the Biggleswade Petty Sessions bound over two of the soldiers for twelve months and returned them to their regiment; the third, who was seen as the ringleader and who had three previous convictions, was committed for Borstal training.[55] But at least as much of the offending by these junior soldiers involved purely military transgressions such as absence and indiscipline.

The Army's initial response was the creation of Young Soldiers' Training Camps staffed by carefully selected personnel; and in many respects these might be seen as the military equivalents of the civilian Borstal training institutions that had been created in the decade before the First World War and that had blossomed to considerable acclaim during the interwar period. The C-in-C Northern Command,

---

[52] MEPO 3/2035, Convicts on Licence Serving with HM Forces: Arrangements for reporting to the Police.
[53] WO 277/7, 69–71.
[54] *Bedfordshire Times and Standard*, 31 May 1940, 5.
[55] *Bedfordshire Times and Standard*, 23 May 1941, 3.

Sir Ronald Adam, played a key role in this response and when, early in 1942, he became adjutant general at the War Office, he was able to take matters further with the creation of Special Training Units (STUs). These units took much of their inspiration from the ideas of psychologists, most notably Cyril Burt, who had made his name in the interwar period with his work on young delinquents. One of the training officers, Joseph Treneman, subsequently explained:

> One-third of [the men sent to the STUs] were already manifestly delinquent, and the other two-thirds must have come from that vast fringe of potential delinquents (possibly two or three times as numerous as those convicted [ . . . ]) who might have been brought before the courts had the arm of the law been longer or more active.[56]

The STUs were considered to be an even greater success than the labour companies in the numbers of young men reformed and turned into good soldiers. The less partisan might suggest that, like other young offenders, those drafted into the STUs simply grew out of offending or that the categories of offending were so vast that some of the young men sent to the units might just as well have been dealt with by their own officers and NCOs.

T. W. 'Bill' Wood was not a petty thief and it would be difficult to label him as a juvenile offender in any way. He was eager to fight for his country and he tried to enlist in June 1940, two months short of his sixteenth birthday. His mother reported him to the recruiting sergeant as underage and he had to wait before joining the young soldiers' battalion of the King's Royal Rifle Corps. Wood was keen; he did not object to tough training or discipline, but disaffection set in when he was one of a squad of young soldiers sent to guard a dummy airfield in Essex. The huts on the airfield were in poor repair; the food was poor and the postal deliveries were uncertain. Worse still, there seems to have been little discipline; there were no parades and the officers were notable by their absence. The young soldiers got bored and hitched their way to London. Wood recalled: 'we were not missed, after all, we were guarding fake aircraft, fake guns, we were probably thought to be cardboard cut-outs.' But when Wood surrendered himself as absent without leave he was sent before a court martial and sentenced to 112 days in Chorley Detention Barracks. After about two months in Chorley he was sent to a Young Soldiers' Training Camp. He arrived with a strained shoulder and an abscess under his arm, but after a spell in hospital he found that, under the liberal regime in the camp, he regained 'health, pride and self-respect'. He transferred to the Royal Engineers and went on to serve in 617 Assault Squadron, fighting across Europe from the Normandy beaches to northern Germany.[57]

There were those who believed that the young tearaway was, potentially, the ideal soldier in the making. What he needed was direction to harness his youthful aggression. Lord Baden-Powell was one of the best-known and most influential spokesmen for this way of thinking, but such sentiments were also found in, for

---

[56] Crang, *The British Army and the People's War* (2000), 81–2; Trenaman, *Out of Step* (1952), 30. Trenaman's book had a preface by Sir Cyril Burt. See also, WO 277/7, 63–8.
[57] IWM (D) 99/31/1, T. W. Wood, 2–3.

example, two books written by Robert Holmes who had served for seventeen years as a police court missionary and probation officer. In 1915 Holmes published *My Police Court Friends with the Colours*, writing, he said, with pride in the valour of these young men, and sorrow at the way in which society had allowed them to grow up in the shameful home conditions that led to their early offences. In the following year, with the more sensational title of *Walter Greenway, Spy*, he wrote with surprise of some of his 'saddest failures'—young offenders whom he had considered incorrigible—who had found in the war 'an opportunity for regeneration.'[58] Sir Basil Thomson, appointed Assistant Commissioner at Scotland Yard in 1913 and head of the Criminal Investigation Department, maintained that in 1915 there were 1,100 habitual criminals serving in the armed forces, and that more than seventy others had been killed. One such had committed murder, had had his death sentence commuted to penal servitude for life, had subsequently been released on licence, and 'was one of the first to answer the call.' Another, whom Thomson claimed to know personally, had won the Victoria Cross for silencing a German machine gun and had later been killed. The man had offended, Thomson maintained, 'through a love of adventure, and [he] was as free of egotism, pose and self-consciousness as any of the men I knew.'[59]

Criminal behaviour in civilian life did not mean that an individual made a poor soldier or sailor. Joseph Sabini, for example, belonged to a family that was notorious for violence in support of its bookmaking activities. He served as an infantryman on the Western Front, was wounded, invalided out of the service, and pensioned. He promptly returned to his family's trade and, in 1922, was sentenced to three years' penal servitude for his part in a gang shooting. Isaac 'Ikey' Bogard, more commonly known as 'Darky the Coon', came from the same tough East End streets as the Sabinis. Before the First World War he acquired a fearsome reputation as a pimp and a thug who regularly, and openly, carried a gun in his belt. After the war he collected 'rent' from market stallholders in Petticoat Lane and in neighbouring Wentworth Street; he provided protection for this rent. During the First World War, however, he had served in the South Wales Borderers and won the Military Medal. During the Second World War he was a stretcher-bearer in the City of London ARP and received a commendation from the king for conspicuous bravery.[60] The piratical Ronald John Chesney followed the finest traditions of the Royal Navy as the small ship that he commanded was blasted to pieces by German gunfire at Tobruk. He strode courageously about the deck, inspiring his men, directed fire against the enemy, and was the last man to leave his floundering

---

[58] Holmes, *My Police Court Friends* (1915a); Holmes, *Walter Greenway, Spy* (1915b), p. v.

[59] Thomson, *Queer People* (1922), 50–2; these pages were reproduced virtually unchanged in Thomson, *The Scene Changes* (1939), 217–18.

[60] Morton, *East End Gangland* (2000), 129, 143, and 152–3; Samuel, *East End Underworld* (1981), 151–2, 158–9, and 320–1. *London Gazette*, 23 February 1918, 7, under the list of men decorated with the Military Medal: '263049, Pte. I. Bogard, S.W. Borderers (Stratford E.)'. My thanks to Stefan Dickers of the Bishopsgate Institute for providing me with additional information on 'Darky'.

ship. But Chesney had already got away with one murder and went on to commit two more, as well as engaging in large-scale racketeering.[61]

Many more men than women appeared before British courts charged with criminal offences during the nineteenth and early twentieth centuries. The female element of the residuum or 'the criminal classes' was the prostitute. While crime was something largely committed by men, and specifically young men, the armed services were reserved solely for men. Women had lived and travelled with soldiers; they had cooked and nursed; sometimes they were wives, sometimes not. Such women were called 'camp followers'; the term acquired negative connotations and became virtually synonymous with prostitute. The manpower demands of the two world wars of the 20th century meant that, in spite of the reluctance of many senior army and naval officers, women began to gain a foothold in the armed services. Initially they were given special ranks that separated their commanders from male commissioned officers and that did not require them to be saluted by men. The women who served in uniform during these wars were often eyed with suspicion and slandered as immoral. Women soldiers of the Auxiliary Territorial Service (ATS) in the Second World War were known as 'the groundsheets of the Army' and 'the Auxiliary Tarts Service'. Until 1941, when they acquired full military status, they were not subjected to military discipline at home, and it was not until September 1944 that those who volunteered for overseas service were subject to such discipline when overseas. Similar problems existed in the Navy. In the summer of 1941, for example, two WRNS were caught attempting to smuggle service tobacco off their base. The major problem for the Admiralty in this instance was how best to punish them; a naval rating guilty of such an offence could be sentenced to five days in the cells but, like the early ATS, the WRNS were not subject to naval discipline and there was no provision for putting them in custody.[62]

The military authorities were determined to keep women out of combat; even those serving in anti-aircraft batteries could do anything and everything but fire the guns. Most women service personnel cleaned, cooked, or worked in administration or in stores; and, as is described below, there were considerable opportunities for theft and fraud in administration, cookhouses, and stores. Service women also committed military offences such as going absent without leave and contravening Section 40; and there were offences unique to women to be found under Section 40, such as wearing stockings inside out, which made them look shinier and more transparent.[63] Unfortunately it is not possible to compare the scale of offending between male and female service personnel as there is no gender distinction in service crime statistics. However the paucity of evidence, the general lack of comment and concerns when confronted with women offenders, suggests that

[61] Tullett, *Portrait of a Bad Man* (1956).

[62] ADM 175/258, Smuggling Offences by WRNS.

[63] IWM (D) 96/34/1, Mrs L. Orde, f. 122. For a general survey of women in the Army see Noakes, *Women in the British Army* (2006).

female service personnel appear, like their civilian sisters, largely to have avoided participation in crime.

The explanation that crime was committed by criminals is, in reality, no explanation. Crime tends mostly to be sporadic, opportunistic behaviour, largely committed by young men; and they appear to grow out of it. There are relatively few people who, either through the contingencies of life experience or through a conscious decision, pursue a career that involves breaking laws on a regular basis. Servicemen are encouraged to be aggressive and their duties can involve violence. The new military family for the young man might also be said to resemble a gang whose members are required to behave by a code that is different from that of civilian life, to obey the gang leaders, and to look out for each other. Some of the offending by service personnel fits with the gang mentality; and still more fits with the run-of-the-mill offending by young men not in uniform.

# 2

# 'A Court of Justice and Not a Court of Law!'

## Courts and Justice in the Services

When 17-year-old Bill Wood was sentenced to 112 days' imprisonment for being absent without leave, he was sent initially to Chorley Detention Barracks. During the Victorian period the armed services, like civilian society, had witnessed an increase in the use of incarceration with a decline of corporal punishment. Civilian prisons were grim in the first half of the 20th century; military prisons appear to have been worse. Until the creation of the STUs, young absentees like Wood were mixed with tough old offenders. Wood remembered Prison Diet 1 (PD1) as inedible; PD2, the punishment diet, was bread and water. Everything had to be done at the double, including the assault course. The latter was made more difficult by the requirement that men wear gas masks and full marching order over their greatcoats as they struggled over the course; some men collapsed. Resistance could lead to a beating; no one dared to complain. The NCOs who ran the centre bullied and shouted at everyone.[1] Rifleman R. L. Crimp painted a similar picture in his diary, admittedly second-hand, after a comrade was sentenced to fifty-six days in the Military Prison in Cairo for trying to dodge the postal censor when he sent a letter to his wife. The corporal, who escorted Rifleman Randall to the prison, expressed fury at Randall's treatment on arrival. He had to double round a yard in full kit being screamed at by a sergeant. He was ordered to halt, put his kit down, then pick it up and run round again for not being smart enough.

> 'Worse than the Nazi SS', says Corporal Furze. 'And that's what we're fighting the bloody war against!' Talk about everyone finding his niche in this Fred Karno Army! It makes your blood boil to think of Randall, a normal bloke not shirking his share of the shite, being kicked around by sadistic thugs whose only virtue is a brutality which is counterpart to the cowardice which keeps them out of the front line.[2]

Wood's and especially Crimp's comments reflect the attitudes of front-line soldiers who knew and depended on their comrades, and who resented those behind the line exerting authority in what seemed like pettifogging and irrelevant ways. There

[1] IWM (D) 99/31/1, T. W. Wood, '"On Tracks" with the Armoured Engineers 1943–1946', f. 31.
[2] IWM (D) 96/50/1, R. L. Crimp, vol 3, ff. 96 and 100; diary entries 16 March and 6 April 1944. Crimp's papers consist of four manuscript volumes; the first of these was edited and published, see Crimp, *Diary of a Desert Rat* (1971). Fred Karno was a popular comedian at the time of the First World War who gave his name to a celebrated soldiers' song: 'We are Fred Karno's Army,/The ragtime infantry;/We cannot fight, we cannot shoot,/What earthly use are we?/And when we get to Berlin,/The Kaiser he will say/"Hoch, hoch! Mein Gott,/What a bloody fine lot/Are the ragtime infantry!"'

does not appear to have been much similar complaint about criminal offences by servicemen tried in civilian courts. Courts martial, however, appeared particularly vexing when the offence was, in the eyes of the fighting soldier, a minor infringement of regulations, and even a court martial for major infringement of regulations could provoke anger and resentment if it was felt that it had been committed with some justification.

## PARALLEL HISTORIES: CIVILIAN COURTS AND MILITARY COURTS

In the same way that most civilian crimes in England, Wales, and Scotland were heard in courts of summary jurisdiction presided over by some kind of magistrate acting without a jury, so most military offences were heard summarily before a senior commissioned officer of the unit in which a man served. Indeed, many petty offences against discipline did not even get this far. Some junior officers on the Western Front considered that their men had been through enough and ignored even serious military offences; a man found asleep on watch might be woken with a cough, with nothing more said.[3] During the Second World War Lieutenant Nicholas Mosley was extremely reluctant to put any of his platoon on a charge and preferred to leave any reproof 'to the verbal pyrotechnics of the sergeants'. Mosley, who had volunteered for service before being called up and who felt that he suffered from two problems—a serious stammer and being Oswald Mosley's son— thought that leaving such matters to NCOs helped him to bond better with his men.[4] Sergeants or senior warrant officers often offered offenders their choice of punishment; they could have a thump administered behind a hut or vehicle shed; or they could be paraded before the company commander, and run the risk of being confined to barracks, or given extra fatigues or a fine. Occasionally the thump behind the hut and aggressive abuse or ill-treatment was excessive, and a few officers and NCOs found themselves before courts martial for striking or ill-treating men under their command.[5] Sometimes the warrant officers punished using very unorthodox methods. At the close of the Second World War, a sergeant major with twenty-one years' service in the infantry, reassigned to an Ordnance Depot at Reading, was reported as setting recruits written lines, in the tradition of public schools, for minor offences.[6]

In his celebrated memoir of the First World War, Robert Graves described how new officers spent much of their time in company or battalion orderly rooms learning how to deal with petty offenders. Very probably with a degree of dramatic licence and temporal elasticity, Graves estimated that, before his battalion went to France, individual cases in the battalion orderly room were dealt with at the rate of

---

[3] Sheffield, *Leadership in the Trenches* (2000), 87–9.
[4] Mosley, *Time at War* (2006), 20.
[5] French, *Military Identities* (2005), 191.
[6] Holmes, *Soldiers* (2011), p. xxii; *Daily Mirror*, 3 May 1946, 1.

three to four minutes each, but that the total proceedings could last for up to four or five hours a day. 'The usual [ . . . ] crimes were desertion, refusing to obey an order, using obscene language to a non-commissioned officer, drunk and disorderly, robbing a comrade, and so forth.'[7] In the orderly room the senior officer would hear the charge and offer the offender the opportunity of opting for a court martial or accepting the officer's punishment. The hope and expectation was that the offender would accept the officer's punishment of a fine, fatigues, or being confined to barracks. Such informal and internal settlements of offences avoided the washing of a battalion's or a regiment's dirty linen in public in a court martial; in some ways it mirrored the choice given to civilians charged with less serious offences of having magistrates decide the case, or risking potentially more severe punishment by taking a chance with a jury in a higher court. The problem was that soldiers were not always aware of their rights and there was no one to advise them. Writing to the editor of the *Manchester Guardian* in 1946, a former captain in the Royal Engineers considered that sergeant majors really ran the orderly room and could make the procedure 'a veritable pantomime [ . . . ] deliberately calculated to make the accused feel ill at ease.' Moreover, in wartime the officer conducting the summary hearing might himself be uncertain of the procedures and if he omitted to mention the accused's right of opting for a court martial 'far too few sergeant majors will remind him of this duty until afterwards, and nothing in military law or the rules of procedure provides a remedy for this injustice.'[8]

Summary punishment awarded in the orderly room might be relatively mild, but it did not necessarily lead to any satisfaction on the part of the accused. In October 1943, in order to spend an extra twelve hours with his family, Gunner Bernard Small took a gamble with tight train connections in coming back from leave. The gamble failed and Small found himself in the orderly room. He thought the officer 'an insufferable egotistic prig' but since this was his first offence and quite a common one, he agreed to accept the officer's sentence. Initially seven days' confined to barracks did not seem harsh, but Small soon found himself subjected to irritating fatigues such as chopping wood and painting steel helmets. On the third day of his sentence the officer expressed surprise that Small seemed 'browned off'. Small responded that he thought his treatment harsh and unjust, and that he had always thought that the 'ideal' was that the punishment should fit the crime.[9] He was probably lucky to avoid another charge. In overseas theatres, the informal resolution of even relatively serious matters could avoid major incidents; and in some instances of this type the suspect was never even brought to a summary trial. A decade after the end of the Second World War, during the EOKA emergency in Cyprus, a soldier caught smuggling guns to Turkish Cypriots was put on the first plane home immediately after the discovery of his offence. He was not prosecuted and nothing more was said about the matter in order to avoid an international

---

[7] Graves, *Goodbye to All That* (1960), 68.
[8] *Manchester Guardian*, 24 April 1946, 4.
[9] Small, *Reluctant Gunner* (1983), 201–5.

incident.[10] The major problem is that such incidents leave no paper trail for the historian to pursue, though anecdote suggests that such solutions were not uncommon.

A similar system existed in the Royal Navy, with petty offenders and defaulters being dealt with by their ship's captain. In the summer of 1940, for example, when four Italian destroyers purchased by the Swedish government were seized by the Royal Navy for fear that they might fall into German hands, several seamen were sent before their captain for looting during the seizure. Their punishments ranged from five days in the cells to the loss of a good conduct badge.[11] Summary trials and summary punishments had expanded enormously in the Navy in the years immediately before the First World War, but there was little information available to men on their legal rights; indeed, seeking to find the extent of legal rights in itself was likely to get a man into trouble. The situation improved during the first war and, particularly after the Invergordon Mutiny of 1931, the Admiralty began to recognize increasingly that it had an industrialized workforce that required management rather than simply orders. An article in the *Naval Review* in 1944 advised young officers that summary justice 'sympathetically and intelligently administered [ . . . ] can be the fairest form of justice.' It argued that the discipline and morale of the ship depended upon it and consequently 'Rule One is: see to it that your summary justice is utterly fair and impartial.'[12] But there were still complaints about punishment imposed by a ship's captain, especially since the loss of badges and medals, and disrating, could affect both a man's promotion chances and his pension.[13] In 1942 Regulating Petty Officer Harry Frederick Houghton lost his long-service medal and a good-conduct badge for returning to HMS *Ramilles* allegedly the worse for drink, fifty minutes late from leave, contravening ship's orders by attempting to enter by the foremost gangway and making an improper remark to a superior. Arguments about Houghton's sentence continued until he left the Navy in 1946. He believed that he should have had the assistance of an officer in dealing with the charges; he also felt that the subsequent black mark against him meant that he never made the rank of master-at-arms, and this ultimately affected his pension.[14] Shortly after the war, Master-at-Arms Norman Wellesly Bullard protested against being brought before a court martial for smuggling cigarettes. Bullard and his defending officer, or 'friend', felt this could have been settled by his ship's captain rather than being taken further. Bullard's conviction for the offence by the court martial led to his disrating to regulating petty officer and the loss of good-conduct medals and badges; a captain's sentence might have been much less and certainly less public.[15] Offences settled informally in orderly rooms and before a ship's captain, for obvious reasons, rarely turn up in the

---

10  Information from an interview with a group of retired MPs, 3 June 2010.
11  ADM 178/218, Thefts from Swedish Ships in British Custody, 1940.
12  Quoted in Prysor, *Citizen Sailors* (2011), 409.
13  Carew, *Lower Deck* (1981), 39–41 and 144.
14  ADM 178/372, Complaints against captain's punishment, 1942–46.
15  ADM 156/298, Smuggling cigarettes, 1948.

official record and never in the official statistics, even when they involved offences that might be considered as crimes in the civilian world.

## COURTS MARTIAL

In England and Wales the more serious civilian criminal offences were heard before juries at courts of Quarter Sessions, at Assizes or, in London, at the Central Criminal Court held at the Old Bailey. The Quarter Sessions were presided over by magistrates, the majority of whom had little or no formal legal training; they were advised on matters of law by a clerk. The Assize courts were presided over by judges who were recruited from leading barristers. This situation was largely paralleled in Scotland by the local Sheriffs' courts and the High Court of Justiciary, which met either on circuit or in Edinburgh. The military equivalents of these higher courts were the courts martial. Just as the civilian accused could, in certain lesser offences, opt to go to have his or her case heard before a jury at a higher court, so service personnel could opt to have their case heard before a court martial. This was the choice offered to Gunner Small, and the choice that had been demanded, unsuccessfully, by Private Heddon twenty-five years before. The difference between the civilian and the military higher courts, however, was that there was no jury of the accused's peers to decide on the evidence presented at a court martial.

In the Royal Navy the system of courts martial was relatively straightforward. Such courts were held when a commanding officer considered an offence to be sufficiently serious as to be beyond his competence. They could also be requested by a petty officer who did not wish to submit to his commanding officer's judgement and who was likely to be disrated if found guilty. The courts were convened by the Crown or its deputy, usually the commander-in-chief, and consisted of between five and nine officers. A sentence did not require the commander-in-chief's confirmation, but it could be revised by the Board of the Admiralty. For the Army, up until the end of the First World War, there were four types of courts martial. The most serious offences, committed either by officers or by other ranks, were heard before a General Court Martial (GCM). This court was convened under the same authority as those for the Navy—that is, technically by the Crown but generally by the commander-in-chief. At home such a court needed thirteen commissioned officers to make up its board; overseas such a court could meet with just five officers. Any decision by a GCM had to be confirmed by the convening authority. The Field General Court Martial (FGCM) was often used in wartime. It required three commissioned officers; in addition it required unanimity for any death sentence. A District Court Martial (DCM) could not try officers and it could not hear the more serious charges. The more rare Regimental Court Martial was similarly restricted in the kinds of cases that it could try, and this particular court was dispensed with in 1920.[16]

---

[16] Smith, 'Military Law' (1969).

There were no permanent court buildings for the courts martial and they could be convened in any suitable hall or structure that was available. There were attempts to ensure that they had all of the aura and dignity of a civilian court, though recalcitrant individuals could cause embarrassment. Again the Australian Imperial Force provides some of the more colourful examples. John Hatherley was a tailor in civilian life. He volunteered and left his native Colac, about 80 miles from Melbourne, early in the First World War; in the autumn of 1916 he was at Codford on Salisbury Plain where he was posted for guard duty at several courts martial. He wrote home to his sister explaining how the proceedings were conducted 'in great style' and with 'great dignity' until

> a hard-faced fellow was brought in. The Officer started to address him but he would keep chipping in; at last the Officer told him to be silent; that did it. He shook his fist at the Officer and yelled out 'I'm going to have my say, you are a bloody bastard, f— you f— you all.' Well Ida if you had been in the room, you could have knocked them all over with a feather [ . . . ]
>
> Another fellow at a Court Martial upset the table with ink, papers and everything else on.[17]

The proceedings of the courts were open and the press had the right to attend. This openness was confirmed early in 1915 following discussion at a court martial in Woolwich convened after trouble at a boxing match involving two sergeants of the artillery.[18] Yet Major Gerald Hurst, a Conservative MP who, in the aftermath of the war, was among those urging reform, estimated that 'no civilian is present as a spectator at 999 out of every 1,000 cases at home, or in any case whatever on active service abroad.'[19] Even a soldier not obviously connected with a court martial might be turned away by the guard on the door. This happened to Private Stuart Dolden in France towards the end of 1915. But Dolden, a patriotic volunteer of 1914, was a solicitor in civilian life and was acting as the 'friend' of a senior NCO on a charge of being drunk while on duty in the trenches.[20] Writing in 1932, T. Hannam-Clark, who had served as a court martial officer on the Western Front at the end of the war, noted that he had never seen anyone not on duty attempt to attend such a court and that there appeared to be a continuing impression that courts martial were secret. 'A Sergeant-Major of great experience has told me in perfect confidence that no entrance is allowed except on business. Perhaps this view was generally prevalent and enforced. But it was quite wrong.'[21] Few soldiers, and few civilians, however, would seek to argue with any guard, let alone any sergeant major 'of great experience' standing at the door of a court.

Naval justice never appears to have been quite as contentious among the general public as that of the Army, yet the supervision of the two systems was similar. The Judge Advocate of the Fleet (JAF), a civilian lawyer, was responsible for the

---

[17] Quoted in Wyeth, *Swords and Ploughshares* (2007), 60.
[18] *The Scotsman*, 19 January 1915, 9, and 21 January, 5; see also, *The Times*, 21 January 1915, 5.
[19] Hurst, 'The Administration of Military Law' (1919), 321.
[20] Dolden, *Cannon Fodder* (1980), 50.
[21] Hannam-Clark, *Some Experiences* (1932), 15.

supervision of courts martial working together with the Chief Naval Judge Advocate, a serving naval officer with legal training. The post of JAF was not seen as a full-time commitment in the first half of the century. In the summer of 1944, for example, there was a minor kerfuffle when Lhind Pratt, the JAF, accepted the full-time appointment of a police magistrate in London. The Home Secretary was surprised when Pratt assumed that he would be maintaining the naval post alongside his new duties in the metropolis. After some airing of opinions and an exchange of letters, it was eventually agreed that he would continue as JAF until six months after the end of hostilities in Europe.[22]

Justice in the Army and, after its independent formation, the Royal Air Force, was overseen by the Judge Advocate General (JAG), a senior civilian lawyer. The men appointed as Judge Advocate General appear to have been much more heavyweight political figures than those appointed to the similar position within the Navy. From 1902 to 1916 the post was held by Thomas Milvain, a lawyer and Conservative MP. From 1916 to 1934 it was Sir Felix Cassel, a barrister and also a former MP who had volunteered and been commissioned on the outbreak of war in 1914; he returned from France the following year initially to act as Milvain's deputy. Cassel was succeeded, in turn, by Sir Henry MacGeagh, another barrister who, as a Territorial Army officer had served on the Western Front until 1916 when he was recruited as a military assistant to the JAG's office. In 1923 MacGeagh was appointed as the head of the new Military and Air Force Branch of the office, which was given responsibility for prosecutions; he was also given the rank of colonel. When he was appointed as JAG in 1934 he resigned his commission; the JAG was, after all, a judicial officer independent of the War Office, though there were suspicions voiced periodically about the extent of this independence.[23]

During the Victorian period the JAG had often been regarded by senior military commanders as something of an imposition. They disliked his insistence on the primacy of judicial authority when they considered the maintenance of discipline to be one of their principal concerns and one that might be impeded by legal niceties. There was some clarification of roles in the aftermath of the Boer War when a greater degree of political authority was asserted over the Army. Henceforth, rather than receiving his authority and commission directly from the sovereign, the commander-in-chief was appointed by the Secretary of State for War. At the same time, the Judge Advocate General was subordinated to the directions of the same Secretary of State. By 1914 the JAG and his deputies were advising on how charges should be framed and on the procedure for courts martial. The requirements insisted upon by the legal officers probably still raised irritation among some senior officers. It was, for example, necessary to prove that individuals accused of failing to perform specific tasks were actually responsible for those tasks and that any objects purloined were the same or similar to objects that had gone missing. It might raise a smile to speculate about how the brigadier general

---

[22] ADM 1/15669.
[23] For these issues, and the development of the JAG's office, see Rubin, 'The Status of the Judge Advocate General' (1994).

commanding Thames and Medway Reserve Brigade in October 1914 received the following response from the JAG's office.

> I am unable to understand how both of the accused can have been in command of the guard, and there is at present no evidence to support the charge against either of them. If it was the duty of either of them to see that the sentries were in fact performing their duties at the time when they were found absent, a charge under section 40 might be brought for neglect of not doing so; or if the accused were acting improperly in going to sleep, a charge in respect of that might be brought. In either case it must be proved that the accused had been ordered to be in command of the guard, if being in command is to form an essential part of the charge.
>
> Unless definite evidence can be produced of some breach of duty the accused should not be put upon their trial.[24]

During the First World War, court martial officers began to be appointed by both the Navy Advocate General's and the JAG's offices to advise the courts on matters of law and procedure. These judges advocate, generally men who had a legal training outside the services as barristers or solicitors, also summed up at the end of serious cases and advised the officers of the court on sentencing. As T. Hannam-Clark put it: 'My position was similar to that of a Judge to a Jury or a Clerk to a bench of magistrates, except that I also took part in deciding the verdict.'[25] But legal niceties raised by men with expertise in civilian law appear to have prompted occasional irritation among some officers, especially those wanting to use their discretion. In 1935 Lord Strabolgi, who had served as a naval officer for seventeen years, explained to readers of the *Daily Mirror* how courts martial were conducted in the Navy.

> Common sense and common justice prevail. Legal quibbles count for little. Civilian lawyers can appear for the defence and frequently do; but I have heard a lawyer who tried to tie a witness up with intricate word-spinning and legal sophistries reminded that a court martial is a court of justice and not a court of law![26]

Given the hierarchy of the services, any junior officer who raised a point of law, especially outside the trial itself, could find himself in trouble. Samuel Elworthy was already a qualified barrister when he joined the RAF during the 1930s. Together with other junior 'officers under instruction', he was ordered to attend the court martial of a corporal accused of desertion. He was shocked at the way hearsay evidence was introduced and when, as part of his training, he was ordered to write an essay on what he had seen, he expressed his concerns. His plain speaking led to him being marched before his station commander for a severe dressing-down. About a month later, however, the JAG reversed the guilty conviction against the corporal and the station commander called Elworthy in to enquire about his knowledge of legal proceedings. Over the next few years, whenever there

---

[24] WO 84/9 fol. 389.
[25] Hannam-Clark, *Some Experiences* (1932), 16.
[26] *Daily Mirror*, 28 February 1935, 12; see also Bourke, *Dismembering the Male* (1996), 96.

was a court martial at the station, Elworthy found himself either prosecuting or defending.[27]

In spite of the possible irritation of some senior officers, the few surviving transcripts of naval courts martial during the Second World War reveal that judges advocate frequently interjected to ensure that legal correctness was observed and understood. Among other things, they warned that leading questions should not be asked, that hearsay evidence was inadmissible and that so too was evidence irrelevant to the charge faced by the accused.[28] The surviving transcripts for Army courts martial are similar. Generally they show a careful observance of legal correctness even when, as in mutiny cases, the verdicts appeared harsh and unforgiving. During a trial for attempted murder in 1941, for example, the Judge Advocate pressured a young officer about how, exactly, he had acquired a statement from the accused. With the *Manual of Military Law* open in front of him the Judge Advocate wanted to know: had the soldier been informed, as the *Manual* required, that he did not have to make a statement but that if he did it would be taken down and could be used in evidence? Was the soldier told that he was under oath? Was the soldier explicitly ordered to make the statement?[29] The young officer probably felt intimidated, but so too did most of the other ranks who found themselves before the senior officers seated before them hearing the case.

At the beginning of the century, soldiers and sailors tried before a court martial were permitted a 'friend' to advise them. In the Navy before the First World War, lower-deck societies were known to engage lawyers for the accused, such was the suspicion of courts martial, particularly by the skilled men working as, for example, engineers on the ships. Initially these 'friends' could do little more than advise an accused on what questions to ask; they themselves were not permitted to cross-examine. It was also known for lawyers to challenge verdicts on legal niceties and, as a result, to get a sentence annulled.[30] On active service, especially close to the front, an Army officer with legal training could be difficult to find and the accused had to make do with whoever could be found to act as his 'friend'. In 1919 evidence was presented to an enquiry into military courts martial that 'in some instances superior authorities have actively discouraged officers from appearing on behalf of accused persons.'[31]

At the conclusion of a court martial, as Hannam-Clark explained, the court martial officer advised on the possible sentence. In turn, the JAG and his deputies also advised the commander-in-chief on the confirmation of sentences and on any petitions received from soldiers concerning their sentence. Petitions, and the recommendations of officers, were the only appeals permitted to soldiers under sentence; and they went no further than the commander-in-chief. In the case of the

---

[27] IWM (S) 3187, Samuel Elworthy, reel 2.

[28] See, for example, ADM 156/235 (hearsay, or could a bosun's mate actually hear an exchange?); ADM 156/250 (for evidence not pertinent to the case); ADM 156/261 (not to ask leading questions).

[29] WO 71/725, FGCM of Pte I. G. C. Smith. For courts martial of mutineers see below pp. 116–19.

[30] Carew, *Lower Deck* (1981), 33.

[31] *Report of the Committee Constituted by the Army Council to Enquire into the Law and the Rules of Procedure Regulating Military Courts Martial*, Cmd. 428, 7.

Navy, petitions and appeals were forwarded to, and decided upon by senior officers at the Admiralty.

The fact that numbers of soldiers were shot for desertion during the First World War contributed to the contentious nature of Army courts martial. The fact that prosecutions were planned within the JAG's office and that this office supplied advice on the confirmation of sentences gave it a more public and, perhaps, a more sinister face than its naval counterpart; it also created difficulty and embarrassment. For this reason, in 1923, the Military and Air Force Department was created under MacGeagh. The new department operated largely independently and was concerned with the preparation of trials; the main office was concerned with judicial matters arising during or after trials. The general public, the press, and many politicians did not grasp these distinctions. Two cases aroused concern during the interwar years: that of Lieutenant Norman Baillie-Stewart—'the officer in the Tower'—charged with supplying military information to Germany; and that of Lieutenant Colonel Herbert Sandford, charged with fraud. A Committee of Enquiry appointed in 1938 found that not one of the seventeen miscarriages of justice alleged within the system of courts martial since 1917 could be sustained, but it also noted that there was a widespread belief that the military department responsible for prosecutions worked hand-in-glove with the civilian legal department of the JAG's office. The committee advised the removal of the prosecutions department from the nominal control of the JAG and recommended making the position of Judge Advocate General much closer to that of a high court judge. The Lord Chancellor was unhappy about the recommendation but the outbreak of the Second World War halted any further deliberation or action.[32]

The evidence from the JAG's correspondence during the Second World War is that there was a determination in his office to maintain the letter of the law and to ensure fairness all round. In August 1944, for example, it was recommended that the verdict passed on a private in the Glosters should be quashed since the court martial was constituted 'otherwise that in accordance with the convening officer's directions' and therefore lacked jurisdiction. In the same month the JAG was critical of the decision by a corps commander to quash the proceedings of the court martial of a gunner who had pleaded guilty to stealing a valise. The corps commander had been informed that there was an inconsistency in the plea.

> The view taken here [ . . . ] is that the statement in mitigation by the defending officer could not possibly be construed as anything but a mitigating address, and even if, instead of reading the observations as a whole, it was decided on the advice of extracts divorced from their contexts [ . . . ] I do not think that any lawyer could say that these extracts constitute a defence to the charge of stealing.[33]

In difficult and delicate cases, such as the prosecution of a corporal in the Catering Corps for indecently assaulting two girls aged under eight years, the JAG's office

---

[32] Rubin, 'The Status of the Judge Advocate General' (1994); *Report of the Army and Air Force Court Martial Committee, 1938*, Cmd. 6200.
[33] WO 81/177, ff. 219 and 302.

recommended first, that an officer experienced in prosecuting at courts martial should be appointed, and second, that if the accused could not pay for professional legal aid, then he should be offered the assistance of a legally qualified officer.[34] In cases such as this, the JAG's office also advised caution and discretion. In November 1939, for example, a private of the King's Own Royal Regiment, who had expressed sympathy for Sir Oswald Mosley, was suspected of having left British Union of Fascist pamphlets and posters in the regimental training centre. The JAG was wary about a prosecution, given that the Fascist movement might well arrange to defend the soldier at any trial. He suggested two alternatives to a court martial: either to discharge the man or, since he was said to have been refraining from his previous political behaviour, 'give him a chance to make good, being suitably watched by the Provost Sergeant or some other responsible non-commissioned officer of the unit.'[35]

The presence of professionals acting for both the prosecution and the defence meant that there was often very little difference between the conduct of serious cases before courts martial and the conduct of serious cases in civilian courts. Private I. G. C. Smith, for example, tried for attempted murder in May 1941, was defended by a junior lieutenant of the Royal Artillery who was also a barrister. Lieutenant Levy put down a marker of his expertise at the opening of Smith's trial by pointing out that he had received very short notice of the date of the trial and had not had time to confer with the accused and prepare his defence. After a thirty-minute adjournment, during which he spoke with Smith, Levy agreed to proceed without further delay. He then went on to show considerable acumen in the way in which he challenged the prosecution's case. In particular he raised questions about the new, American rifle recently issued to Smith's unit, and with which Smith had wounded his fellow soldier. The rifle had a different loading action from that of the ordinary British Lee Enfield, and its safety catch was on the opposite side.[36] But officers like Levy were not always readily available, especially when overseas near a front line.

Some of the defending officers who did not have legal training might have resented the role; others appear to have thought it an interesting challenge. The lack of legal training could have been the prompt for Major G. G. Raphael of the Judge Advocate General's Branch in Scottish Command writing to his superiors early in the Second World War asking what advice he should give defending officers about putting a soldier's character before a court martial. The advice of the more experienced judge advocates was that it was neither necessary nor wise that even a judge advocate should be advised of an accused's bad character 'having regard to the fact that they are supposed to be as impartial as possible and go into closed Court with the members when they retire to consider their finding.' Raphael was also advised:

> Whenever you have reason to think that the defending officer does not know the results of putting in issue the character of the accused, when he has a bad character, see

[34] WO 84/71, f. 98.      [35] WO 84/53, 216–18.      [36] WO 71/725.

the defending officer as a matter of routine before the Proceedings open, and point out to him that, if his man has a good character, he is wise to put it in issue, but if he has a bad character, refer him to the rules of evidence relating to this matter.[37]

The situation might be complicated by the class divide between enthusiastic young officers acting for the defence and the fact that the individuals prosecuted, as with many of those accused before the civilian courts, came from poor backgrounds, lacked education, were sometimes inarticulate, sometimes stupid, sometimes naïve. Early in 1943, Lieutenant Harold Mitchell, serving with the Ox and Bucks in the Middle East, found himself appointed to defend two privates at a Field General Court Martial. Their offences were, respectively, drunkenness and striking a superior officer. Mitchell was excited; imagining himself to be the great, early 20th-century barrister Sir Edward Marshall Hall, he carefully studied the evidence, looking for inconsistencies and omissions. He was then rudely brought down to earth when he met the accused.

> For one insisted on pleading guilty, and the other told me a story that he 'couldn't remember' a thing that had happened—he must have gone into a species of trance. Fancy trying to get—not an hysterical jury—but the hard-bitten President of a F.G.C.M. to believe such a ridiculous story! Talk about bricks without straw.[38]

The officers who sat in judgement during a court martial were sworn not to disclose the votes or opinions of any of those sitting alongside them. There is little evidence about how they made their decisions, but there was the suspicion that, given the hierarchical nature of the armed services, the junior officers sitting as members of the court usually followed the lead of their superiors. Major Gerald Hurst gave examples of senior officers 'whose preconceptions of what punishments should be awarded, and of what the Court's findings should be' were well known. Members of a court martial who crossed such officers could find themselves labelled as 'too kind-hearted to be efficient disciplinarians' and have their careers checked. But, while he argued for greater transparency and openness, Hurst also thought that courts worked reasonably well and fairly, and there are many examples of officers using discretion rather than the full force of the law in coming to their decisions.[39] Lt. Col. J. W. Allen was appointed permanent president of courts martial for the 33rd Division on the Western Front for a short period at the end of 1916. He believed that it was his task 'to help the accused as much as possible'. In a letter home he described one man sent before his court from his old battalion; the man was 'rather a rotter' but Allen believed that the charge levelled against him was far too severe, and he appears to have exerted his authority to ensure a verdict of not guilty.[40] Stanley Brook described court proceedings from late 1917 or early 1918

[37] WO 81/168, f. 436.
[38] IWM (D) 97/7/1, W. H. Mitchell, letter of 31 January 1943.
[39] Hurst, 'The Administration of Military Law' (1919), 324–5; for examples of the use of discretion, particularly where the death penalty was involved, see, Bourke, *Dismembering the Male* (1996), 95–7.
[40] Brotherton, Liddle Collection, (GS) J. W. Allen, letter 406, 22 November 1916.

that appear to have been designed by the court's president to prevent junior officers from simply following the opinions of their superiors. Brook was a veteran of Gallipoli and later had been invalided from the Western Front with trench fever. Posted to Doncaster with a battalion of the King's Own Yorkshire Light Infantry, he found himself appointed to a court martial hearing the case of a Regular Army lieutenant who, possibly as the result of shell shock, had gone absent without leave and had been arrested in Paris wearing a major's tunic with decorations to which he was not entitled. The court comprised a major general, who was the president, four lieutenant colonels (including Brook's CO), two majors, a captain, and Second Lieutenant Brook himself. The general listed the officers in reverse order of seniority and, after clearing the court, required them to give their verdicts in that order. Whether or not this was the general's intention, this ensured that a junior officer did not feel compelled to follow the verdict of his immediate superior. Brook was also relieved that the captain had only an acting rank, and that he had received his commission after Brook, which meant that the captain had to cast the first vote.[41] According to Lord Strabolgi, this form of voting was the usual practice in the Navy.[42]

It might well have been the case that the professional officers who dominated at the beginning of both world wars generally took a tougher line than those serving only for the duration of the conflict. But there could also be divisions among the professionals sitting on the same case. In 1943 E. A. Arderne, then a lieutenant colonel, was appointed president of a court martial called to adjudicate on a mutiny involving fourteen NCOs and men. Four other officers joined Arderne to judge the case: two full colonels from the staff and two lieutenant colonels who, like Arderne, came from the battle area. The men were found guilty; the three lieutenant colonels voted for the death penalty; the two staff officers for prison sentences. 'When we voted for the death sentence', explained Arderne, 'we knew, of course, that they would never be shot. We simply wished to show that we considered death was a fitting punishment for the crime and that we would be satisfied if it was carried out.' The staff officers were probably more political animals, remembering the impact on the general public of such sentences during the First World War and recognizing that, whatever a battlefield commander believed about the necessity for examples, death sentences would not play well with the Army's reputation. The mutineers were given prison sentences and Arderne lamented that 'they would spend the rest of the war in safety and comfort. When peace came they were certain to get a suspended sentence under a general amnesty.'[43]

Lieutenant Colonel Martin Lindsay had a similar attitude. He lamented that the 'thirty-odd toughs' who came back from Durban with him in 1942 could not have been shot. 'They were all serving sentences of penal servitude for desertion, rape, arson and similar serious crimes, and then proceeded to beat up their guards and burn part of the ship.' Lindsay was sympathetic to men who genuinely lost their

---

[41] IWM (D) 06/61/1, S. G. A. Brook, no folio numbers.
[42] *Daily Mirror*, 28 February 1935, 12.
[43] IWM (D) 97/7/1, Brigadier E. A. Arderne, 'An Army Life, 1918–1944', f. 69.

nerve in battle but when, as president of several courts martial in Northern Europe in the concluding months of the war, it came to sentencing men for desertion, he calculated how much a sentence would be reduced. 'So if you think a man should get, say, four or six years, you pass a sentence of ten or fifteen respectively.' Even then it was likely that the man would only serve a few months. Lindsay was shocked and annoyed when, a few weeks before the war ended, the Army began confirming sentences in full rather than reducing them. He feared that a man with a good record, but who had cracked and deserted before a recent battle and who he had sentenced to ten years in the estimation that he would serve perhaps three or four, would now have to serve his full sentence.[44]

## 'HEADS WE WIN, TAILS YOU LOSE'

Lt. Col. J. W. Allen believed that 'the British Tommy is a fine fellow in his own way. They would steal the buttons off the next man's shirt and yet they would do anything for him if he was wounded.' He intensely disliked having to punish men and hoped that the prisoners brought before him could 'never accuse [him] of not being just to them in seeing that all the evidence they can produce is brought out.'[45] Nevertheless there was a general belief among both soldiers and sailors that examples were made by courts martial to enforce discipline regardless of the facts of a case and it was this in particular that led to feelings of injustice. The fact that sentences by a court martial were subject to confirmation was little consolation and the situation was aggravated by the lack of any system of appeal. Writing shortly before the First World War, Sergeant Robert Edmondson, who himself had twice faced a court martial, summed up the governing maxim of military law as: 'Heads we win, tails you lose.' Possibly soured by his own experiences, he was highly critical of both the courts and the officers that presided: 'poorer in natural intelligence, less educated, and more full of themselves and of their own importance than any other class of persons I have had any personal knowledge of.'[46]

Concerns about the fairness of courts martial and their verdicts were not confined to NCOs and men. In April 1916, Lieutenant John Theodore Foxell of the Royal Engineers was stationed in Poperinghe, Belgium. On 29 April he recorded in his meticulously kept diary that one of the sappers under his command was under close arrest on a charge of attempted rape. The man, allegedly, had merely lifted a Belgian girl of around ten or eleven years old off a ladder in a billet. The girl was frightened and had run to her mother. The mother had reported the incident to a Belgian gendarme who, in turn, had called the British Military Police and, on the instigation of the Assistant Provost Marshal (APM), the man had been put in the cells. On hearing the news, Foxell went immediately to the APM who

[44] Lindsay, *So Few Got Through* (1946), 24, 225, and 262–3.
[45] Brotherton, Liddle Collection, (GS) J. W. Allen, letters 160, 3 September 1915, and 406, 22 November 1916.
[46] Quoted in Skelley, *The Victorian Army* (1977), 139.

told him that 'this sort of thing is all too common, and one must make an example.' Foxell, and other junior officers, knew the sapper to have a good character, but when Foxell protested to his superiors, 'they said it was not his character but his little hobbies they did not like.' Foxell was unimpressed with this 'poor form of humour.' At the sapper's court martial, Foxell acted as the prisoner's friend, and other junior officers attended and spoke up for the accused. Nevertheless, Foxell concluded: 'The court were out to make an example—as the APM predicted—and they meant to find my man guilty. All the time they acted as though they were counsel for the prosecution.' The court accepted the evidence of the Belgian mother 'with avidity' and ignored all else. The sapper was sentenced to forty-two days' Field Punishment No. 1 and, though the verdict was subsequently quashed, this was after the man had served more than half of his sentence.[47]

An even more damning indictment was thrown at the whole structure of courts martial three years later. George Black, a peacetime barrister and former governor of the Yukon who had served as a captain in the Canadian Machine Gun Corps, was detailed by the Agent General of British Columbia to defend the troops from British Columbia charged with mutiny following the Kinmel Camp riots of early 1919. Of fifty men tried for the offence, thirty were found guilty and imprisoned. Black was incensed by the entire proceedings which he believed were motivated by 'vengeance' rather than 'justice', and he wrote a furious letter to Sir Robert Borden, the Canadian prime minister, insisting that Borden's government press for the men's freedom. As the letter addresses a variety of complaints against the system, it is worth quoting at length.

> Courts Martial are for the most part not comprised of persons competent to administer justice. They usually have no knowledge of law, and though sometimes advised by a Judge Advocate, he has not the authority of a Judge directing a jury, and in many cases has had very little experience. Officers may sometimes get a fair trial before a Court Martial, other ranks frequently do not; officers constituting Courts Martial are seldom able to hear and consider a case with open minds. They are so imbued with ideas of discipline and of the absolute subordination of those of lesser rank and with the practice of at all costs upholding the action or statement of an officer or O.C.C. [sic] as against the Private soldier that they are prejudiced and unfit to be judges. In some cases exaggerated ideas of their own importance as officers so fogs their vision and warps their judgement as to make them positively dangerous where it is necessary to weigh evidence and pronounce upon the guilt or innocence of accused persons.
>
> Court Martial for the trial of 'other ranks' should have at least a proportion of their numbers of the same rank as the accused, this is provided for in the trial of some officers.
>
> Only a majority verdict is required to convict before a Court Martial not, as before a Jury, a unanimous verdict. The accused, although liable to the death penalty, has no right to peremptory challenge. The precedence and influence of seniority which prevails among and dominates military officers is not discarded by officers comprising Courts Martial, but follows them into Court, robs the junior officers of their

---

independence and keeps them subservient to the will of others superior in rank though frequently inferior in intelligence and possessing but narrow vision.[48]

There was very probably Canadian pride and some legal jealousy in this protest, yet the potential problems of military hierarchy and class attitude cannot be so easily dismissed. The 1919 enquiry into courts martial gave the system a clean bill of health, but a minority report from three Members of Parliament who sat on the committee (Horatio Bottomley, Major C. Lowther, and Stephen Walsh) considered that there had been insufficient investigation of cases of alleged miscarriages of justice.[49]

Beliefs that military authority and hierarchy were unfairly enforced through military courts resurfaced during the Second World War, and many soldiers thought that there was a general presumption of guilt before a trial started. Four young Scots sentenced to three years' penal servitude by a court marital in France in December 1939 protested that their case was 'cut and dried' before they even appeared before the court. They had enlisted together on 23 October, had spent their first ten days of Army life in their civilian clothes, and the journey that took them to France lasted nearly a week. They claimed that they could not yet tell one NCO from another; that was why they had refused a sergeant's instructions and why, already very drunk, they had sought to leave their billet to get even more drunk. Some of their complaints were acknowledged and the initial sentence was reduced to one year with hard labour.[50] Nearly three years later a soldier in North Africa complained: 'The court tried to give the impression that they were considering my generosity [in pleading guilty], but it was evident that everything had been decided in advance.'[51] There were also complaints that the courts went out of their way to protect officers. Sergeant Jeffrey Hall considered that the court martial of his unit's chief clerk was engineered because 'he would not say "yes" to everything.' He believed also that the verdict was rigged and that evidence involving the culpability of a senior officer was closed down by the president of the court.[52] Similarly, Signaller Ken Beaufoy believed that the court martial of one of his mates for being absent from a guard post was dropped when the defending officer asked about other defendants in the case. The implication of the question was that, rather than a solitary private, there should have been officers on duty supervising a sensitive map room in Belgium on the eve of the German winter offensive in the Ardennes in 1944; and since no officers appeared to have been on duty or in the vicinity, the case was allowed to drop to save embarrassment and, perhaps too, the court martial of officers.[53]

---

[48] IWM (D) MISC 155 Item 2426, Black to Sir Robert Borden, 21 June 1919. Black appears to have inserted an extra 'C' in 'O.C.' for Officer Commanding.

[49] *Report . . . into the Law and Rules of Procedure Regulating Military Courts Martial*, 7.

[50] WO 71/691.

[51] IWM (D) 98/35/1, A. R. Graydon; and see in general, Connelly and Miller, 'British Courts Martial' (2004).

[52] IWM (D) 01/57/1, J. W. Hall, letter of 23 June 1942 (f. 87).

[53] IWM (D) 96/46/1, J. Corbett, recollections of Ken Beaufoy, no folio numbers.

Similar accusations of unfairness were made about courts martial in the Navy and the system gave them added force when the offence was one that might have been heard in a civilian court. In August 1944, for example, Lt. Commander Clifford Hall was tried before a court martial in Alexandria on charges of fraud and currency trafficking. Hall was a financier and there was no question that he had made money from deals conducted in Greece. Several of his activities were distinctly dubious, and he pleaded guilty to some of the charges against him, but he was able to hire a barrister for his defence in the shape of D. N. Pritt, King's Counsel, MP for North Hammersmith and Soviet fellow-traveller. After the trial, Pritt requested a meeting with the JAF to protest about aspects of the proceedings. The Admiralty agreed to the meeting on the grounds that, if they refused, Pritt was certain to raise the matter in Parliament. The minutes of the meeting show Pritt deploying his usual legal style of scoring points against the system. Courts martial, he suggested, were useful for some things, but not for others, and among the others was the trial of his client:

> this court consisted of 5 people who were at once judges and jurymen. As judges they had the same qualifications as every juryman, as jurymen they had a little less than the ordinary qualifications of jurymen as they had specialised lives remote from finance [ . . . ] With regard to the Prosecuting Officers, I suppose I might be frank about them.
>
> There were two prosecuting officers a Captain and a Lieutenant Commander. The Captain did not speak more than 3 or 4 sentences the whole time he was there and he was the superior officer of the Deputy Judge Advocate. The other prosecuting officer a Lt. Commander was a gentleman of considerable vigour and not very much experience, he was said to be a bar student. Apart from the lawyers hired for the defence (it would be wrong of me to describe these as poor stuff, but they were actually regarded by the court as 'hired for the defence'), the only lawyer for miles was the Deputy Judge Advocate General, an Englishman, Lt. Commander, a man of the highest possible integrity, a member of the Scots Bar with not much experience at all.

Pritt succeeded in getting the Admiralty to admit that it had no claim on money deposited in Hall's name in an Egyptian Bank, but that was as far as he got. The Admiralty stuck to the court's decision and Hall was left to serve a two-year sentence in a civilian prison.[54]

But while there were complaints and concerns about courts martial during the Second World War, there were also instances in which, even when the offence was one concerning military discipline, the courts rigorously observed the letter of the law and rejected charges brought by senior, experienced officers. Jim Carradice was conscripted into the Gordon Highlanders early in the war. He had a poor opinion of the Regular sergeants and senior NCOs in his battalion, and the loathing appears to have been mutual. Much of the old military hierarchy had a poor opinion of the material sent to them by conscription. Carradice, however, showed promise on the firing range and, while undergoing training, he was offered promotion to lance corporal and the opportunity to become a major's batman. He refused both,

---

preferring to stay with his new comrades, and within minutes of his refusal the company sergeant major had him on a charge of being improperly dressed—a bootlace had appeared from under his gaiter—and the same major who had offered him the position of batman sentenced him to seven days' confined to barracks. This possibly made Carradice a marked man for the NCOs and a few weeks later he was charged with disobeying an order—he had looked for somewhere to put down a mug of tea when ordered to put it down rather than immediately obeying the instruction. He was also alleged to have used obscene language. Carradice refused to accept punishment from his CO and demanded a court martial. The CO 'warned me of the consequences of a court martial, particularly that in wartime I could be hung if I was proved guilty. I think he stressed the point to make me frightened.' Carradice thought correctly since disobeying an order and obscene language were not capital offences. He recalled his response as being: 'They do not make a habit, Sir, of hanging innocent people in this well-kept country of ours.' The comment probably served only to increase his superiors' annoyance and loathing; and so too did his persistence in insisting on a court martial on the five or six occasions that he was summoned into the CO's presence during the thirty-two days between his arrest and trial. But Carradice was lucky in that his platoon commander was a conscript like himself who sympathized and who persuaded him to accept a similar young officer, a solicitor in civilian life, to conduct his defence.[55]

Carradice sketched a vivid picture of the court martial itself and of the atmosphere that must have overawed many young soldiers. He and his escort marched in.

> We were halted and ordered to face three judges, not one of them was less in rank than a brigadier, and they were seated behind a highly polished, long, oak bench. On its surface were piles of papers, documents and copies of 'The King's Rules and Regulations.' Behind them were about twenty or thirty young lieutenants and cadets, who were seated on plush, red, upholstered chairs.

But the court rapidly showed itself to be fully cognizant with the rules of evidence. When a regimental sergeant major (RSM) from Carradice's unit began his evidence with the fact that he had eighteen years' service, the court upheld the defence officer's prompt interruption that such statements were irrelevant to the matter in hand and instructed the sergeant major to stick strictly to the facts of the case. Twenty members of Carradice's platoon spoke up as witnesses in his defence. The court found him not guilty. Carradice declined bringing a charge of 'discrimination' against the NCOs but, while his popularity with his fellow squaddies was high, he was marked out as a barrack-room lawyer among the senior officers. The CO was unhappy; the adjutant awarded him the thirty-two days' pay held back while he was in the cells, sent him on leave, and promised him the opportunity of a transfer to another unit. Carradice joined the Argyll and Sutherland Highlanders, among whom he won his corporal's stripes in Italy and was then severely wounded.

---

[55] IWM (D) 78/71/1, J. Carradice, 'My Damaged Brain', chapter 4 *passim* for all of this and the story of Carradice's court martial.

## BOBBIES, REDCAPS, AND OTHERS

Service personnel who committed criminal behaviour in homes, streets, pubs, and other places of entertainment on the home front were no different from other members of the public and came under the jurisdiction of the civilian police just as they had done in earlier periods. Raids looking for absentees and deserters often involved both civilian and military police; one provost based in London in the Second World War thought that the civilian police gave his men additional authority in pubs in a 'rough neighbourhood'.[56] During the two world wars, when it was known that the services were filled with respectable volunteers and conscripts, there appears to have been rather more sympathy among the general public for service personnel in trouble with the police on the streets. In the spring of 1941, for example, two Metropolitan Police constables created a furore attempting to move a soldier, too drunk to stand, along Oxford Street to West End Central Police Station, a distance of a little over 400 yards. The wife of Major Sir Jocelyn Lucas, MP, demanded that the constables hire a taxi. She even offered to pay for it, but found herself under arrest charged with obstructing the footway and causing a crowd to gather; the charges were eventually dropped.[57] But for the soldier, sailor, or airman, there were many other agents of discipline than the civilian bobby and, like the courts martial, these often seemed pettifogging, unjust, and high-handed.

A unit's non-commissioned officers were the first line for enforcing discipline and dealing with petty offences. At the beginning of the century the larger ships in the Royal Navy were policed by the ship's corporals, popularly known as 'crushers', who were responsible to the master-at-arms. The master-at-arms himself was known as the 'jaunty', but not to his face. The ships' corporals subsequently acquired the rank of regulating petty officer, but this did little to improve their popularity among the ratings, and the pejorative label of 'crusher' continued to be employed. George Clarkson, a ship's carpenter who rose to the rank of petty officer, considered that the crushers were always ready to take a bribe to drop a charge and might even expect payment to ensure that a man received his legitimate leave pass or 'liberty ticket'. The Navy also deployed men ashore as shore patrols, checking men's liberty tickets, ensuring good behaviour and, where necessary, assisting any civilian police having problems with boisterous or drunken sailors.[58]

In the Army, serious offences missed by, or beyond the remit of NCOs were dealt with by the Regimental Police, who had responsibility only within their own unit. Beyond the Regimental Police were the Military Police, and similar enforcement institutions also existed in the Royal Navy Regulating Branch and the RAF Police. The members of these bodies, while not sworn in as constables like the

---

[56] Brotherton, Liddle Collection, (ARMY 184) G. St. George Stedall, see reports in files 2 and 3.

[57] MEPO 3/1966, Arrest of Lady Lucas regarding a protest over police handling of a drunken soldier.

[58] McKee, *Sober Men and True* (2002), 35–6; IWM (S) 679, George Michael Clarkson, reels 4–5 and 26–9. Bill Glenton describes 'crusher' and 'jaunty' as still in use towards the end of the Second World War; Glenton, *Mutiny in Force X* (1986).

civilian police, could take action against personnel from another service found committing an offence. The overall command of Military and RAF Police was in the hands of a provost marshal, a rank that went back to the Middle Ages. At the beginning of the First World War the Army's provost marshal held the rank of colonel; from 1915, and thereafter, he was a brigadier. At the beginning of the war each division had an assistant provost marshal (APM) with the rank of major. The Military Police units in the different arms were divided into provost companies and the other ranks were always on the first rung of the NCO hierarchy; thus the lowest rank in the Military Police was a lance corporal—though not necessarily always in receipt of a lance corporal's pay—to ensure that he had authority over the lowest-ranking soldier.[59]

There were two branches to the Army's police in 1914, both of which had been created during the last quarter of the 19th century: the Military Mounted Police and the Military Foot Police. They were not amalgamated into the Corps of Military Police until 1926. Their principal tasks were to assist the civil police in garrison towns and to enforce military law and crime prevention among the Army community. For the Navy, in contrast, the assistance of the civil police in sea ports generally fell to shore patrols from ships, a task that was rarely popular with the men ordered to undertake it. The exigencies of the Great War led to a significant escalation of tasks for the Military Police at, and immediately behind the front. In particular they had to control traffic to and from the front, and to look out for stragglers, absentees, and deserters; often they also had to receive and manage prisoners-of-war. The APMs and their deputies were responsible for liaising with local authorities, which included the local police. From a few hundred in 1914, the MPs reached 25,000 men at their peak during the war.

The number of MPs was around 4,000 on the eve of the Second World War. The planners had recognized the need to prepare for war, and particularly the need to ensure the smooth running of military transport in an increasingly mechanized conflict. Scouts from the Automobile Association were encouraged to join a Supplementary Reserve from 1938. In the spring of 1942, in an article for the popular photojournalism magazine *Picture Post*, it was stated that three-quarters of the work of the Military Police consisted of road traffic duties; 'like the London "bobby" [the MP's] chief duty is to keep the traffic moving and wave the army on its way.'[60] Initially little consideration was given to the problem of conventional crime by soldiers. A small detective unit appears to have existed briefly within the British Army of Occupation in the Rhineland between 1919 and 1926. In 1939 the High Command of the Army was shocked by the scale of criminality among the British Expeditionary Force and requested a senior officer of the Metropolitan Police to make an assessment of the problem and suggest a remedy. Chief Inspector

---

[59] As with military criminal justice in general, the Army is much better researched in the respect of its police than the Royal Navy or the Royal Air Force. The information in the following paragraphs draws heavily on Crozier, *History of the Corps of Royal Military Police* (1951); Lovell-Knight, *Story of the Royal Military Police* (1977), which itself draws heavily on Crozier; and Sheffield, *History of the Royal Military Police* (1981).

[60] Hastings, 'An Army Redcap' (1942a).

George Hatherill's report led directly to the creation of the Special Investigation Branch (SIB), and in February 1940, twenty detective officers of the Metropolitan Police, led by Superintendent Clarence Campion, who was given the rank of major, were sent to France to investigate thefts from Army stores.[61] The other services followed with their own, similar SIBs. A second, significant change to the service police during the Second World War was the appointment of women police, which was necessitated by the significant recruitment of women into the forces. The consensus among the new women service police was that most of the offending with which they had to deal related to absenteeism and conduct against good order and discipline. This, as the first training officer of the ATS Military Provost put it, 'could include almost anything, drunkenness, wearing your stockings (they looked shinier and more transparent) inside out, smoking with your cap on in the street, wearing your cap indoors, and going arm in arm with a soldier.' But, as one of the ATS police lance corporals remembered: 'The girls used to see the red hat in the distance and had buttoned up their jackets and put the caps on long before they reached us so there wasn't much to do except to be seen.'[62]

The red cover over the top of the peaked cap gave the Military Police officer a distinctive appearance. The RAF Police had a similar cover, but white. The covers provided the police with their more respectable nicknames: 'Snowdrops' for the RAF; 'Redcaps' for the Army's police. Among the rank and file, however, the Redcaps were generally rather more disparagingly referred to as 'Cherry Nobs' or 'monkeys'; and they were often accused of high-handed behaviour and, in consequence, disliked.[63] Major George Cornwallis-West of the Grenadier Guards, who was briefly married to Jenny Jerome and hence stepfather to Winston Churchill although only two weeks older than the future wartime leader, was declared medically unfit for active service in 1915 and was appointed, instead, as assistant provost marshal with jurisdiction over Surrey and Middlesex. Cornwallis-West noted the other ranks' dislike of the Redcaps; he also remarked on the unpopularity of APMs amongst some young officers, especially those recently returned from the front on leave and who objected to what they considered to be provosts wasting

[61] *The Times*, 6 February 1940, 10. Campion was killed during the Dunkirk evacuation. Not all SIB officers were former police detectives. Jack Chadwick served as a naval rating during the First World War and was invalided out in 1926 when he took a job in the Post Office. He volunteered for the SIB in the Second World War, supervised a district stretching from South Shields to Glasgow before being attached to the Guards Armoured Division in North Africa. IWM (Sound) 10918, Jack Chadwick.

[62] IWM (D) 96/34/1, Mrs L. Orde, f. 122; IWM (D) MISC 236 (3354) 'Accounts of Service with the ATS Provost', L/Corp. Dorothy French.

[63] The term 'monkey' is not mentioned in the official histories and its origins have generated some debate among former members of the corps. Some have suggested that it originated in the eighteenth century when a military provost executed a monkey in either Aberdeen or Hartlepool; the monkey was suspected of being a Frenchman and a spy. It has also been suggested that the term originated during the Egyptian campaign of 1885, when the red pillbox hats worn by NCOs of the Military Foot Police were noted as resembling the red caps worn by the monkeys of organ-grinders in the souk. Equally, it has been pointed out that the 'police' of the wicked witch in the film of *The Wizard of Oz* were monkeys. *RMP Old Comrades Link Up Newsletter*, 51 (September 2011) and 52 (October 2011). My thanks to Bob Eggelton, editor of the *Newsletter*, for this information.

time over trivialities. Cornwallis-West claimed that he attempted to prevent trouble in advance by using light-hearted banter to discourage such front-line officers from wearing 'yellow ties and mauve socks' with their uniforms. But he had no truck with drunkenness in public.[64] It was probably much the same with many of the Redcaps in their dealings with ordinary Tommies. But Tommies were sometimes inclined to respond to Redcap interference with violence; indeed one Tommy appointed as clerk to an APM on the Western Front confessed to coming very close to striking the man: 'If only one could say something to such buggers. I am personally getting fed up with his numerous references to the old regulations etc.'[65] In June 1919 the *News of the World* reported that members of the Black Watch were on the lookout for Military Police to beat up after one of their boy bandsmen had been reprimanded for eating fish and chips.[66]

Just as civilians could take the part of servicemen who got in trouble with civilian police, so too they occasionally objected to what they saw as high-handed behaviour on the streets by the Military Police. In May 1918, for example, a Military Police sergeant approached a corporal in the streets of St Albans for being improperly dressed. An old soldier took the corporal's part: 'Leave him alone, he is doing nothing to you.' A large crowd assembled, siding with the old soldier and the corporal against the MP.[67] Just over two months later there was a larger, more serious disturbance in Bedford when a drunken soldier was arrested and the Military Police had to call on the assistance of the local police to get him off the street and into the civilian police station. A rumour spread in the town that the soldier's war wounds had had to be restitched as a result of his manhandling, and this led to more trouble. No one appears to have been charged as a result of the disorder but, in a speech at the town's police court, the mayor condemned 'the disgraceful scenes'. The local APM thanked the mayor for his words and for the support of the civilian police; he also reported that eleven of his men had been injured.[68]

Hostility to the Military Police was equally apparent during the Second World War. To many servicemen the service police epitomized pointless spit and polish. They disliked the way that MPs hovered around railway stations checking leave passes. Denis Argent, a journalist who had worked for Mass Observation and who, during the war, initially served in a noncombatant bomb disposal unit of the Royal Engineers, described one comrade as referring to Redcaps as 'Gestapo'. He also described how, when his unit's lorry drove past two Redcaps in Luton, the men let fly with 'a volley of raspberries [ . . . ] it's almost impossible for soldiers to resist handing redcaps a large razz.'[69] MacDonald Hastings's article for *Picture Post* appears to have been designed to assuage such feelings. He and his photographer were given privileged access to the MPs' training and the article stressed the

[64] Cornwallis-West, *Edwardian HeyDays* (1930), 293–4.
[65] Brotherton, Liddle Collection, (GS 1569) T. Tarlton, 5 July 1918.
[66] *News of the World*, 8 June 1919, 5.
[67] AIR 1/558/16/15/56, Weekly Intelligence Summary, GHQ Great Britain, March–June 1918.
[68] *Bedfordshire Times and Independent*, 2 August 1918, 2.
[69] Malcomson and Malcolmson, eds., *A Soldier in Bedfordshire* (2009), 116, n. 44 and 132.

difficulties and necessities of the job; but many service personnel remained unconvinced, and wrote to the editor saying so.[70] A sub-Kiplingesque doggerel of the war also reflected the dislike:

> You look so fierce and terrible
> As with your lead, indelible,
>> You write my misdeeds in your little book.
> Because my boots are dirty
> You get quite annoyed and shirty
>> And make me out to be a bloomin' crook

The tone of the final verse, however, suggests that the piece did not have its origins among, and probably was not recited by either Regular Army squaddies or conscripts:

> Yet on the Dunkirk beaches, you
> Kept calm and knew just what to do,
>> And we for you had admiration deep.
> But tonight I have a date, sir,
> And I'm going to stay out late, sir,
>> So please, dear Red Cap, just go home and sleep![71]

Aggression and bullying by service police occasionally backfired, especially on, or close to the front line. Two spit-and-polished Military Policemen took exception to the slovenly, unwashed infantrymen sprawled across the street of a recently captured town and brewing tea. What they did not know, as they ordered the men to get up, smarten up, and look like 'British soldiers', was that the men they were addressing, who wore no badges of rank, included a senior NCO who outranked them. It provided the perfect opportunity for jeering at authority, followed by the production of pay books to demonstrate the infantry NCO's superiority of rank.[72] Nor was it only the other ranks that took exception to pettifogging police officers. On 3 August 1944, Lieutenant Colonel Martin Lindsay noted in his diary a visit to his front-line infantry battalion from an APM.

> [He] asked if we didn't know that it is forbidden to use crops for camouflage purposes and lining the bottom of our dugouts (for warmth). The Adjutant tartly replied that he was our first visitor from any kind of Corps H.Q. They still seem to think that we are out on an exercise.

Another of Lindsay's officers expressed annoyance at an APM who impeded him on a champagne-buying expedition to Paris, on the grounds that his pass did not authorize him to enter the city. The APM was branded as 'the worst kind of Englishman—the Englishman abroad!'[73]

---

[70] Hastings, 'An Army Redcap' (1942a); and for replies highly critical of this account, also using the label 'Gestapo' to describe MPs, see *Picture Post*, 2 May 1942, 3.

[71] 'Red Cap', in Page, ed., *Kiss Me Goodnight Sergeant Major* (1975), 58–9.

[72] Longden, *To the Victor the Spoils* (2004), 193–4.

[73] Lindsay, *So Few Got Through* (1946), 38 and 147.

Sometimes it was not aggression, bullying or attempts to enforce pettifogging regulations that generated resentment: interservice rivalry would suffice. Dulcie Lamb remembered how WRNS objected to ATS Redcaps searching them when suspected of smuggling goods in Egypt at the end of the war; the situation was resolved by bringing in police from the WRNS.[74] Moreover, like all police officers, Redcaps and other service police had discretion. Major C. H. Butt recalled some tough MPs in Rome confronting a number of 'sharp-end' infantrymen who were with a group of prostitutes. The confrontation exploded into a fist-fight, which the MPs won, but then, not wishing to see the infantrymen facing charges of consorting with prostitutes, the MPs 'forgot' about it.[75]

## PUNISHMENT

As discussed in the previous chapter, the use of capital punishment in the military was significantly restricted after the First World War. Moreover, most executions during the Second World War were carried out by the hangman, rather than by firing squad. A notable exception occurred in 1945 when, as one of his last acts as an artillery officer, the future leader of the Conservative Party and prime minister, Edward Heath, found himself in charge of the execution by firing squad of a Pole guilty of rape and murder. It is unclear whether the Pole was a soldier or one of the displaced persons, a former slave labourer, of the sort that wandered through Germany after the collapse of the Third Reich often seeking revenge. The lack of official evidence from the case has led some to question the story, though, as with the lack of some court martial evidence from the First World War, it is quite possible that the paperwork was lost in the chaos at the end of the war. Heath did not mention the experience for many years, but subsequently claimed that the profound impact of commanding the firing squad influenced his subsequent stance in opposition to capital punishment.[76]

The executions for desertion during the First World War aroused anger and disgust among the public, most notably at the time with *John Bull*'s furious front page 'The Tragedy of a Boy Officer' in February 1918. The editor, Horatio Bottomley, used the article to demand a reform of the system of courts martial and followed the story up with another sensational front page and the headline challenge: 'Let Them Prosecute Me.'[77] But before this well-known incident there

---

[74] IWM (D) MISC 236 (3354), 'Accounts of Service with the ATS Provost', Corp. Dulcie Lamb.

[75] IWM (D) 02/19/1, C. H. Butt, 26–7.

[76] Ziegler, *Edward Heath* (2010), 46. Captain Michael Bendix of the Coldstream Guards was a staff officer at the end of the war. He recalled: 'The nastiest job I ever had to do was to arrange for a gunner to be executed by firing squad for raping a German girl. The awful thing was that he had a DCM and an MM, but even so justice had to be done.' IWM 98/3/1 Extracts from the Memoirs of Captain Michael Bendix, 34. Was this Heath's soldier? Heath was also an artilleryman.

[77] Sellers, *For God's Sake Shoot Straight* (1995), chapter 7. Dyett was only the second officer to be shot for such an offence during the war. There was a strong sense of injustice among the other ranks that it was only men from the non-commissioned ranks who were executed in such circumstances. It is also notable that Dyett had requested a transfer to sea duties because, after a brief period in the Royal

had been another outcry, taken up by the press and leading to questions in Parliament, against the punishment introduced to replace flogging. Field Punishment No. 1 could be awarded for a range of offences from drunkenness to, as in the case of Lieutenant Foxell's unfortunate sapper, attempted rape. The convicted man was required to carry out hard labour, usually harsh fatigue duty for a period of up to three months and, where possible, he could be imprisoned. But he was also to be tied up for two hours a day, for three consecutive days out of four, for a period of twenty-one days in all. It was this tying up, and the manner of it, that particularly infuriated soldiers. Men were sometimes tied to the wheels of a gun or limber with their arms, and sometimes their legs, outstretched; soldiers called it 'crucifixion'. On the eve of the First World War the JAG was advising on charges against two artillerymen for allegedly fostering a mutiny 'to resist their superior officers and prevent soldiers who had been sentenced to Field Punishment from being made to undergo that punishment.'[78] Charles Keller, who had three years' service with the Royal Horse Artillery before the outbreak of war, recalled:

> The thing that bothered us a lot was to see British soldiers tied to the gun wheels in the barrack square where people passing the gate to stop and watch [sic]. They were there as punishment for various crimes [ . . . ] The people of Le Mans raised strong objection to this form of punishment, seeing men spreadeagled to the gun wheels. They took this to be a mockery of the Roman Catholic religion in some way.[79]

But it was not just civilians in France who were shocked by the punishment.

By the end of 1916, stories of 'crucifixion' involving members of Kitchener's New Army were filtering back to the home front. The public appears to have been unaware of, or uninterested in the punishment before the war; perhaps those who had heard of it generally ignored it on the assumption that it was inflicted on dangerous, drunken old sweats. Indeed, as late as the 1960s, a battalion commander from the Second World War could write a book on military morale arguing that, with reference to the tough, pre-1914 Tommies 'one cannot believe that tying them up for two hours to a gun wheel did them very much harm'.[80] Such punishment inflicted on patriotic volunteers, however, was viewed very differently. Robert Blatchford's campaign was launched in October 1916 with an article in the *Illustrated Sunday News* under the sensational headline: 'Why "Crucify" Tommy?' The article was the cue for a flood of petitions from different organizations and letters to MPs and the War Office, protesting about the punishment. The outcry led the War Office to design a standardized system for tying men to fixed points which was introduced in January 1917: there was to be no restriction to the

Naval Division on the Western Front, he recognized that he could not stand the strain of trench warfare.

[78] WO 84/9 f. 358.

[79] IWM (D) 02/55/1, Charles Robert Keller, f. 27; and see also Brotherton, Liddle Collection, (GS) H. N. Edwards. Edwards first saw the punishment inflicted on seven men who fell out exhausted during a gruelling march in August 1915. 'I was ashamed of my country when a party of French soldiers passed through the wood and saw it.'

[80] Baynes, *Morale* (1967), quoted in Oram, *Military Executions* (2003), 46.

offender's breathing, there was to be at least six inches play between the man's arms and hands and the object to which they were tied, and his feet were not to be tied more than twelve inches apart. The issue was raised again at the end of the war; popular interest had waned but Haig and most Army commanders believed that the punishment was essential to maintain morale and to keep men in line. Without Field Punishment No. 1, insisted Haig, 'recourse to the death penalty would have to become more frequent.' Nevertheless, the regulations continued to be revised and, at a meeting in March 1923, the Army Council resolved that the form of punishment should disappear from the Army's penal code.[81]

The Navy had a punishment that could be equally as gruelling. The 10A, or simply 'Number 10', which took its name from a section of the *King's Regulations and Admiralty Instructions*, was a punishment awarded by a ship's captain. It involved deprivation of the ship's grog ration and the right to smoke; meals were restricted to half an hour under the eye of a sentry and there were ceaseless extra fatigues such as scrubbing the deck with holystone—known as 'the Bible'. Some commanders could make the Number 10 extremely severe. One novice seaman on a warship in Scapa Flow, who claimed not to have known the bugle call for muster, was said to have been required to holystone the deck from 4.30 a.m. to 9.00 p.m.[82]

But while the death penalty, field punishments, and the Number 10 could excite discontent among service personnel and outcries among civilians, since the late 19th century punishment for serious military offences had, like that for serious civilian offences, increasingly involved some form of prison sentence. Any sentence of more than fourteen days passed on a sailor meant incarceration in detention barracks. In 1909 the Royal Navy introduced a sentence of 'detention', which was designed to reduce the stigma of prison for those offenders henceforth referred to as 'men under detention'. The men wore uniform and were supervised and drilled by petty officers in the detention barracks. The detention barracks were said to be places where they 'tamed lions'. Everything was done at the double and tasks were often pointless, such as loading rubble into a wheelbarrow, moving it fifty yards, emptying it, and then repeating the task to take the rubble back to where it had started.[83] Similar practices were followed with soldiers serving sentences in military prisons, though there were progressive moves to abolish the pointless, largely unproductive tasks of picking oakum and shot-drill with more productive labour and with elementary schools for the soldiers. But many service offenders, and most commonly those serving sentences for civilian offences, were sent to civilian prisons.

All prisons were harsh institutions. A sufficient cluster of imprisoned service personnel could present a threat within a civilian prison. They might establish a group identity through their membership of the service family and unite in order to demand their rights or better treatment. In the spring of 1919, for example, there

---

[81] WO 32/5460, Field Punishment No. 1; see also, WO 32/5461, Enquiry into Field Punishment No. 1, 1919, and WO 32/5462, Revised Rules for Field Punishment No. 1, 1923.
[82] McKee, *Sober Men and True* (2002), 37–9; Brown and Meehan, *Scapa Flow* (2008), 10.
[83] Brown and Meehan, *Scapa Flow* (2008), 68; McKee, *Sober Men and True* (2002), 40.

was trouble at No. 7 Military Prison Camp Calais as 420 men assembled to protest about conditions, food, and treatment. The Riot Act was read but a few men persisted to hold their ground and complain. Some of these men were shipped back to Britain to serve their sentences and trouble flared again. Major-General Wyndham Childs, the deputy adjutant general who subsequently became assistant commissioner of the Metropolitan Police, considered them to be 'the scum of the Army and deserving of little if any consideration.' But the governors of Dartmoor and Portland Prisons, where the trouble occurred, together with a prison inspector who was also a retired colonel, took the liberal view of the majority among the leaders of the prison service in the early 20th century. They believed that the men had some justification, not least in that they were owed some clarification of their release dates now that the war was over. Moreover, it was suggested, continued incarceration could turn them into hardened offenders rather than enabling them to return to civilian life as responsible, orderly men. The War Office agreed to review all of the cases and, in their annual report for 1920, the prison commissioners noted that large numbers of the soldiers had since been discharged from the civilian prisons.[84]

The expansion of the armed forces at the beginning of the Second World War, with the corresponding increase of service offenders, led to the Army taking over three civilian prisons and establishing a series of new detention barracks. The Army's facilities were also used by the RAF. The Royal Navy had four detention quarters. There were various other prisons across the world, such as the one in Cairo to which Rifleman Crimp's comrade was sent. These prisons were often criticized for harsh regimes. There were scandals over the treatment of the prisoners, which led to public hostility towards the Military Provost Staff Corps that supervised the military prisons and detention barracks; but, as with the service police, much probably depended on the discretion and attitude of the staff involved and the involvement and authority of the officers in overall charge.

After being wounded by mortar fire, Guardsman Len Waller was listed as unfit for active service. He was made acting corporal and posted to a punishment centre situated in what appeared to be a medieval prison in Sicily. There were ten men on the staff: an RSM, eight corporals, and a cook. 'We'd all been downgraded unfit and none of us would ever have dreamed of volunteering for prison duties. But here we were, in charge of a bunch of blokes like ourselves—only they'd been caught and we hadn't.' He also described one of his fellow corporals bringing in a prostitute one night and putting her in the cell with a 'model prisoner' who was serving seven years for killing a warrant officer.[85] Bill Wood recalled his arrival at Chorley Detention Barracks in 1942: 'I arrived at Chorley station in handcuffs [ . . . ] and I can still remember the torrent of abuse the lassies from Lancashire poured on my escort who, as it happened, had been very kind and generous to

---

[84] WO 32/5480, Imprisonment of Military Prisoners in Civil Prisons, 1919; *Report of the Commissioners of Prisons for 1920*, Cmd. 972, 24.
[85] IWM (D) 87/42/1, L. Waller, 'When Bugles Call', 68–9.

me.'[86] At roughly the same time Macdonald Hastings, who had earlier urged the readers of *Picture Post* to 'spare some of your sympathy for the Redcaps', was given privileged access to the 'Glasshouse' in Aldershot Barracks. The intention was clearly that he and his photographer should attempt to do for military prisons what they had attempted to do for the Military Police.

The Glasshouse, so called because of the glass roof that covered the three storeys of the Aldershot Military Detention Barracks, had been built in 1870. By the beginning of the 20th century its name had become a synonym for Army prisons. Hastings and his photographer produced a sympathetic article that denied any brutality in the regime.

> The most severe punishment—rarely administered and then only under medical supervision—for insubordination inside the Glasshouse is bread and water and solitary confinement for a maximum of three days. The crimes for which a punishment is considered necessary are crimes for which, in any Continental army in wartime, the culprit would be shot. Lesser punishments are deprivation of mattresses or library books. Reports that prisoners are physically knocked about by members of the prison staff—however justified such a measure might seem—are nonsense. In fact, there has been only one case of this happening in a detention barracks since the war. The offending NCO was court-martialled, reduced to the ranks, and sentenced to six months' detention himself. And, whatever you may hear to the contrary—and however much an outsider might wonder that at a time when this country is fighting for its very existence, military offenders are still treated with reasonable consideration—such are the facts.

It is a moot point that, at that time, offenders in continental armies were shot for such offences, and other 'facts' in Hastings's piece were challenged by some *Picture Post* readers who had experienced military detention.[87] Moreover the hostility towards members of the Military Provost Staff Corps did not diminish. The officer defending two senior NCOs of the corps charged with the manslaughter of a detainee, William Clayton, in the spring of 1943, urged Chatham magistrates to have the case dealt with as quickly as possible. 'There is feeling in the town. These men do not like going about there.'[88]

Rifleman William Clayton had been sent to Fort Darland, one of the new detention barracks at Gillingham in Kent, early in 1943. Clayton, aged 40 years, had reported sick on several occasions and had been excused Physical Training. On 17 March he protested that he could not march and, during an ensuing confrontation with RSM James Cullinay and Quarter Master Sergeant Leslie Salter, he was allegedly beaten by both NCOs; a few minutes later he was dead. The post-mortem investigation revealed considerable injuries to Clayton's face consistent with being punched, but the cause of death was found to be pulmonary tuberculosis

---

[86] IWM (D) 99/31/1, T. W. Wood, '"On Tracks" with the Armoured Engineers 1943–1946', f. 31.

[87] Hastings, 'Inside the Glasshouse' (1942b); for readers' letters about the piece see, *Picture Post*, 20 June 1942, 3.

[88] *Manchester Guardian*, 6 May 1943, 6.

complicated by blood flowing into the lung cavity. The naval surgeon who conducted the post-mortem believed that the tuberculosis could have been missed in an ordinary examination because of a thickened plural membrane; it would have been found by an X-ray. There was concern about the fact that a man who was seriously ill could have been in the Army, let alone subjected to the tough regime of a detention barracks. There was evidence too that Clayton was deaf and one NCO reported him as 'always obedient and seemed to do his best to carry out orders.' Salter, however, told the court at the Kent Assizes where he and Cullinay stood trial for manslaughter, that he did not think Clayton was ill. 'I thought him more a defiant character.' The jury took less than half an hour to bring in their verdict of guilty.[89] Clayton's death led to a Committee of Enquiry established by the prime minister.

The committee noted that, at the time of their deliberations, the various military prisons and detention barracks in Britain housed upwards of 5,200 inmates: about 750 were naval ratings and marines, 800 came from the RAF, and the rest were soldiers. Overall they considered that the Army prisons were tougher than detention barracks, but the hardest institutions of all, and ones which had not raised any outcry, were those run by the Royal Navy. In the latter, men had to sleep on bare boards without blankets for at least the first two weeks of their incarceration. The committee did not report finding much evidence of 'chasing' or bullying, though it considered that, given the large number of NCOs with authority in these establishments 'a few bullies will inevitably be found'. The inquiry's report was not a whitewash and it made a series of recommendations for increasing staffing levels, improving sick quarters and sanitation, and extending opportunities for general education and training. The latter sprang from surprise at the poor educational attainments of the men in custody.

> A surprising number of soldiers and sailors under sentence are in varying degrees illiterate, and many are in one way or another antisocial, with distorted ideas of the meaning of citizenship and with remarkable ignorance of world affairs and lack of general knowledge.

At the same time it is significant that the committee readily accepted the warnings of the prison and barrack commandants that of the ninety-one men who complained formally and in private about ill-treatment or injustice, 'the vast majority came [ . . . ] from men of the recidivist type who are, as might be expected, the troublemakers of these places.'[90] Poor educational attainment was identified as a problem shared by many of those in prison since the 19th century. It appears to have been a problem among many in the services, especially among the Victorian soldiery branded as drunken, dangerous libertines. But it was also another way of

---

[89] *Manchester Guardian*, 6 May 1943, 6; 25 June, 6, and 26 June, 7 and 8; *The Times*, 6 May 1943, 25 June, 2, and 26 June, 2.

[90] *Report of the Prime Minister's Committee of Enquiry into Detention Barracks, 1943*, Cmd. 6484, 8, 9, and 11.

suggesting that crime in the services was essentially the work of criminals who had found their way into the ranks.

If a disproportionate number of young men in trouble with the criminal justice system of the armed forces were noted as having poor educational attainments, this was no different from offenders in the civilian world. But, as in the civilian world, the situation in the armed forces was not static. While there were Regular officers who appear to have come close to the parody of the crusty blimp that opposed change, there were significant developments in the criminal justice system of the services in the first half of the 20th century. Change was apparent before the outbreak of the First World War, but the influx of patriotic volunteers and then conscripts helped to accelerate this. The poorly educated Regular might have resented the court martial system and the severity of Field Punishment No. 1 or the Navy's Number 10, and the better-educated artificers in the Royal Navy particularly had been campaigning for greater rights and fairer treatment before 1914. But the enormous influx of respectable volunteers and conscripts—men who would not normally have joined the services—meant that the services suddenly had to cope with more articulate men, some with experience of trades unions, and many who could see no reason why service courts and service law should be any different from their civilian counterparts. Moreover the families and friends of these men quickly learned about, and expressed concerns about what they saw as injustice. While the precise impact is difficult to measure, these new pressures on the services contributed to change. But it would be wrong to think that all change was the result of wartime expansion of the services. Military officers were as much a part of the civilian society that they served as soldiers, sailors, or airmen; and as such they absorbed ideas current in that society. It was, after all, senior servicemen who attempted to organize fair voting procedures for courts martial, and a general who developed the Special Training Units for young soldiers seen as potential delinquents.

# 3

## 'Law Makes Crime'

### What Difference Does War Make?

At the beginning of 1916 a headline in *The Times* declared 'No Prisoners. No Quarter Sessions.' The article following explained that the Quarter Sessions that should have been held at Croydon on the day before had been abandoned because there were no prisoners for trial. It was the same in Bedfordshire, Northampton-shire, and Southampton. A few months later the paper reported that there had only been one prisoner at the Portsmouth Quarter Sessions, and he had pleaded guilty.[1] Towards the end of the following year, reflecting on the annual report of the prison commissioners, *The Times* commented on what seemed to have been a great reduction in crime over the previous decade. 'The total per 100,000 of the population, which was 586 in 1904–5, fell to 281 in 1914–15, while for the year under review it is estimated at 118 only.' In addition, there had been a steady decrease in the numbers held in convict prisons: 'on 31 March last there were [ . . . ] 1,402 males, as compared with 2,504 at the beginning of the war and 2,879 10 years ago.' Yet between these good news stories there was another in July 1917, beginning 'Law makes crime.' This lamented the fact that attempts to avoid conscription under the new Military Service Acts had led to an upsurge in offending. There had been thefts of, and trafficking in medical exemption certifi-cates, varieties of fraud including simulated or 'artificially induced symptoms of tuberculosis, synovitis, and debility', faked deafness and paralysis. Yet the number of convictions for these frauds did not appear to have impacted greatly on what *The Times* saw as the overall decrease in crime.[2]

Two important points have already been emphasized: first, that most of the people accused of criminal offences during the 20th century, as in other centuries, were young men; and second, that young men tend to be the backbone of a state's armed forces. It has also been noted that, at least since the early modern period, contemporaries tended to consider that criminal offences declined at the outset of a war and increased at the end. When the First World War began, the collection of criminal statistics in Britain was a hundred years old; since the 1850s the statistics had included crimes reported annually to the local police forces. The English and Welsh statistics were sent to the Home Office each year where they were collated and published among the parliamentary papers with an introduction drawing

---

[1] *The Times*, 8 January 1916, 3, 11 January, 5, and 7 April, 5.
[2] *The Times*, 9 July 1917, 4 and 16 October, 3.

attention to such trends as appeared significant. The statistics for Scotland were sent to the Scottish Home Department in Edinburgh, where they were similarly collated, assessed, and published with an introduction. The two sets of statistics contained slightly different content, which makes direct comparison difficult; not only do they reflect the different offence categories of two different legal systems but, whereas in Scotland all crimes and offences known to the police were recorded, in England and Wales it was only the crimes that were indictable that appeared in the official statistics. An interdepartmental committee, which was convened in the mid-1950s to draw comparisons between the English and Welsh and the Scottish statistics, found it most sensible to limit itself to reporting broad trends rather than attempt direct annual comparisons.[3]

There are other, more general problems with crime statistics which have long vexed criminologists, historians, and statisticians over the years. How, for example, can allowance be made for the 'dark figure' of crimes never reported? And how can any assessment take account of the possible agendas of police institutions?[4] Yet these official statistics are, by and large, all that remain for assessing the broad patterns of criminal offending during the 19th century and first three-quarters of the 20th; and, as a consequence, they constitute the best starting point for assessing what, if anything, the broad impact of the two world wars may have been on crime—in other words for doing something similar to the interdepartmental committee of the 1950s.

Broadly the official statistics for England and Wales suggest a general levelling out of criminal offending in the second half of the 19th century, followed by a gradual rise in the first decade of the 20th century, increasing slightly in the interwar years and then beginning a very significant rise during the late 1950s. The statistics for Scotland are more erratic. In contrast to those for England and Wales, they were significantly lower during the interwar years than they had been at the beginning of the century; from the mid-1930s they began a steady rise, but it is only in the three years before the outbreak of the Second World War that they began to overtake the levels of offending reported to the police in the first decade of the century. In 1937 the Scottish Office noted that this was the result of an upsurge in miscellaneous offences, specifically road traffic offences, betting and gaming, breaches of the peace and drunkenness—the two latter being commonly linked.[5]

The periods of the two world wars suggest slight changes in the overall trajectory of the statistics, but the patterns are different for each conflict and for each country. During the First World War the statistics for England and Wales and those for Scotland show a downturn which might suggest that some young men were drawn out of usual patterns of criminal offending by the circumstances of international conflict. But in 1917 the prison commissioners for Scotland warned that

[3] Lodge, 'A Comparison of Criminal Statistics' (1956–7).
[4] For discussions of these problems see Emsley, *Crime and Society... 1750–1900* (2010a), chapter 2; and Emsley *Crime and Society in Twentieth-Century England* (2011), chapter 2.
[5] *Report on the Criminal Judicial Statistics for Scotland for 1937*, Cmd. 5877, 5–6.

the fall in the numbers of committals [to prison] cannot be merely attributed to the absence on service of a large proportion of the floating population, for the number of women offenders has diminished as well as that of males.[6]

Moreover, in Scotland, in contrast to the overall pattern in that country and in contrast to England and Wales, in 1917 the figures for persons disposed of for offences against property both with and without violence, increased to a number above the pre-war average.[7] During the Second World War there was no general downturn apparent in the figures. In England and Wales the statistics continued to increase; a peak was reached in 1948, after which the figures temporarily fell back, though remaining significantly above pre-war levels. In Scotland the pre-war increase continued until 1940, after which the numbers fell slightly. After 1942, however, the Scottish figures remained well above those for most of the interwar period, though not above those of the three years immediately before the war.

Within these broad trends there appears to be other contrasts between offences in England and Wales and in Scotland. The Scots seem to have suffered more property crime and there were more convictions for drunkenness. The figures for drunkenness fell during both wars; they increased a little after 1945 to remain at almost twice the level of those for England and Wales. Possibly related in part to the problems of drink, the statistics for Scotland also showed a greater problem with offences against the person, but a decision in 1945 to reclassify many assaults as 'breach of the peace' contributed to a decline in the numbers recorded for these offences. A decade after the reclassification the numbers convicted of offences against the person in Scotland were roughly the same as the numbers convicted in England and Wales—around twenty-six individuals annually for every 100,000 in the population.[8]

The extent to which men recruited into the British armed forces brought broad traditions of offending with them, and the extent to which they were socialized into new behaviours by new peers and new military institutions is ultimately unanswerable. Such figures as exist for the armed forces are thinner than the official Judicial Statistics of the component parts of the United Kingdom; there is no record of crimes reported to the Military Police, particularly the SIB, or to regimental officers, and no record of the offences dealt with in the orderly room. Such statistical evidence as remains is fragmentary and, in the case of the two world wars, it is not precisely the same. The extensive statistical tables constructed for the Army during the First World War give the total number of courts martial, with convictions and acquittals, including those of officers, other ranks, and the few civilians caught up in the military net by virtue of the area in which they were when an offence was committed. There is, in addition, an annual breakdown showing the number of courts martial held at home and held abroad. The committee appointed to inquire into courts martial statistics during the Second World War gave an

---

[6] *Annual Report of the Prison Commissioners for Scotland for the Year 1917*, Cd. 9604, 3; and see also *Annual Report of the Prison Commissioners for Scotland for the Year 1918*, Cmd. 78, 3.

[7] *Report on the Criminal Judicial Statistics for Scotland for the Year 1925*, Cmd. 3007, 7.

[8] Lodge, 'A Comparison of Criminal Statistics' (1956–7).

**Table 3.1** Court Martial Trials of Other Ranks at Home and Abroad in the Two World Wars

| Offence | 4 August 1914 to 31 March 1920 | 1 September 1939 to 31 August 1945 |
|---|---|---|
| Total | (298,310 trials) 266,513 convictions | 210,029 convictions |
| Miscellaneous Military Offences | 49,712 | 23,085 |
| Miscellaneous Civil Offences | 3,040 | 6,041 |
| Desertion | 38,584 | 30,740 |
| Absence Without Leave | 87,131 | 75,157 |
| Mutiny | 1,807 | 800 |
| Cowardice | 541 | 167 |
| Striking and violence | 13,084 | 6,053 |
| Threatening, insubordinate language | 29,975 | 5,263 |
| Disobedience | 11,439 | 11,416 |
| Quitting/sleeping on post | 8,790 | 3,854 |
| Drunkenness | 39,906 | 3,812 |
| Offence against inhabitant | 1,704 | 572 |
| Theft | 9,322 | 18,599 |
| Fraud | 950 | 852 |
| Indecency | 270 | 790 |

*Sources: Statistics of the Military Effort of the British Empire during the Great War*, London, 1922, Part XXIII, Section 2 and WO/277/7 Brig. A. B. Macpherson, *Army Discipline*, Appendix 1(a)

annual breakdown of such trials in the Army and RAF for the nine years following 1 September 1938. But the statistics presented by Brigadier A. B. McPherson in his analysis of Army Discipline during the Second World War are less full than those for the earlier conflict; in particular, they include only convictions for other ranks.[9] None of these military statistics, like their civilian counterparts, can be used to suggest anything like the actual level of criminal offending by men on active service. However they do reveal the kinds of offences that military officers considered sufficiently important to bring before the courts, and they are as near an indication as can be found anywhere of the pattern of military offences committed by soldiers and the number of criminal offences that were tried by courts martial. Tables 3.1 to 3.3 are constructed from these statistics. The first of these provides the broad comparison of the convictions of other ranks at courts martial during the two wars. Tables 3.2 and 3.3 give the annual breakdown of selected offences, together with an indication of whether the trial was held at home or overseas.

The figures in these three tables are raw and take no account of the size of the Army. In both wars all of the services grew significantly, and the Army most of all. By the end of 1914, volunteering had brought its numbers up to almost one and a

---

[9] *Statistics of the Military Effort of the British Empire during the Great War, 1914–1920*, Part XXIII, Discipline; WO 93/50 and WO 93/51, Statistics—Military Effort, 1914–1920; *Report of the Army and Air Force Courts-Martial Committee*, Cmd. 7608; WO 277/7, *The Second World War 1939–1945: Army Discipline*, compiled by Brig. A. B. McPherson.

Table 3.2 Court Martial Convictions (Selected Offences) of Other Ranks by Year, 1 October 1914 to 30 September 1919

| Offence | 1914–15 | | | 1915–16 | | | 1916–17 | | | 1917–18 | | | 1918–19 | | |
|---|---|---|---|---|---|---|---|---|---|---|---|---|---|---|---|
| | Home | Abroad | Total | H | A | T | H | A | T | H | A | T | H | A | T |
| Striking or violence | 1,968 | 713 | 2,681 | 1,314 | 1,607 | 2,921 | 1,035 | 1,483 | 2,114 | 785 | 1,913 | 2,698 | 487 | 1,140 | 1,527 |
| Insubordination | 2,442 | 119 | 2,561 | 3,640 | 81 | 3,721 | 5,902 | 146 | 6,048 | 4,130 | 142 | 4,272 | 1,861 | 140 | 2,001 |
| Theft | 679 | 350 | 1,029 | 810 | 643 | 1,453 | 969 | 574 | 1,543 | 1,279 | 1,592 | 2,871 | 654 | 1,221 | 1,875 |
| Fraud | 97 | 7 | 104 | 155 | 11 | 166 | 170 | 12 | 182 | 212 | 10 | 222 | 111 | 16 | 127 |
| Drunkenness | 2,138 | 6,372 | 8,510 | 1,442 | 9,849 | 11,291 | 1,062 | 7,222 | 8,284 | 487 | 6,518 | 7,005 | 289 | 3,427 | 3,716 |

Source: Statistics of the Military Effort of the British Empire during the Great War, London, 1922, Part XXIII, Section 2

**Table 3.3** Court Martial Convictions (Selected Offences) of Other Ranks by Year, 1 September 1939 to 30 August 1945

| Offence | 1939-40 | | | 1940-1 | | | 1941-2 | | | 1942-3 | | | 1943-4 | | | 1944-5 | | |
|---|---|---|---|---|---|---|---|---|---|---|---|---|---|---|---|---|---|---|
| | Home | Abroad | Total | H | A | T | H | A | T | H | A | T | H | A | T | H | A | T |
| Striking or violence | 242 | 308 | 550 | 769 | 178 | 947 | 617 | 343 | 960 | 447 | 556 | 1,003 | 447 | 776 | 1,223 | 283 | 1,092 | 1,375 |
| Threatening/insubordinate language | 139 | 230 | 369 | 707 | 149 | 856 | 475 | 271 | 746 | 458 | 494 | 952 | 446 | 643 | 1089 | 263 | 988 | 1251 |
| Ill-treating a soldier | 34 | 31 | 65 | 112 | 18 | 130 | 78 | 48 | 126 | 64 | 75 | 139 | 40 | 104 | 144 | 30 | 131 | 161 |
| Theft | 461 | 178 | 639 | 2043 | 143 | 2186 | 2739 | 491 | 3230 | 2840 | 1326 | 4166 | 2468 | 1374 | 3842 | 1639 | 2897 | 4536 |
| Fraud | 55 | 16 | 71 | 146 | 14 | 160 | 148 | 35 | 183 | 86 | 48 | 134 | 87 | 57 | 144 | 72 | 86 | 158 |
| Falsifying an official document | 17 | 8 | 25 | 83 | 1 | 84 | 113 | 10 | 123 | 92 | 36 | 128 | 73 | 108 | 181 | 39 | 143 | 182 |
| Drunkenness | 145 | 409 | 554 | 402 | 153 | 555 | 182 | 70 | 252 | 99 | 630 | 729 | 51 | 714 | 765 | 31 | 926 | 957 |

Source: WO/277/7 Brig. A. B. Macpherson, *Army Discipline*, Appendix 1(a)

**Table 3.4** Court Martial Convictions (Other Ranks, Selected Offences) per 100,000 men 1914–18

| Offence | 1914–15 | 1915–16 | 1916–17 | 1917–18 |
|---|---|---|---|---|
| Striking or violence | 129 | 97 | 63 | 64 |
| Drunkenness | 422 | 376 | 219 | 177 |
| Theft | 51 | 47 | 38 | 71 |

*Source*: As Table 3.2

**Table 3.5** Court Martial Convictions (Other Ranks, Selected Offences) per 100,000 men 1939–45

| Offence | 1939–40 | 1941–2 | 1942–3 | 1943–4 | 1944–5 |
|---|---|---|---|---|---|
| Striking or violence | 61 | 48 | 37 | 45 | 47 |
| Drunkenness | 61 | 11 | 27 | 28 | 33 |
| Theft | 71 | 140 | 154 | 142 | 156 |

*Source*: As Table 3.3

half million. By the end of 1916 it was approaching three million men and, following the introduction of conscription, it grew to just under four million. In September 1939 there were just under 900,000 men in the Army; two years later there were roughly 2.3 million, rising to 2.7 million in 1943 and 1944, and reaching 2.9 million by the summer of 1945. When the raw figures for convictions at courts martial are reduced to convictions per 100,000 of men serving in the Army, see Tables 3.3 and 3.5, the numbers appear to tumble considerably, and distinctions between the two world wars become apparent. Given the rapid changes in the size of the Army no figures for 1940–41 have been given.

The most striking thing, though perhaps the thing that might most obviously have been assumed, is the fact that the majority of courts martial dealt with offences committed against military law. The figures imply a less rigid approach to discipline during the Second World War; there were, for example, fewer convictions for striking a superior and for insubordination during this war, and 'ill-treating a soldier' appears as a distinct and separate offence. Noticeable for both wars is the statistical increase in courts martial as the wars drew to an end and in the months following victory in Europe. Brigadier McPherson concluded:

> Whenever fighting is continuous, and particularly in operations which are being successfully conducted, it has been found that the incidence of serious crime diminishes. The converse is also true. Similarly in the case of units billeted behind the line near to large towns or cities, it may be expected that, during long spells of inactivity, offences such as drunkenness and insubordination will tend to increase.[10]

[10] WO 277/7, 37.

Yet the year following 30 September 1917 witnessed the savage fighting of Passchendaele and the Ludendorff Offensive; while the year following 1 September 1944 saw British troops heavily engaged in Northern Europe and Italy as well as in the Far East. Some criminal and military offending probably was the result of inactivity and boredom, yet the final year of both conflicts were not the periods of maximum inactivity and boredom. Moreover, there are several other questions that might be posed from McPherson's figures. The greatest number of thefts tried by courts martial during the war occurred in the period September 1944 to August 1945; of these 1,639 were on the home front and 2,897 overseas. It is possible that, with a fluid front, long and mobile lines of communication and supply, soldiers thought that there were greater opportunities for getting away with plunder. Equally it might be that some men reasoned that being held behind the front line on a Section 41 charge was preferable to being sent forward into action, with the consequent risk of death or injury as, first, the fighting intensified and then as the war drew to a close. Similarly, some men might have committed offences at home to avoid being sent abroad to the front line.[11] Finally there is the question: what percentage of the thefts that led to courts martial in Europe after May 1945 were an indication of the frustration of men still in uniform, wanting to get out of it and to go home now that the war was over? Answers to all of these questions can be hazarded, but they can never be certain.

There were always a few miscellaneous military offences that would probably never have been considered as offences outside of the armed forces. Men disliked the fact that the letters they wrote to family and friends were read by the officers acting as the postal censors. In December 1943, for example, two soldiers in Sicily were arrested by men from the SIB for forging postal censors' signatures on nine separate, private letters.[12] But a favourite method of circumventing the censor was to get a friend who was going on leave to take letters with him and to post them in an ordinary letter box when he got away from barracks, if posted in the British Isles, or once he set foot on British soil if he had been serving overseas. Any man who sent a letter in this way was liable to a court martial. In the spring of 1940 a gunner in an anti-aircraft unit wrote detailed descriptions to his mother and a girlfriend of working the range-finding equipment during an air raid on a naval base in the north of Scotland. The detail was such that anyone with sufficient inclination could have identified the base and noted the number of dummy ships that he described. Both the gunner, and his comrade who had promised to post the letters 'south of the border', were prosecuted under Section 40.[13] This was also the offence for which Rifleman Randall was sentenced to fifty-six days' detention in the Military Prison in Cairo in April 1944. Randall's battalion had served in the Western Desert since 1941 and the offending letter was written in March 1944 as the battalion prepared to move to Italy. His comrade, Rifleman Crimp, noted how the offence was regarded as too serious to be dealt with by the company or battalion

---

[11] See, for example, *Evening News (Portsmouth)*, 1 February 1945, 8.
[12] CRMP Archive, SIB Crime Book, Sicily 1943, no. 21.
[13] WO 84/56, 1–3.

commander, and the outrage felt by the men at Randall's sentence. 'Evidently the authorities are taking a serious view of circumventing the censor and want to make an example.' Crimp thought that this might be because of the impending Second Front, but it did not stop the ill-feeling, especially when the news came back about Randall's reception at Cairo's military prison.[14]

Other offences such as abusing or striking an officer or NCOs might have appeared in the civilian statistics as threatening behaviour or under one of the categories of assault. In civilian life abusing a superior because he was newly appointed, or had not seen as much service, might have cost a man his job but, if no form of violence was involved, it is most unlikely that it would have led to any form of trial. The continuing levels of confrontation between officers and men may have reflected the frustration of men who in some instances had significant artisanal skills and who had depended on their union to protect these skills in the civilian world. Similarly, a Regular serviceman with such skills could have had links with unionized civilian counterparts. Such men resented being ordered about by those that lacked their skills either in non-commissioned or commissioned rank. They also resented class distinctions, rigidly adhered to by many Regular service officers; engine room artificers in the Royal Navy, for example, had their claim for commissioned officer rank rejected in 1919 on the grounds that 'an officer did not work with his hands'. Often it was when men had drunk too much that resentment exploded into abuse or a blow but, while the levels of confrontation remained similar, the incidence of drunkenness resulting in courts martial was far smaller in both the Navy and the Army during the Second World War than during the First.[15] For the Army there were nearly ten times fewer cases of drunkenness that led to convictions before Army courts martial in the Second World War. The contrast in the scale of these figures is not easily explained; possibly more offenders were hauled before their officers for summary punishment, for which no records remain. It is equally impossible to assess whether some units—for example those principally recruited from Scotland with its high statistical pattern of drunkenness offences—were any worse than others.

Heavy drinking and drunkenness had been among the accusations levelled at the Victorian soldier, and it was one of the major reasons for stigmatizing him. Heavy drinking and drunkenness were also seen by many Victorians as a root cause of criminal offending. From the 1870s, however, the situation appears to have been improving in the Army, with a better diet, improved education, greater recreational facilities, and the creation of a vigorous Army Temperance Association.[16] Courts martial hearing cases of drunkenness among soldiers steadily decreased; and so too did the number of fines for drunkenness imposed by commanding officers, even

---

[14] IWM (D) 96/50/1, R. L. Crimp, vol. 3, ff. 96 and 100.
[15] For a brief survey of these issues as they affected the Royal Navy, see Sears, 'Discipline in the Royal Navy' (1991).
[16] Skelley, *Victorian Army* (1977), 64–5, 128–32, and 160–3; Snape, *Redcoat and Religion* (2005), 114–15.

though from 1907 men became liable for such fines on their first and second offence.[17]

The majority of the drunkenness offences during the First World War were listed as having been tried overseas: 33,994 out of 39,906, or 85 per cent. There is no indication of how many of these were committed on the Western Front, but this high incidence of drunkenness might have been a reflection of the long absences from home and family, the nature of industrial warfare, and the availability of French 'plonk' and *eau de vie*, the former in particular being a beverage that was quite new to the average Tommy. It is also possible that on the Western Front, away from the new restrictions on licensing hours and the rising prices of the Home Front, soldiers seized the opportunity for consuming alcohol.[18] Moreover heavy drinking, and the camaraderie that surrounded it, had long been part of British male culture, and in addition it provided a way to alleviate the pressures and the hideous memories of the battlefield.

Paul Fussell, the celebrated literary critic, who wrote an important analysis of British literature during the First World War and who served as an American infantry officer in northern Europe during the second, noted a much greater preponderance of poetry commenting on drinking, drunkenness, and hangovers in the second war. Peter A. Saunders's 'Tripoli' is a far cry from Owen, Rosenberg, Sassoon, and company:

> I've a mouth like a parrot's cage
> And a roaring thirst inside,
> My liver's a swollen, sullen rage –
> Last night I was blind to the wide.
>
> Canned as an owl, last night,
> Drunk as a fiddler's bitch,
> Oiled and stewed and pissed and tight,
> Sewn up, asleep, in a ditch.[19]

Such literature might have reflected a much greater awareness and a greater acceptance that men drank to solve the problems of boredom and fear; and this, in turn, might have led to a greater leniency when dealing with drunkenness in the services between 1939 and 1945. In both world wars some magistrates accepted drunkenness as an excuse for other offences such as theft.[20] The smaller number of convictions for drunkenness by courts martial during the Second World War conceivably reflects the overall decline in drunkenness among the civilian population; though there is a problem here in that a decline in civilian drinking could equally have led to higher standards and more of a clampdown in the armed forces at the summary, orderly room, or ship's captain level. As in the First World War,

---

[17] *The General Annual Report on the British Army for the Year Ending 30 September 1911*, Cd. 6065, Part VI, Tables 2 and 5.

[18] Bowden, 'The New Consumerism' (1994), 244.

[19] Fussell, *Wartime* (1989), 97.

[20] See, for example, *Evening News (Portsmouth)*, 27 September 1918, 4, 10 February 1945, 5, and 5 March, 4.

the majority of the Army's courts martial convictions for drunkenness, 2,902, were abroad, and only about a quarter, 910, were at home. But of course, drunkenness at home could be brought before a civilian court and there is no way of distinguishing between the number of service personnel and the number of civilians brought before civilian magistrates for drunkenness during the conflicts.

The majority of the convictions for drunkenness during the Second World War also occurred abroad and, once again, the novelty of foreign drinks might have played a part. But this 'novelty' must not be overemphasized. The explanation of men getting drunk at the beginning of the campaign in Sicily and Italy might be justified by the heat, the lack of beer, and the need to take long drinks, but this is hardly an explanation for drunkenness during the bitterly cold winters of 1943–4 and 1944–5. Italians complained rather of allied troops '*in cerca di vino e signorine*'; probably success in the pursuit of wine fired up the pursuit of women.[21] There might have been grounds for a similar argument about ignorance of the strength of local drink in Normandy in the summer of 1944; but men were only likely to have confused calvados and cider by accident on the first occasion, and they were happy to drink whatever could be purchased from bars or liberated from French and Belgian cellars, and captured German messes.[22] But in both wars, even when added together, the total convictions for drunkenness, for the abusing or striking of senior officers, and for theft did not reach the figures for the number of service personnel convicted by courts martial for absence without leave or desertion.

Desertion and absence without leave had been major problems for the Victorian and Edwardian Army and Navy. At the turn of the century, between 1,600 and 2,300 men deserted annually from the Royal Navy. Between 1,500 and 2,000 men, the equivalent of two or three battalions of infantry, went before Army courts martial each year charged with desertion. The majority of the men accused appear to have been young soldiers, in their first year or two of service, who were having difficulty getting accustomed to the life.[23] The scale of such offending was similar in the mass armies of the two world wars. Desertion and absence without leave account for rather more than 40 per cent of the Army courts martial during the First World War, and a little over one half of the convictions in the Second. The problems became especially acute as the wars ended and men appear to have become increasingly fed up with military discipline. Between 1944 and 1945, desertion and absence accounted for almost 60 per cent of the convictions before courts martial. The situation was considered to be particularly serious among infantry units fighting in Italy in the last year of the war. During the first nine

[21] Williams, *Crime and Disorder* (forthcoming, 2013).

[22] In an article on 'Apple jack' the D-Day veteran and *The Guardian* London editor Gerard Fay noted how Normandy veterans would remember the local apple brandy, Calvados. He went on: 'The first court martial I sat on in France was over a man who had drunk what he thought was half a pint of cider but it was Calvados. He then unfortunately joined in a French political meeting which was setting the stage for the arrival of General de Gaulle in Bayeux. More unfortunately still there was an *agent de police* standing behind him who understood English, so he was taken into custody for using grossly insulting and obscene language.' *The Guardian*, 26 November 1960, 14. For a general account of drinking in the 21 Army Group after D-Day see, Longden, *To the Victor the Spoils* (2004), chapter 3.

[23] Carew, *Lower Deck* (1981), 63; Skelley, *Victorian Army* (1977), 130–2.

months of 1944, 1,289 out of 1,981, or 65 per cent of the Army's court martial convictions in Italy were for desertion and absence without leave; another 1,091 men were listed as absent in the period 21 August to 1 October.[24] The position in Northern Europe seems to have been little better. From the beginning of January until the end of May 1945, courts martial were convened for 1,512 soldiers, according to the monthly returns of the Judge Advocate in Montgomery's Army; 975 of these, 46.5 per cent, involved absence without leave or desertion.[25]

When men deserted, the difficulties they had surviving, particularly in a foreign land, meant that they could easily get sucked into criminal behaviour. Major General Wyndham Childs insisted that, during the First World War,

cases occurred in France where soldiers deserted from their unit and made their way to the Base, where they lived—mostly by robbery and violence—a life of drunkenness and immorality. The death penalty was a necessity when dealing with such men and nobody had the slightest sympathy when they met their fate.[26]

This may be true, yet remarkably few of the men shot for desertion during the First World War appear to have been in this category. It was usually possible for a brief period to find food and shelter with different units on the excuse that a soldier had become temporarily separated from, or was travelling to join his own unit. During the Second World War, soldiers near the front would help out men who they thought were separated from their units and, perhaps also, those who they might suspect to be deserters; in addition, Black GIs were said to be particularly sympathetic to men in British uniforms. If a man had money he could buy goods in NAAFIs, and one of the best ways of making money was to engage with the black market; large towns in liberated areas became centres for such dealing. In April 1944, RSM Woodmansey of the Coldstream Guards went looking for deserters from his unit in Salerno. An archetypal guards' warrant officer, he was appalled by the lack of discipline in the town—men could not produce passes, they were slovenly dressed, failed to salute, and enjoyed joy riding with women civilians. He considered that many deserters had become long established in the town, knew their way around, and were now living with civilians. He and his party caught the two guardsmen they were seeking, but another three that they recognized disappeared among the backstreets of the slums. Woodmansey claimed that Army trucks, laden with goods and carrying civilians, could be seen regularly on the road to Agropoli between midnight and 3.00 a.m. His report was forwarded to two senior officers who protested that it was exaggerated, that the Military Police were overstretched rather than lax, and that anyway more than 300 deserters had been apprehended in Salerno in the previous two months.[27]

The problem in Italy appears to have been compounded by the overthrow of Mussolini in July 1943. Many of the British PoWs held by the Italians avoided

---

[24] WO 204/6713, Lt. Gen. R. L. McCreery, 'Crime in the Eighth Army,' 22 October 1944; and see, in general, Peaty, 'The Desertion Crisis in Italy' (2002).
[25] WO 171/4456.
[26] Childs, *Episodes and Reflections* (1930), 143–4.
[27] WO 204/6714, Copy of a Statement by RSM Woodmansey, and replies.

falling into German hands and melted away from Italian custody as the Italian troops guarding them also melted away. The majority of those close to territory occupied by the allies had reported to the British authorities by August 1944, but the provost marshal in Italy believed that around 200 had no such intention. 'Most of these [ . . . ]', he wrote, 'have been in Italy some considerable time and may be found in civilian clothes, possibly married to Italian women, speak the language of Italy and generally live the life of an ordinary Italian civilian.'[28] The court martial record of Sergeant J. Foxall has survived and, while it does not fit the stock story in every respect, it is nevertheless illustrative of the problem. Foxall had been captured in North Africa in the summer of 1942. He was moved to a prison camp in Italy and the following summer he was one of the men handed over to the Germans. He made three escapes and was twice recaptured. He explained:

> I intended to make my way to the Allied line which I thought to be somewhere near Perugia. On my way towards Perugia I met some people working in a field who took me to a house [ . . . ] [Subsequently] I used to sleep in the woods and only called at the house for meals. I had decided that it was best to wait for the advancing Allied troops rather than try to get through the German lines and risk getting captured a 4th time.

But the owner of the house had a daughter; Foxall fell for her and was concerned that he might be sent back to England before he received her parents' consent and before he could marry her. British troops arrived in the district, and Foxall did not report to them, deciding to stay with the Italians. He was betrothed to the young woman on Christmas Day 1944 but, a few weeks later, Foxall was picked up by Military Police. His future father-in-law spoke up for 'Giacomo', as he was known in the village. Foxall pleaded guilty at his court martial and was sentenced to eighteen months' hard labour, which was promptly commuted to '12 months' detention'.[29] Other absentees and deserters might also have lived and worked as ordinary Italian civilians, but in both Italy and Northern Europe the senior provosts believed that long-term deserters survived by stealing War Department property, or scrounging from other soldiers, by moving around in stolen vehicles and by selling in the booming black markets. Drives were mounted against deserters in liberated areas, and failure to net many offenders was put down to too many people being 'in the know'.[30]

Civilian criminal law defined offences such as theft and various forms of assault; military law defined offences that related largely to matters of discipline within the services. The statistics give an idea of which offences were the most prevalent and, in some instances, which kinds of individuals were the offenders. The statistics also underline the different priorities of civilian and military law. What they do not provide is any clear indication of how far war and, particularly, the recruitment of large numbers of the most crimogenic section of the population influenced the

28 WO 204/6713, provost marshal in Italy, 31 August 1944.
29 WO 71/958.
30 WO 204/6713, Plan for Special Drive against Absentees and Deserters, 24 August 1944; WO 171/4475, Combined Check on Absentees and Deserters, 14 February 1945.

overall patterns of criminal offending. Generally speaking, the military is well organized and well resourced but, particularly during a war, it can find itself functioning in conditions in which some, often many elements of civilian order have fallen apart, are not functioning well or, compared with the military, are relatively powerless. Such circumstances provide opportunities and temptations for people to take advantage and to commit crimes. The focus needs now to shift to specific forms and to specific instances of crime for a more detailed picture of illegal behaviour among individuals and groups of service personnel.

# 4

# 'The Biggest Thieves in the World'
## Service Personnel and Property Crime

On 16 May 1946, A. Norman Schofield spoke to the Rotary Club in Watford. Schofield was a professional local government officer who had been town clerk of Watford for several years; he was subsequently to move to Southampton, to be President of the Society of Town Clerks and, in 1966, he was appointed to the Press Council. His talk to the Rotary Club concerned his wartime service in the Middle East; he was a firm pro-Zionist but, while he was impressed with the intelligence of the Jewish independence movement, he feared that, without the protection of the British Army, the Jews would all be ejected from Palestine or killed. During the war, as a lieutenant colonel, Schofield had acted as president of the military court in Jerusalem and, at the end of the talk, he was asked about the extent to which Arabs were thieves. His response to his fellow Rotarians was the quip that British soldiers were 'the biggest thieves in the world'. Such a comment was meat and drink to sections of the national press. Interviewed by the *Daily Express*, he was unrepentant.

> I have sentenced a number of British soldiers who stole arms from their unit armoury and sold them to local inhabitants. I gave one seven years for that. Soldiers often trade arms with their women friends. I can't think of a worse type of crime, for they would probably be used against their comrades. I have watched military police rounding up British soldiers who have raided the Arab orange groves to steal fruit. That was done on a big scale. You've no idea what the troops get up to. I have seen them steal handfuls of nuts from Arab stalls—and I've defended one who stole £100 from the Army Post Office. I do not think that the soldier in Palestine was worse than elsewhere. Officers have told me how British troops in Germany drove cattle over the frontier to sell to the Dutch.

The evening before publication, the *Express* sought a statement from the War Office and were told: 'As the department which deals with disciplinary matters is closed, we cannot comment yet.' It appears that they never did comment. Schofield's interview with the local press was a little more restrained. 'Perhaps I might have used such alternatives as "scrounging" or "winning", but the fact remains they are synonymous for "thieving".' He also told the local paper that while he had received one anonymous letter of protest, he had received dozens of letters, telegrams, and phone calls expressing agreement with his comments and congratulating him on his outspokenness.[1]

---

[1] *Daily Express*, 18 May 1946, 1; *West Herts Post and Watford Advertiser*, 23 May 1946, 7.

## QUARTER-BLOKES AND PETTY THIEVES

Theft and the handling of stolen goods were the most common categories of offence in the civilian criminal statistics during the 20th century; from the beginning of the century to the beginning of the 1960s, they constituted around two-thirds of the total number of recorded crimes. During the First World War, the number of offences recorded in the theft and handling category declined a little; during the Second World War a steady increase detectable in the interwar period was, more or less, maintained. Separating out any effects engendered by war is a problem. First and foremost, the civilian statistics provide no indication of the number of offenders who were serving in the forces or who were veterans. Equally frustrating, the thefts appearing in the court martial statistics show no distinction between petty and major offences. The detail offered in memoirs, press reports, and trial records do not help to construct any measurement of the scale of offending, but they do underline the complexities and the parallels with the civilian world. Some thefts were committed by men new to the services who had never committed an offence before, and who suddenly found opportunity and temptation. Others were committed by Regulars who, in wartime, found new opportunities and temptations.

Some service posts always provided the chance for appropriating goods for personal profit. The quartermaster sergeant—the 'quarter-bloke'—who was responsible for a unit's clothing, equipment, and food, including rum and tobacco, is, perhaps, the best example. Ronald Skirth, who served briefly as a 'temporary unpaid Quarterbloke' considered himself to be 'reasonably efficient'. He refused to let anything leave the stores without a 'chit' signed by an officer, unless he withdrew it himself. 'It didn't seem right that I should do extra work without financial reward, so I used the opportunity to look after No. 1.'[2] Skirth's profiteering, however, seems to have been restricted to getting himself a better quality uniform, less like the 'wire wool' usually issued to the rank and file, and acquiring an officer's camp bed. T. Hannam-Clark, a court martial officer from the First World War, recalled that

[T]he job [of quartermaster sergeant] was reputed to give, in wartime, many lucrative chances, below the counter, illicitly to add to his pay, quite generous though it was. One way was to exact a bribe from a man before he received clothing or other article of government store to which he was absolutely entitled. It was said, I know of one, that unless a man paid a recognised sum for his leave pass he was told it was lost; and to any complaint through higher authority the reply was given that the man had positively received and probably lost it. The Quarter-bloke was reputed, too, to 'knock off' or make 'savings' in the rations, or the margin allowed for dividing up, and sell them for his own pocket. He was a man, it was said, who rarely missed his opportunities.

---

[2] Skirth, *Reluctant Tommy* (2010), 152–3.

Hannam-Clark was involved in the court martial of several quarter-blokes, one of whom was found guilty of regularly sending his wife large quantities of Army foodstuffs as well as soap, scrubbing brushes, razors, and stationary that she might sell on.[3]

While a quarter-bloke suspected of appropriating goods from his stores was most likely to appear before a court martial, many thefts by servicemen were heard before the civilian courts. It is possible that the strict discipline and rigour of an Army barracks or training area, the drill, the training, the Blancoing of belts and webbing, polishing boots, and cleaning rifles, restricted some of the opportunities and the time available for minor larcenies. Yet some service personnel still found time to commit petty thefts that were largely indistinguishable from those committed by other young men who were not in uniform. Occasionally, as in the civilian world, thefts were little more than pranks or were motivated by some quirk. In January 1945 two young able seamen took pin-up photographs from a show case outside a cinema in Portsmouth. They pleaded guilty, said that they had thought the photos would look good in their barrack hut, and explained that they had been drinking before the offence. They were given good character references and the magistrates dismissed the case, advising the seamen 'to leave other people's goods alone in future'. A few months later another able seaman, a Cambridge graduate who had just been selected for promotion to sub-lieutenant, admitted to Chatham magistrates that he had stolen two pairs of women's knickers and asked for another thirteen offences to be taken into consideration. 'I did not mean to do it', he had told the police, 'I have a kink.' He thought that he was suffering from 'pressure of work and sexual inhibition.' The magistrates remanded him on bail for a medical report.[4] Yet, as in the civilian world, most thefts were opportunist, petty, and generally squalid.

Some young servicemen stole from the civilians on whom they were billeted. Two privates of the Royal Army Service Corps (RASC), for example, appeared before the Hertfordshire Quarter Sessions in February 1941, charged with stealing a purse containing nearly £4 from a house in Lidlington, Bedfordshire. One of the soldiers had been billeted with the family and knew that, every Friday, the householder gave his wages to his wife, and that she put them in her purse on the mantelpiece.[5] In spite of the fears that led to the development of the STUs, when such offenders were prosecuted and found guilty in the civilian courts, they were often treated with considerable leniency. Moreover, possibly drawing on the kind of ideas expressed by Baden-Powell about harnessing the energies of young tearaways, some such offenders were willingly accepted back into the services.

---

[3] Hannam-Clark, *Some Experiences* (1932), 7–8. Dishonest quarter-blokes did not, of course, purloin goods from their own stores only. Signaller Arther Howes recalled a quarter-bloke court martialled and reduced to the ranks for taking petrol in Egypt towards the end of the First World War. Brotherton, Liddle Collection, (E/PAL) A. Howes, 29–30.

[4] *Evening News (Portsmouth)*, 6 January 1945, 4; *Chatham, Rochester and Gillingham News*, 11 May 1945, 9.

[5] *Bedfordshire Times and Standard*, 14 February 1941, 8; and for a similar theft see *idem*, 24 May 1940, 9.

A succession of cases brought before the Bedfordshire courts in 1940 are illustrative of this. In April a young soldier from the Bedfordshire and Hertfordshire Regiment appeared before magistrates in the Bedford division charged with stealing the handbag of the local woman on whom he had been billeted. He had a record and had been sent to an approved school on three occasions, but his commanding officer spoke up for his character as a soldier. The magistrates decided to bind the soldier over and send him back to his regiment 'to give him another chance to recover his character.' But he was also required to help buy a new handbag for his victim and to repay the stolen money. A similar case was heard at the Beds Assizes towards the end of May; the judge bound over the offending soldier for twelve months and sent him back to his regiment saying 'the Army was the right place at present for a young man of his age.' Seven teenage soldiers who, as a group, had stolen from shops in Cranfield the following September, were treated similarly; and so were four more who stole cigarettes and chocolate from a NAAFI in December. On the latter occasion, however, it appeared that two of the offenders had lied about their age on enlistment and, being only 15 years old and 16 years old respectively, they were dismissed from service. The victims in these petty thefts were mainly civilians; but other thefts, in which the military was the victim, appear to have been prompted by the abundance of service provisions.[6]

At the beginning of the First World War, the theft of Army food appears to have gone under the euphemism of 'fraudulent misapplication'.[7] But by the time of the second conflict, the Judge Advocate General's office was quite comfortable with the word 'theft'. Many thefts were small and in the context of the war emergency the prosecutions can seem petty. Early in 1916, for example, Guardsman Ernest William Glithero saw a leg of lamb in a dustbin near the cookhouse at Victoria Barracks, Windsor. In Glithero's eyes the meat looked fit to eat; he picked it up, took it to the kitchen and found himself charged with theft. At his court martial, Guardsman Alfred Waklin, also of the Coldstreams, reported seeing what he thought to be good meat in the dustbins on several occasions. Captain C. L. Gordon, however, who was prosecuting the case, insisted that 'even if the meat was found to be in the dustbin it was Government property and the accused had no right to it.' The court agreed and Glithero was found guilty.[8] For a soldier from a poor background, such an attitude must have appeared incomprehensible, especially when people's food was restricted because of the war. Nor was food the only luxury that the services appeared to have in abundance. In 1919 an issue of sheets to soldiers for the first time tempted at least one soldier to try to take his two sheets home to his wife.[9] But not every theft—or 'fraudulent misapplication'—was the product of a belief that good food should not be wasted or that a good wife deserved good sheets. Early in 1916, Private William George Baston, a cook at the

---

[6] *Bedfordshire Times and Standard*, 1940, 5 April, 11; 24 May, 9; 20 September, 2 and 6; 4 October, 7; 13 December, 6.

[7] WO 84/9, ff. 405, 407, 417, and 434.

[8] *The Times*, 28 February 1916, 5. Glithero's sentence was not given in the report as promulgation had to await the decision of the JAG on the proceedings.

[9] *Aldershot News*, 2 January 1920, 5.

Connaught Hospital, Aldershot, was found guilty at the local Police Court of stealing over £2-worth of groceries and passing them on to a woman who appears to have been his landlady. A few months later, Corporal Edwin Loynd of the Royal Flying Corps was found guilty at the same court after having used a service lorry to deliver nearly eight hundredweight of coal to the house of another local woman.[10]

Any serviceman who had grown up during the Depression and whose family was experiencing the difficulties and privations of wartime rationing was, during the Second World War, likely to be tempted by the vast quantities of foodstuffs that he saw stacked in the cookhouse stores. In October 1939, for example, a bombardier stole two tins of herrings, a tin of salmon, four tins of sardines, and a tin of preserved milk from his regimental cookhouse in Golders Green; the charge was framed under Section 41. But there were other appropriations that cannot be easily explained or partially excused by servicemen from poor backgrounds suddenly seeing military abundance and trusting that no one would miss a few tins.[11] In April 1944, for example, a captain in the Scots Guards was caught taking books from the University of Naples; he intended to ship them home to England. That same month a corporal serving in the Army Dental Centre at Catania in Sicily used his situation to steal false teeth and sell them to a local dentist.[12] There were others who stole much bigger quantities of War Department or Admiralty goods, usually with the intention of selling their haul on to others: large meat thefts are an obvious example. It was also possible to take, and sell on, from vehicle parks and petrol dumps. From the early months of the Second World War, increasing numbers of offenders were caught offering fuel to garages at a good price.[13]

## THINKING BIGGER: THE BLACK MARKET

Shortly after his arrival in Haifa in September 1942, Craftsman Thomas Henry Bell of the Royal Electrical and Mechanical Engineers joined with two fellow soldiers, Danny Simpson and Jimmy McElroy, to 'acquire' tyres that they then sold to an Arab gang in the town. Bell appears to have had no previous criminal career; he had been born in Bishop Auckland in 1918, the son of a black American seaman who was killed during the first war. His upbringing had been hard; but so had that of many others. He had joined the Royal Engineers Tunnel Works before the war, volunteered for full-time military service in March 1940 and for overseas service shortly afterwards. The profit from selling tyres was insufficient for Bell and his mates and they decided to graduate to armed robbery. Their first couple of attempts were shambolic failures. In their next and final raid, on a jeweller's shop, they panicked and fled empty handed. During his flight, Bell shot both a man who

[10] *Aldershot News*, 21 January 1916, 2 and 16 April, 7.

[11] WO 84/53, f. 158; for similar offences see WO 84/53, f. 229, and WO 84/71, ff. 117, 152, 181, and 185.

[12] WO 84/71, f. 276; CRMP Archive, SIB Crime Book, Sicily 1943–4.

[13] See WO 84/53, 259–60, for an example of the theft of beef; WO 84/53, ff. 30–1 and 43, for examples of the theft of petrol.

had given chase from the jeweller's and a sergeant from a Palestine Anti-Aircraft Battery of the Royal Artillery. The sergeant was killed; Bell was found guilty of murder by court martial and hanged; there appears to be no record of the trial of Simpson and McElroy.[14]

Everywhere servicemen developed their opportunities for working with the local black market or for selling, on their own account, petrol, tyres, spare parts for vehicles, and even the vehicles themselves to anyone who could pay. Sometimes they were deserters; sometimes they worked in conjunction with local gangs, and in such instances they could become embroiled in local forms of offending. In September 1944, the SIB in Sicily arrested a private of the Argyll and Sutherland Highlanders who had been absent since the previous May. He was living with an Italian woman; interrogation also revealed that he became involved with a 'Black Market' gang who used him as an 'English Policeman'.

> On Sept. 1st. 1944, he went to an office in Palermo, after having received instructions from one of the civilians. There he obtained 10,000 Lire by presenting himself as a 'Policeman', also producing a revolver, from a civilian who was supposed to be in possession of 'Black Market' corn. Later that day he attempted the same ruse at a baker's in the same town, but this failed and brought about his arrest.

Private Mitchell appears to have got himself involved with one of the local mafia families that specialized in 'protection' and extortion. His arrest also brought about that of seven locals, charged with harbouring him as a deserter, and of an additional five for being involved in his attempted robberies.[15]

A major problem in Rome during the months after its liberation was that men, especially officers, would unthinkingly take vehicles—jeeps, reconnaissance vehicles, wireless trucks, even armoured cars—and park them in the street outside restaurants, brothels, and other places of recreation and amusement. Within minutes the vehicles were either stolen, or gangs of civilians and allied deserters had stripped them of all their tools and wheels. Captain C. H. Butt, a provost in the city, described the offenders as having 'a drill' enabling them to 'remove all four wheels in as many minutes.'[16] Sergeant Arthur Bastone, an MP in liberated Rome, recalled that in order to limit the scale of theft, jeeps were ordered not to carry spare petrol cans, except when on special duties. Similarly, the number of spare tyres was reduced from one per vehicle to one for every five vehicles. The scale of the profit that some criminal entrepreneurs in khaki could make was illustrated by another of Bastone's recollections. One evening a patrol by some of his colleagues stopped a smart sergeant who, for some reason, struck them as suspicious. The sergeant had a letter, signed by a general, stating that he must be allowed to proceed to his unit with all haste and without impediment but

> when made to turn out his pockets, he had books of blank passes, company rubber stamps, blank 'Priority 1' flight tickets, and thousands of pounds in Italian lire, French francs and several North African currencies. They [the arresting MPs] started looking

[14] Rubin, *Murder, Mutiny and the Military* (2005), chapter 3.
[15] CRMP Archive, SIB Crime Book, Sicily, 1944, nos. 272 and 273.
[16] IWM (D) 02/19/1, C. H. Butt, 6–7.

at the money to see if it was genuine, and he said it's all good money, I'm too smart to have forged money on me. His story was that he had been absent since long before Alamein, and had been flogging (selling) [sic] army equipment, from Egypt to Algiers, and had a bank account in every country he had been in, including Italy.

He said you will never trace them because I have no written records, and they are all in different names. He said that he went to France [ . . . ] to see if it was ready for 'picking'. It was not ready in his opinion.

It was on his return from France, with a Priority 1 air ticket, that he had bluffed a general into providing the letter that authorized him to proceed without hindrance. The arresting MPs handed him over to the SIB.[17]

The selling or bartering of military equipment was a common offence. The First World War was barely a month old when the chairman of magistrates in Gosport Police Court thought it necessary to warn the public against buying anything from soldiers.[18] The East End terror, Arthur Harding, served prison sentences in preference to serving king and country in the First World War, but he recalled acquaintances urging him to join them in the Royal Army Veterinary Corps. They assured him that he could become a sergeant and, like them, make a lot of money by selling horses to Belgians.[19] Robert Graves's first independent command was at Rhyl towards the end of 1917, looking after the remnants of a battalion engaged in camp duties. One night they were descended upon by 3,000 Irish troops on leave from France and heading for home. These men were held up for four days by the presence of U-boats in the Irish Sea, and they became rowdy and insubordinate. They were issued with blankets from the quartermaster's stores, a large number of which appear to have been sold to local civilians for beer and cigarettes. A court of inquiry followed and Graves was able to exonerate himself from blame for the loss of the blankets by pointing out that the blankets were issued without his author-ization, and by revealing further some dubious behaviour on the part of another officer.[20] Rather more serious entrepreneurial activity occurred during the guerrilla conflict in Ireland that followed the First World War. Here some British troops sold guns and ammunition to the IRA, not out of any ideological commitment, but simply to make money.[21]

There was a ready market for military clothing and equipment on the home front during the Second World War, and there could also be illicit exchange or selling of various goods among soldiers from different units.[22] Martin Lindsay enjoyed a good dinner in the front line on 20 July 1944 when one of his men exchanged a Gordon Highlander's cap badge with a drunken Canadian for four gallons of wine. Lindsay knew that his quartermaster would replace the cap badge. The wine,

[17] IWM (D) 01/32/1, A. L. Bastone, 1944, f. 23; 1945, f. 10.

[18] *Evening News (Portsmouth)*, 18 September 1914, 3; and the warning was repeated, see 6 October 1914, 3.

[19] Samuel, *East End Underworld* (1981), 171.

[20] Graves, *Goodbye to All That* (1960), 222–3.

[21] Sheehan, *Hard Local War* (2011), 54–5.

[22] For the sale of military clothing and equipment in London see Brotherton, Liddle Collection, (ARMY 184), G. St. George Stedall.

presumably, had been previously liberated from the French. Other goods, such as wristwatches and fountain pens, were liberated from the enemy dead or from prisoners of war. Luger pistols were greatly prized, particularly by American soldiers, and British squaddies found that they could sell them to GIs for as much as £10.[23] Most of this selling and exchange, while frowned upon officially, appears generally to have been ignored.

The economic and social disruption at the end of both wars, together with the continuing abundance of military supplies surrounding men who were fed up, bored, and wanting to go home, provided other opportunities for profiteering. T. Hannam-Clark, serving as a court martial officer in the area round Tournai recorded that, following the armistice in 1918, considerable profits were to be made from trafficking lorry-loads of sugar and tobacco across the Franco-Belgian border.[24] Early in 1919, Gunner Charles Keller found himself as part of the Army of Occupation in Cologne. The privations of the blockade meant that the Germans were keen to buy from the Tommies soap, chocolate, cigarettes, and anything else that they lacked; and the Tommies were happy to oblige.[25] But an appalling winter and the collapse of the German Mark increasingly limited this form of exchange and, in spite of regulations against fraternization, the British soldier found that they could exchange goods for sexual favours. Not only were women prepared to prostitute themselves, but even some parents were prepared to offer their daughters to soldiers for the necessaries of life.[26] When the Army of Occupation left for home at the end of 1929, the radical German weekly *Die Weltbühne* estimated that they were leaving 8,000 illegitimate children. Obviously not all of these children were the result of sexual favours being offered for the necessaries of life. Other sources suggested that the Army's conduct had been good and appreciated by the locals. A correspondent for the *Daily Herald*, for example, described Rhinelanders as waving the men off with affection.[27]

The privations and shortages in southern Italy at the time of the allied landings in 1943 drove thousands of women to prostitute themselves for food and also fostered a massive black market. It was estimated that about 45 per cent of all supplies reaching Italy and destined for the allied armies were stolen and resold on the black market. The situation was aggravated by corruption that reached to the top of the allied military government. Colonel Charles Poletti, a former lieutenant governor of New York, served first as the US Army's senior civil affairs officer in Palermo, and then as the regional commissioner for Campagnia. Poletti was supposed to clamp down on corruption, but he appears rather to have participated, and he chose as his guide and translator in the region Vito Genovese, a former New York mobster who had come to dominate the rackets in Naples.[28] Poletti might have been duped by local criminals and, given the allies' total ignorance of the

[23] Lindsay, *So Few Got Through* (1946), 24 and 216–17.
[24] Hannam-Clark, *Some Experiences* (1932), 21.
[25] IWM (D) 02/55/1, C. R. Keller, f. 97.
[26] Jeffery, '"Hut ab" "Promendade with Kamerade for Schokolade"' (2005).
[27] *Daily Herald*, 30 October 1929, 5; and see also 10 September 1919, 3, and 16 September, 4.
[28] Newark, *Lucky Luciano* (2011), 204–7; Dickie, *Mafia Brotherhoods* (2012), 350–68.

workings of the mafia brotherhoods, certainly many senior officers were; but petty pilfering and profiteering by the fighting soldier pales into insignificance besides racketeering on the scale deployed by Sicilian and Neapolitan gangsters during the Liberation.

Towards the end of the Second World War the men of Rifleman Crimp's battalion, quartered close to Florence, became disaffected when they heard that their battalion, which had fought together since the early stages of the North African campaign, was to be broken up. Everyone, Crimp recalled, set about selling off surplus kit before it had to be handed in to the quartermaster's stores, and there were plenty of takers among the local Italian community. Civilian clothes were almost unobtainable and the locals had plenty of money stashed away. Squaddies found they could sell shirts, trousers, pullovers, and greatcoats. A blanket fetched 2,000 lire, a pair of boots 3,000 lire, and this money could be spent in the NAAFI or on leave in the locality, allowing pay to be saved or simply sent home. The Regimental Police were rapidly directed to focus on the prevention of such sales.[29] But even Regimental Policemen were tempted to get in on the act. Guardsman Len Waller was posted to Como as a Regimental Policeman in October 1945. Como was, by then, a centre for black-market activity in Northern Italy, not least because of its proximity to Switzerland. Before long, Waller found himself 'up to [his] ears in corruption' like everyone else, and the Regimental Police 'were an important part of the whole crooked set up [ . . . ] if I'd gone against them they'd have made things very unpleasant.' In addition to the usual merchandise of everything from cigarettes to tyres, army blankets were 'high on the shopping list'.

> But they were too scarce to be exchanged for anything as sordid as lire. A girlfriend who's been inclined to shilly-shally would throw in the towel for a present like that. A few weeks later, you'd see her going to Mass in a smartly tailored coat or costume made from your grey army blanket.[30]

And it was not only Italian women who wore such clothing. Early in 1946, Kenneth Ryland, serving with the Military Police in Flensburg, noticed that a young German woman who acted as an interpreter in the NAAFI was wearing a coat and trousers tailored from British army blankets.[31]

## FRAUDS AND RACKETS IN A RUINED EUROPE

As the Second World War drew to its end, the dislocation on continental Europe extended the opportunities for currency frauds and racketeering as well as large-scale thefts and fencing. In the spring of 1945, the SIB in Naples were co-operating with the Italian *Guardia di Finanza* in investigating currency fraud.[32] There

---

[29] IWM (D) 96/50/1, R. L. Crimp, vol. 3, entry for 15 March 1945.
[30] IWM (D) 87/42/1, L. Waller, 'When Bugles Call', 83.
[31] IWM (S) 27312, Kenneth Albert Ryland, reel 4.
[32] CRMP Archive, SIB Crime Book, Naples, 1945, no. 266.

appeared to be no shortage of money in some quarters, but across the ruined continent many goods were in short supply. From the end of 1944, the Belgian government expressed concern about the way in which the liberators were involved in smuggling. Wine, spirits, and perfume in particular were reported as being transported from France in army lorries for Belgian entrepreneurs to sell on to those who could afford them. Bank notes were similarly transported at the behest of speculators and black marketeers; it was even alleged that some of the fraudsters, lacking the appropriate identification papers, were allowed to travel in military vehicles, sometimes wearing military uniform. There was particular anxiety about what could happen if these stories were widely circulated, since the Belgian population was constantly being told that a shortage of transport made it impossible to import foodstuffs into the desperate country. The 21st Army Group was responsible for the north of Belgium on a line running from Douai to Tournai and it agreed to establish permanent Military Police control points on the five major roads running across the frontier, together with temporary checks on the minor roads. But initially there was still a war on and there was no question of stopping convoys but only individual vehicles; moreover individuals were only to be searched if there was a strong suspicion that they were involved in illicit behaviour. Such regulations were continued in the weeks following the German surrender.[33] In The Netherlands, the problems were such that, in July 1945, it was felt necessary to deploy additional Military Police. The war diary of the senior provost branch noted that there was 'a great deal of Black Market in WD Petrol and Foodstuffs going on that has been unchecked for some considerable time.' The Netherlands Police were considered to be seriously lacking in resources; assistance was offered and close co-operation was established with them. But the problems continued and in early September spot checks were begun on vehicles crossing the frontier with Germany. Indeed, wherever there was a frontier, MPs were stationed to look out for smuggling and black marketeering.[34]

Quite how many service personnel profited from the black market and from smuggling, and to what extent, must remain an open question. John Gray, a serious-minded socialist who drove a tank in the Fife and Forfar Yeomanry, recalled how the black market in Germany promised money 'beyond our wildest dreams'. Gray was by no means a serious offender, but by trafficking cigarettes for German Marks he was able to purchase goods such as sheets, towels, and baby powder to take home.[35]

RAF aircrew found opportunities for making money on the side as they ferried new or replacement aircraft, former prisoners, and varieties of legitimate cargo across Europe and beyond.[36] Service personnel from all arms found that the shortage of medical equipment and supplies in Germany could be met by

[33] WO 202/740, Discipline—Smuggling, January–May 1945.
[34] WO 171/4475, Provost Branch, Lines of Communication, 1945. Kenneth Ryland's Military Police unit was based on the border with Denmark. IWM (S) 27312, Kenneth Albert Ryland, reel 4.
[35] IWM (S) 20202, John Gray, reel 10.
[36] Hodgkinson, *Best Foot Forward* (1957), pp. 211, 219–22, and 225.

smuggling some of Belgium's surplus of thermometers, and by stealing and smuggling penicillin from military stores. The premium on cigarettes, chocolate, and coffee in Germany could be met by barter. Looting became largely irrelevant when soldiers could exchange a week's supply of cigarettes for a Leica camera, or a tin of coffee for a good gold watch. Such goods might also be sold for Reichsmarks; the German money was then exchanged for British postal orders at British Army Post Offices and sent home. The enormous number of postal orders being sent to Britain in this way prompted an enquiry followed by a control on their issue; from January 1945 a postal order had to be entered in a man's pay book as a debit and, in consequence, men could no longer purchase postal orders for more money than they were actually paid. But resourceful soldiers found their way around this and black marketeers seemed also to have unrestricted access to £1 and ten-shilling notes, and the smuggling of these notes back into Britain began to affect the value of sterling. At the end of 1945, Metropolitan Police detectives combined with the SIB to investigate the German black market and, as a result, old German banknotes in the British zone of occupation were replaced by a special issue from the military government. Probably few of the service personnel involved in this considered their activity to be seriously criminal, and they were quite open about what they were doing in letters home.[37] The law made no distinction, but clearly many of the perpetrators did.

Yet there were some who saw these activities as seriously corrupting and as a potential threat to civilian life when the men came home. Squadron Leader 'Dickie' Leven was disturbed and depressed by what he found when commanding an RAF staging post in Berlin. He had already suffered what appears to have been a degree of post-traumatic stress disorder following bombing raids on Germany early in the war. He had been shocked by drunken sailors leering at and pursuing girls in Mediterranean ports; and the extent of the black market and of corruption provided a dystopian climax to his war. He seized 10,000 cigarettes on his base, but found no one to prosecute. A raid on three suspect houses yielded nothing, as someone appeared to have tipped off the suspects well before the police arrived. Worse still: 'I discovered that Air Marshals and Generals were organising high-powered looting, and making themselves a fortune. One Air Marshal, who was knighted, collected yachts near Schleswig and sent them back to members of the Cabinet.'[38] Elsewhere among the personnel involved, there were a few criminal entrepreneurs on the grand scale.

John Donald Merrett, better known as Ronald John Chesney, was a singularly nasty individual who generally hid his unpleasant nature behind ebullience and charm. At the end of the 1920s he had been tried for the murder of his mother and for fraud; he got away with the former and served a spell in prison for the latter. On his release he changed his name to Chesney, made a good marriage and spent the latter part of the 1930s enjoying a hedonistic lifestyle on the Mediterranean littoral.

---

[37] Williams, *Contraband Cargoes* (1959), 273 and 279–80; Longden, *To the Victor the Spoils* (2004), 202–3; Allport, *Demobbed* (2009), 170–1.
[38] IWM (D) 05/59/1, R. Leven, vol. 1, 145 and 160–1.

In 1940 he joined the Royal Navy and, during the siege of Tobruk, he commanded a schooner running supplies in to the garrison. The command suited Chesney's piratical appearance; he was a big man, with a big beard and a big smile—he even sported an earring. In addition to the official supplies, Chesney also carried gin, whisky, and other things that the garrison wanted and was prepared to pay for; and on the return trips he carried anything that he knew he could sell for cash in Alexandria. Like a good pirate captain, Chesney was courageous. As noted earlier, he fought heroically as his ship was blasted by German fire when Tobruk fell. He escaped from German captivity, was recaptured by the Italians, but then persuaded them that he was seriously ill and was repatriated. At the end of the war he found himself in northern Germany, principally at Buxtehüde, a short drive from Hamburg. Here he organized a massive black-market enterprise dealing in everything from chocolate and cigarettes to arms and penicillin. The police came near to catching him but, on demobilization in May 1946, he volunteered for and, amazingly, was accepted into the Control Commission for Germany. From his position on the commission he was able to continue his racketeering until, towards the end of the year, he found himself before a naval court martial charged on three counts of stealing and using a Royal Navy car. From that time onwards, things went from bad to worse for Chesney; eventually he committed suicide in Germany while on the run from the English police for having murdered his wife and another woman.[39]

A similarly striking example of a criminal-military entrepreneur, this time in khaki, is the man identified only as 'Turner' who was interviewed by John C. Spencer for his doctorate and who was then included in his subsequent book on crime and the services. At the time of the interview, Turner was serving a five-year term in Dartmoor; his wartime criminal behaviour had led to him being ostracized by his family and his mother had moved house for shame. Before the war, at the age of 17 years, Turner had been put on probation for the relatively minor offence of stealing a bike, but thereafter, as a lorry driver, he had showed himself to be a good worker. After call-up on the outbreak of war, he had served in an Army bomb disposal unit, first in England and then, following the allied invasion, in Belgium. Like the incompetent and murderous Craftsman Thomas Bell, he had no serious criminal record before the war. But here any similarity ended. In Belgium, Turner deserted and became engaged very successfully in black-market activity in Brussels. He linked up with a gang in Paris involved in the theft and selling on of military vehicles. His offences ranged from Calais to Toulouse and from Antwerp to Graz. Together with the former manager of a NAAFI canteen, he established a nightclub in Cannes and from here he was involved in an organized crime network that trafficked in Swiss currency and arms for Yugoslavia.[40]

Chesney and Turner were smart entrepreneurs running racketeering businesses. Elsewhere sensitive young men who would probably never have dreamt of committing a criminal offence found opportunities for fraud; and they justified their behaviour

[39] Tullett, *Portrait of a Bad Man* (1956).
[40] Spencer, *Crime and the Services* (1954), 133–4.

with excuses that would not have stood up as a defence in court, and that grate on the modern ear. Keith Douglas, a poet and artist with a cavalier attitude towards authority and an intense dislike of military discipline, left a highly regarded memoir of his time as a tank commander during the battle of Alamein. When one pair of his spectacles was lost and another pair broken, he was sent back to Alexandria to get his eyes tested and to purchase some stores. Not all of the purchases were above board.

> We drove the truck into the docks and arranged to fill the spaces under the seats, etc., with orange, gin, liqueurs, cigarettes and cigars; sitting on these, we drove out past the sentry and the Egyptian police, congratulating ourselves on getting English gin for 7s., and defrauding the Egyptians who had lived upon us for so long.[41]

## WORKING IN PACKS

Other groups of servicemen committed offences acting as a unit, in many respects like the working-class groups, such as dockers, who used the opportunity of their job for enhancing their pay through what they might characterize as perks. Indeed, dock work by soldiers led to precisely the same problems, not least because the soldier dockers were often also peacetime dockers. When Chief Inspector Hatherill of the Metropolitan Police investigated the crime problem in the British Expeditionary Force at the end of 1939, he noted that in the ports of north-west France 'the greater part of the military forces [ . . . ] are composed of labour companies, most of which have been drawn from the dock labour class of Manchester, Liverpool and Glasgow.'[42] There were similar problems found at home ports later in the war, in spite of the fact that they were patrolled by special units of Military Police. At Southampton in October 1944, for example, forty-six men from 902 Company, Dock Operating, Royal Engineers were investigated for 'Larceny, Receiving and Improper Possession of Army Clothes, Rations etc.' Thirty-five of these were dealt with by their commanding officer while the remaining eleven were sent for trial. There were similar charges against men in London, at Grimsby, Hull, Glasgow and—presumably as an indication of the truth of the old adage 'if you cant beat 'em, join 'em'—even a Redcap of 174 Provost Company was charged with larceny and receiving NAAFI whisky at Dent's Wharf, Middlesbrough.[43] Other specialist groups seem to have stuck together and hunted in packs. Robert Graves described as 'notorious thieves' the tunnelling companies, usually composed of peacetime miners, whose grim and dangerous wartime task was to dig under German trenches to plant mines or to dig counter-tunnels against such German attacks. 'They would snatch things up from the trench and scurry off with them into their borings; just like mice.'[44]

---

[41] Douglas, *Alamein to Zem Zem* (1969), pp. 78–9.
[42] CRMP Archive, Hatherill Report, 3 January 1940, 8.
[43] CRMP Archive, SIS Ports (UK), Register of Charges, From 14-9-44 to 19-9-45, and SIS Ports (UK), Crime Register, From 17-1-45 to 21-11-45.
[44] Graves, *Goodbye to All That* (1960), 103.

But there were also units with no particular peacetime specialism that simply became notorious for their behaviour. Some salvage companies were accused of helping themselves to the civilians' furniture during the First World War while, according to *John Bull*, there was a racket involving the looting of men's civilian clothes when they were parcelled up to be sent home after uniforms had been issued.[45] Martin Lindsay had several run-ins with a notoriously light-fingered Irish battalion. Before the D-Day landings, when this battalion had been based close to that of Lindsay, some of its men had rifled the bedrooms of Lindsay's officers while they were out watching a boxing competition. They had also stolen kit from his quartermasters' stores, a battalion cash-box and a NAAFI safe. Early in 1945, Lindsay's Highlanders replaced the same Irish battalion in a Belgian village, where a deputation led by the local *curé* showed him around houses that had been ransacked by the unit. 'I remember being asked at a dance what their regimental crest is,' Lindsay commented, 'and my partner's peel of laughter when I replied that it should be a couple of jemmies and a broken lock.'[46]

Particular moments also provided particular opportunities for some small groups to profit. The Blitz, for example, offered temptations to those ordered to guard or to clear up war-damaged buildings. Following an air raid on Ashtead at the end of August 1940, thirty men from the Royal Norfolk Regiment were sent to cordon off an area of damaged houses where there were also suspected to be some unexploded bombs. Over the following three days the unit acquired drink and various items of civilian property, leading to prosecutions before courts martial.[47] Early the following year some thirty members of the Pioneer Corps deployed in London to clear debris left by air raids and to demolish unsafe buildings, decided to turn the situation to their personal advantage by stripping lead from the roofs of houses. The lead was then transported in Army vehicles to a scrap-metal dealer's yard and the money that he paid for it was pooled and divided equally. Sergeant George Gallon, who was said to be the instigator, was sentenced to three years' penal servitude at the Old Bailey; Sergeant Henry Collier got twelve months; twenty-six pioneers got six months each and another four were acquitted. The civilian scrap-metal merchant, who collapsed when sentenced and had to be carried to the cells by prison officers, was sentenced to fifteen months.[48]

Appropriating goods as part of a group was one thing, taking from a member of the immediate service family was something else. While the old dock communities had no problem with theft from cargoes—from the bosses who could afford it—they had no truck with an individual who stole from a member of the community. It was the same with anyone who stole from a service comrade except, it seems, when service kit was involved. A chaplain on the Western Front was shocked when someone he knew, who had had a blanket stolen, made good his loss by stealing another comrade's blanket. Equally shocking, when a battalion moved into a

---

[45] Van Walleghem, *De oorlog te Dickebusch* (1964–67), vol. 1, 168; *John Bull*, 6 January 1917, 23.
[46] Lindsay, *So Few Got Through* (1946), 163.
[47] WO 71/1050.
[48] *The Times*, 29 March 1941, 2; *Daily Mirror*, 29 March 1941, 3.

forward trench line as a reserve, they promptly rifled the packs left behind by the battalion that had just gone over the top; they were particularly keen to get new razors.[49] 'If you were stupid enough to lose a piece of equipment,' explained Len Waller, 'you made sure that you damn soon replaced it with one pinched from one of your mates.'[50] The purloining of a piece of kit, however, was generally regarded as quite different from taking a man's private property or money. Frank Day, a volunteer of 1915 who rose to the rank of sergeant in the Royal Engineers, was robbed twice by comrades. The first time, in barracks at Chatham, he and other victims had no idea who the thief was but thought that it was no one in their room. On the second occasion, in Egypt, Day had a suspect; he told his mother that he intended to confront the man, but there is no follow-up in his letters home.[51] In a ship's mess, petty thieves were generally dealt with, often roughly, by their fellow ratings; and it was usually the same in barracks.[52] But there were instances when senior officers became involved and rough justice by a man's comrades became more difficult. In March 1941, Leading Aircraftsman A. E. Cross was due for some leave in Egypt; he was especially keen to see the pyramids and the sphinx. He carefully laid out his best uniform but, while he was showering, his wallet was taken from his uniform pocket. Cross guessed that the culprit was one of two, or both men leaving his squadron for Suez. His station adjutant checked train times and, finding that the Suez train had not yet left, he sent Cross and two RAF Whitecaps to the railway station in a staff car. Cross's wallet, together with the missing pay book of another airman were found on one of the men. Cross's mates had a whip-round and produced £30 for his leave; the money in his wallet was required as evidence for the court martial. They also offered to deal with the offender. Their offer was rejected, but the CO drew his revolver, 'waved it under the prisoner's nose and stated that, had we been in the desert proper and not a base station, he would willingly have shot him himself.' The offender was found guilty at his court martial and sentenced to six months. At the end of his sentence he was sent back to Cross's squadron, which no one in the squadron thought a good idea; strings were promptly pulled and the offender was sent to another squadron far out in the desert.[53]

## WHITE COLLAR: KHAKI COLLAR

Many of the offences that came under the category of fraud were of a kind that would, in the civilian world, be labelled as white-collar crime. Early in 1914, for

---

[49]  Pym and Gordon, *Papers from Picardy* (1917), 50–1.

[50]  IWM (D) 87/42/1, L. Waller, 'When Bugles Call', f. 17.

[51]  Brotherton, Liddle Collection, (EP 015) F. D. Day, letter 8 and letter 119.

[52]  McKee, *Sober Men and True* (2002), 146–7; Prysor, *Citizen Sailors* (2011), 411–12. For a discussion of theft from comrades in the post-war Army, and the platoon's usual response of beating the offender, see Hockey, *Squaddies* (1986), 128–30.

[53]  IWM (D) 96/58/1, A. E. Cross, 'Chronicles and Memoirs of a Desert Airman', 18–19. For other examples of men being prosecuted before courts martial for stealing from comrades see WO 84/71 ff. 46 and 139.

example, and well before the outbreak of war, a fleet paymaster was found guilty of embezzling over £13,000 and sentenced to three years' penal servitude. Several other officers were reprimanded for not maintaining a proper surveillance of his accounts. Shortly afterwards, on a much smaller scale, a petty officer was found guilty at Devonport of fraudulently converting to his own use £12 collected for charity at a dance; he was given one year's detention and disrated.[54] Towards the end of the following year, Captain Herbert Wynne Taylor faced a court martial convened in Lewisham Town Hall. He was acquitted of converting to his own use money to be used for his men's billets; no decision was reached on a second charge of misappropriating public funds; he admitted borrowing £60 from a fellow officer to meet his private expenses and to being careless with account books.[55] NCOs entrusted with money to pay certain bills, or to reimburse others, also sometimes appropriated the money for their own use.[56]

Similar opportunities were exploited in the Second World War. In April 1940, for example, a battery sergeant major was brought before a court martial in Ipswich for fraudulently misappropriating money from his regimental mess.[57] Four years later an able seaman was prosecuted similarly for stealing £65 from the wardroom mess of his ship, an offence compounded by him going absent without leave and having various fraudulent leave certificates and warrants in his possession. The seaman, only 20 years old when the offences were committed, had a clean record and his character and conduct were described as very good. He was acting as the ship's quartermaster at the time of the offences and, like some of his young civilian counterparts, he appears to have yielded to a moment's temptation when a large amount of money was put into his hands.[58] Rather less allowance can be offered on behalf of an infantry major tried by court martial in Leeds in April 1941 on a series of charges relating to billeting, catering, and transport frauds. Among other things he was accused of employing a woman who could not type as a typist and of putting his daughter on the payroll before she was actually employed. He had allegedly stopped a shilling a month from his men's pay for amenities and damage repair and entered into an agreement with some caterers for supplying his men's dinners at one penny less than the official allowance. In the following year a court martial in Liverpool led to the dismissal of a lieutenant in the Royal Army Service Corps who had made a fraudulent statement and drawn allowances to which he was not entitled.[59]

Bureaucratic institutions like the military, wherein so much behaviour and so many transactions require some form of written authorization, lay themselves open to a degree of fraudulent behaviour by individuals seeking to turn an illegal profit or simply to help themselves or their friends. During the First World War there was

[54] *The Times*, 10 February 1914, 6, 18 February, 4, 17 April, 13 and 18 April, 4.
[55] *The Times*, 4 November 1915, 5.
[56] See, for example, WO 84/12, to Major General commanding Portsmouth Garrison, 19 June 1916; WO 84/17, to Brigadier-General commanding . . . Northampton, 4 February 1918.
[57] WO 84/56, 42–4.
[58] ADM 178/343.
[59] *Manchester Guardian*, 22 April 1941, 8 and 24 August 1942, 2.

trading in travel warrants and discharge papers, sometimes forged. In the summer of 1916, for example, one soldier in the Tyne Garrison was charged with forging a discharge certificate and another with the theft of a Railway Warrant Book and fraudulent use of the warrants for travel.[60] Two years later, an investigation into the supply and use of drugs that rendered men unfit for military service in a battalion of the Royal Fusiliers, unearthed a regular traffic in forged Army Discharge Certificates. In addition to the certificates, the two suspect sergeants had a box and attaché case full of railway warrants and passes.[61] George Cornwallis-West described using undercover Military Police officers to expose and prosecute a corporal in Hounslow Barracks who, for a fee, was supplying fraudulent warrants to enable men to avoid conscription by travelling to Ireland.[62] The shambolic demobilization at the end of the war provided further opportunities for such offending. In addition, demobilized soldiers could draw a form enabling them to surrender their greatcoats to railway companies for £1. One individual was found selling the forms for 5 shillings each.[63] Similar sorts of white-collar offences were prosecuted during the Second World War. In November 1939, for example, a private in the RASC faced fourteen charges of forging warrants to travel on buses around Camberley and Aldershot. In August 1944, the JAG prepared a case against a sergeant and a gunner based in England for the theft of combined leave passes and railway warrants.[64] Most of these service fraudsters committed relatively small-scale offences involving travel warrants and leave passes, but a few had grander aspirations and hoped for considerable profits.

The laying of mines off the coasts at the start of the Great War led Lt. Col. Frederick George Scott of the Tyne Electrical Engineers to propose the formation of a special unit to watch out for loose mines that could endanger shipping off the north-east coast. The Royal Marine Submarine Mining Corps was formed early in 1915 under Scott's command. It was a relatively small unit reaching around 300 men at its peak in the summer of 1917. Membership of the corps had benefits; there were special rates of pay; since the tasks were local and local men were recruited, generally the men were able to live at home; above all, membership of the Submarine Miners kept men away from the Western Front and other dangerous theatres. Scott was authorized to recruit the men personally and, shortly after conscription was introduced, rumours were circulating that places in the corps were available for a fee. The police employed a decoy to meet first with Private Hyman Cohen and then with Captain John Moralee; it was agreed that the decoy would be recruited into the corps for the payment of £400. A deposit of £100 was paid in appropriately marked notes. At the Newcastle Assizes in November 1917, Cohen and Moralee pleaded guilty; Cohen was sentenced to eight months' imprisonment and Moralee to twelve. Scott, who appears to have been attempting other, similar

---

[60] WO 84/12, to Brigadier-General commanding . . . Tyne Garrison, 13 July 1916, and to Staff Captain . . . Tyne Garrison, 19 August 1916.
[61] AIR 1/558/72093, Appendix 'B'. Intelligence Summary Period 2.6.18–9.6.19.
[62] Cornwallis-West, *Edwardian Hey-Days* (1930), 297–8.
[63] AIR 1/552/72346, Intelligence Summary, 24 March 1919.
[64] WO 84/53, 90–3; WO 84/71, f. 63.

frauds for both financial profit and social advantage, pleaded not guilty, but the jury found against him and he was sentenced to eighteen months. All three men had to pay £200 towards the costs of the prosecution.[65]

There were also opportunities, taken by some, for defrauding or stealing from the dead and wounded, and from servicemen's parents. Harold Jago was responsible for checking the contents of parcels sent home to relatives containing the valuables of his dead and wounded fellow soldiers. In April 1917, at a civilian court in Winchester, he was given eighteen months' hard labour for stealing from those parcels. Later that year Private Thomas Johnson was given two months' hard labour at the North London Police Court for visiting the parents of soldiers at the front and saying that they required money and goods which he would forward to them.[66] The parcels sent to troops proved an irresistible temptation to a few of those charged with handling them. Sergeant George Airton recalled two men court-martialled and given fourteen days' Field Punishment No. 1 for stealing parcels in Egypt early in 1915.[67] At the Hertfordshire Quarter Sessions at the beginning of 1941, Private Victor Holloway, a Regular soldier, was sentenced to two years' imprisonment for opening his comrades' letters and parcels and stealing cheques and postal orders.[68]

Military service also provided the opportunity for men, and their wives, to make fraudulent benefit claims. Sapper James Riley appeared at a special juvenile court in Bedford in November 1915, charged with making a false declaration to get an allowance. Riley had enlisted in June, just before his fifteenth birthday, claiming to be 19 years old. On enlistment he had been asked if anyone was dependent on him and had replied that he gave his mother twelve shillings a week from earnings of fourteen shillings a week as a moulder. In reality he earned just four shillings a week, or 5s. 4d. with overtime, and had no dependents. The deputy clerk of the peace for Bedfordshire was concerned that such cases were becoming frequent, but was also sympathetic and urged the bench to pass a light sentence. Riley was fined five shillings, and the bench warned that: 'No other person would receive such lenient treatment.'[69] The allowances paid to the wives of soldiers also provided opportunities for fraud. The wife was the usual offender in such cases, but husbands might also be complicit. In May 1915, for example, Evelyn Mabel Ollerenshaw appeared at Bow Street Magistrates' Court on a charge of fraudulently collecting two allowances by claiming to be the wife of two members of the Brigade of Guards. The magistrates were sure that both of the guardsmen were complicit.[70] A stronger case of male complicity, or rather inducement, led to the court martial of

[65] ADM 178/26; *The Times*, 8 November 1917, 5, 9 November, 3, 10 November, 3, 12 November, 4, 18 November, 4 and 19 November, 4.

[66] *The Times*, 17 April 1917, 3 and 29 December, 3.

[67] Brotherton, Liddle Collection, (GS) G. B. Airton. Airton actually writes of 'punishment Class 1'.

[68] *Bedfordshire Times and Standard*, 14 February 1941, 8.

[69] *Ampthill and District News*, 13 November 1915, 3.

[70] *The Times*, 31 May 1915, 3; see also WO 84/9, f. 366 for the case of an unmarried sergeant in the Army Service Corps making a false statement that he had been married in 1912. It is unclear who the sergeant was intending should receive the allowance.

Sapper George Ellison in March 1940. Ellison had joined the Royal Engineers in July 1939, gone absent without leave from Shorncliffe and enlisted in the RASC in Sheffield the following October. He had then induced his wife, who lived in Sheffield, to draw two family allowances of thirty-two shillings a week for his serving in both units.[71] Others, like the underage Sapper Riley, claimed that their wages in civil life were higher than they were so as to obtain a bigger allowance for their dependents—in the case of an ATS private the dependent was her mother.[72]

## MISCELLANEOUS OFFENCES

Service personnel had access to, or knowledge of sensitive information that could be of value to an enemy. There were relatively few prosecutions under the Official Secrets Act and those in peacetime often became *causes célèbres*, such as the prosecution of the novelist Compton Mackenzie in 1932 for his war memoir that discussed his time in counter-intelligence. The prosecution might well have been designed to dissuade more prominent individuals from using information that they had acquired in office. Mackenzie's response was a comic novel, *Water on the Brain* (1933), which described a secret service that, in order to remain a secret service, considered that it must remain totally secret from everyone. More serious, in the year of Mackenzie's novel, Lieutenant Norman Baillie-Stewart of the Seaforth Highlanders was charged with ten offences under the Official Secrets Act, brought under Section 41 of the Army Act, for supplying information to the German government. Baillie-Stewart was held in the Tower of London awaiting trial, and photographs in the press of 'the officer in the Tower', together with tantalizing accounts of his romantic involvement with a woman in Berlin, ensured that the case received wide publicity, little of which put the Army, or the JAG, in a favourable light.[73]

The trials of Mackenzie and Baillie-Stewart were both held in camera. Wartime trials for offences against the Official Secrets Act were generally much more low-key and received little if any publicity. The service personnel who appeared before courts martial on charges framed under the Act rarely seem to have been motivated by political ideology. A few men sold information for money. Private Erik Kemp, for example, was sentenced to three years' penal servitude for passing information to Japanese representatives in Hong Kong in the summer of 1940; and, a few months later, Gunner Frank Gardner was sentenced to seven years' penal servitude for a similar offence in Singapore.[74] Fusilier Michael Hopper came from a poor, working-class background. On the eve of the Second World War he had met two men who were beginning to establish themselves as writers and who encouraged him to develop his own writing skills. Left to his own devices following call-up,

---

[71] WO 81/168, f. 246.     [72] WO 84/71, ff. 226 and 292.
[73] Vincent, *Culture of Secrecy* (1998), 170–1 and 182–3; Rubin, 'The Status of the Judge Advocate General' (1994), 247–9.
[74] WO 71/1042 and WO 71/1056.

Hopper decided to ignore their advice about writing short stories portraying working-class experience, and to write a big book about the war. To this end he began making notes and collecting maps, and in August 1940 he found himself charged with possessing documents and information that might be useful to an enemy. The court martial was lenient and gave him just thirty-five days' detention.[75] Private John Downie was less fortunate. He had been attached as a clerk to the 20th Guards Brigade serving with the British Expeditionary Force in 1940 and was evacuated with them from Boulogne. As a clerk in the brigade headquarters he subsequently had sight of the report on the defence and evacuation of Boulogne; he made a copy of much of it. He also collected a variety of other documents, including a report of the shooting down of British aircraft, various letters, aerial photographs, and maps. Like Fusilier Hopper he claimed that he wanted to write about the events, but he had no witnesses to comment on his literary potential. Downie was sentenced to two years' imprisonment with hard labour, to be followed by a dishonourable discharge.[76]

Other men wrote letters telling of their exploits and, as noted earlier, tried to avoid the postal censor; sometimes the content, and the avoidance, may have been to impress their wife or girlfriend. CSM Garnet Harvey of 136 Section, Intelligence Corps, might also have been out to impress some acquaintances—mainly women—but he was certainly silly when he showed off his copy of the Black List. This list contained the names of individuals who were suspect and not permitted entry into the country; witnesses remembered seeing the names of Baillie-Stewart and Unity Mitford on the list. Harvey was also charged with giving civilians, again mainly women, lifts in his Army car—'joy riding' was the popular contemporary term.[77]

Joy riding and taking a means of transport without the owner's permission were offences committed by young men in civilian life and there is little surprise in finding young servicemen doing the same. On at least one occasion during the First World War, joy riding involved the theft of a horse; and bicycles as well as cars were also taken, often to get back to camp.[78] Many of these cases appeared in the civilian criminal courts, but when military vehicles were involved the accused faced a court martial; the charge was commonly framed under Section 41 of the Army Act.[79] It was also an offence to use service vehicles for personal purposes, especially if the takers—like two troopers of the 3rd Hussars in November 1939 and a second lieutenant in the Royal Artillery five months later—were unfortunate enough to damage it.[80] Captain H. A. McCaffrey of the Royal Army Medical Corps decided to use an Army car for taking women out, and compounded the offence by ordering a lance corporal to tell a false story to superior officers. The Army decided to throw the book at the captain and, in addition to charging him with the above offences, he

[75] WO 71/696.     [76] WO 71/698.     [77] WO 71/1059.
[78] *Evening News (Portsmouth)* 7 November 1914, 3; 6 October 1939, 3, and 8 November, 2 and 4; *Chatham, Rochester and Gillingham News*, 16 March 1945, 8.
[79] WO 84/53, 61–2, 110–13, and 265–8.
[80] WO 84/53, 194–5; WO 84/56, 66–7, JAG's Office: Court Martial Charge Books, 17 April–2 June 1940.

was also prosecuted for the theft of War Department petrol while driving his lady friends around.[81] McCaffrey was not the only officer charged with taking lady friends for drives in military vehicles; nor was he the only man who found himself charged with the theft of petrol as a subordinate charge to the illicit use of a military vehicle.[82]

The detailed, qualitative evidence of property crime among Britain's mass armies suggests, unsurprisingly, that theft and fraud was much like that in the civilian world. Young men yielded to temptation and committed petty thefts; some saw opportunities for benefit fraud and others for turning bureaucratic regulation to personal advantage. Economic disruption provided considerable opportunities for involvement in war-induced black markets—at home and abroad—on active service; usually this was petty and on a relatively small scale, but a minority of daring and unscrupulous individuals engaged in major racketeering. Perhaps, as Dickie Leven complained, the powerful and influential were in the best place to make some of the biggest profits. But few of the offenders could be classed as serious, or even petty criminals before the war brought them into the armed services.

Taking a comrade's kit might be excused, but his personal property was sacrosanct within the tight community of the immediate service unit—the surrogate family. Service personnel depended upon each other, especially in, or close to the front line. But this also meant that a unit could work together against outsiders to commit property crime, whether it was small groups of dockers and miners who did similar jobs in the services to those that they did in peacetime, or whether it was groups that took advantage of situations and who could, it would seem, take advantage of the non-participants to remain silent out of unit solidarity. Looting by units involved in policing during the Blitz, or tidying up afterwards, appears sometimes to have fallen into this category. Looting at the front can be seen in many instances as the desire for little luxuries to add to basic rations to make a temporary respite more comfortable. Early in 1945, as Lt. Col. Martin Lindsay's Gordon Highlanders fought their way deeper into Germany, he confided to his diary the problems generated by looting and his officers' solutions.

> Difficulties arise over such articles as cars, food, luxuries like eggs and fruit, prohibited articles such as cameras and shotguns, and wine. We have more or less come to agreement amongst ourselves that we are going to take only:
>
> (a) What is necessary to make ourselves more comfortable, such as bedding or furniture.
> (b) Luxuries that the Huns can well get on without, e.g. eggs and fruit, but not food such as poultry.
> (c) Forbidden articles we want for our own personal use, such as shotguns, cartridges, cameras, field glasses.
> (d) Wine (which is mostly looted from France already).[83]

All in all, a pretty comprehensive list.

---

[81] WO 84/70.  [82] See, for example, WO 84/71, ff. 11, 15, 31, 78, and 108.
[83] Lindsay (1946) *So Few Got Through*, p. 264.

# 5

## 'I Didn't Like the Officer [ . . . ] and I Don't Like You'

### Crimes Against the Person

C. V. Hearn, a civilian police detective both before and after the Second World War, served with the SIB during the conflict. His wartime memoir described the chaotic state in the south of Italy during the allied campaign and occupation. Two chapters of the book, with dialogue that reads at times like that of a 'B' feature gangster movie, focus on his unit's struggle with the so-called Tiger Gang. According to Hearn this gang was run by a deserter from an anti-tank regiment, 'Tiger' Williams. His lieutenants were half a dozen other deserters and, at its peak, the gang was said to have had some seventy members, at least a third of whom were native Italians. It specialized in armed robbery, large-scale shop-breaking, and larceny. It had its own territory, feeding and clothing the inhabitants of a town and three villages. 'Tiger' and his principal lieutenants were finally caught when they went into Bari to have their photos taken, but not before a gunfight with Hearn and his men in one of the town's main piazzas. Property worth upwards of £7,000 was recovered in the subsequent mopping-up operation. Following a court martial, Williams was sentenced to six years for attempting to kill Hearn and four years for other offences; his confederates received from two to eight years.

The area where Williams and his gang were active was not one of the most notorious areas for Mafia-type groupings such as Sicily, Naples, or the mountains of Calabria. The history of these groupings is only gradually being uncovered and, even if their reach did not spread into the district around Bari, it seems unlikely that Williams could easily have attracted a significant number of Italians into his gang. More likely, perhaps, he developed links with Italians who were happy to use him as they used each other, and to provide information to get rid of him when it suited their interests. The allied armies had little understanding of the way in which the Mafia, the Camorra, or the 'Ndrangheta functioned. But while Hearn might have added some extra colour and misunderstood criminality in the *mezzogiorno*, there is plenty of evidence to suggest that, in Italy particularly, deserters became involved in banditry and brigandage. Generally they appear to have worked in rather smaller gangs than that described by Hearn, and the gangs were made up of men from different armies and nationalities. They engaged in highway robbery and moved around in stolen vehicles; and it was their use of these vehicles that often led to their arrest since they generally kept to the roads and they needed petrol.[1]

Some property crimes are, by definition, violent, but the situation involving allied deserters and native Italians in Italy from 1943 to 1945 appears to have been exceptional.[2] There were violent property crimes committed by service personnel elsewhere. Robbery, by definition, is a violent offence, and even on the Home Front there were reports of men in uniform robbing other servicemen and civilians. Wellington Arch was the smallest police station in London, but covered a central area around Green Park and Piccadilly. A surviving Occurrence Book for the station contains reports of seven such robberies between August 1942 and August 1945, when the attacker (or attackers) were identified as servicemen. In April 1944, for example, a woman walking along Knightsbridge with her husband was robbed by a soldier; the husband, possibly terrified of the assailant, excused his failure to defend his wife by claiming to have drunk too much.[3] But robbery, though it rose during these war years, was a relatively rare form of theft.[4] Most thefts were non-violent. Nineteen thefts of lady's handbags, for example, were reported at Wellington Arch during 1944 and 1945; none of these appears to have involved any violence and they were described simply as 'larceny'. This was the most common offence reported at the station but, while such small larcenies also constitute the largest proportion of offences in the Criminal Justice Statistics, it is crimes of violence that generate most space in the media and that attract most concern.

Violence is part of the soldier's trade. As described above in the introduction, from at least the 18th century, the ideal of masculinity in Britain, and elsewhere in western society, was gradually restructured to focus less on a man's physicality and strength and more on good works, probity, and restraint. Those who readily resorted to violence were deemed uncivilized; and while the powers of continental Europe required annual tributes of conscripts from their citizenry, the British depended on a volunteer Army that, in contrast to its Navy, was commonly derided as recruited from roughs. There was something of a softening in this attitude towards the soldiery by the beginning of the 20th century, and this accelerated with a much wider range of recruitment during the two world wars. But the patriotic volunteers of 1914, the men who, between 1939 and 1945, wormed their way out of reserved occupations to serve in the forces, and the conscripts of both world wars, were put into institutions that demanded and developed an aggression and toughness that were undoubtedly necessary in the context of war, but which appeared to run counter to the more gentle and restrained masculinity that had been evolving over the preceding centuries. The novelist and Vietnam veteran Karl Marlantes has warned that modern 'warriors

---

[1] Hearn, *Foreign Assignment* (1961), chapters 9 and 10; WO 204/2492 Italy: Internal Security. For the criminal groupings of Italy during the Liberation see Dickie, *Mafia Brotherhoods* (2012), 350–68.

[2] There was a bandit problem in Belgium at the end of the First World War; however, there does not appear to be any evidence of British deserters playing a role in this. My thanks to Antoon Vrints of the University of Ghent for information on this point.

[3] MPHC, Occurrence Book Wellington Arch Police Station (available online at www.open.ac.uk/Arts/history-from-police-archives).

[4] The Judicial Statistics record 685 robberies in 1942, 730 in 1943, 821 in 1944, and 1,033 in 1945.

[. . .] suffer from their compromises with, or outright violations of, the moral norms of society and religion.'[5]

There had been efforts to limit and humanize war in the century before the outbreak of the First World War, most notably through the Red Cross and the conventions issued as a result of international conferences at The Hague in 1899 and 1907.[6] Aggression was meant to be confined to the battlefield and the moment of battle. Often it was not. Men might surrender, but they were not always taken prisoner; and even prisoners in the immediate aftermath of battle were not safe. At least two British officers, one of them holding the temporary rank of brigadier, were found guilty by courts martial and dismissed for assaulting captured German aircrew shot down over the south of England in 1940 and 1941. The killing of prisoners during and immediately after a battle unquestionably occurred in both world wars; sometimes officers and NCOs stepped in to prevent it, sometimes they were complicit. The killing and brutal treatment of Nazi personnel worsened considerably after British troops entered Belsen.[7]

## DRINKING, FEUDING, AND FIGHTING

As well as fighting the enemy, soldiers, sailors, and airmen also fought each other; and as often as not they fought as a group in their platoon, company, regiment, ship, or squadron community. Ships' crews fought the crews of other ships, or men from different home ports. Such fights were generally followed by a dressing-down from the ship's captain as battered, bruised, and hungover men mustered the morning after; the dressing-down could be more severe if the crew had lost the fight.[8] Soldiers fought men from different regiments over arguments, incidents, and slights long gone but long remembered. 'Even the Black Watch had a stain on its record,' recalled Robert Graves,

> and everyone knew about it. If a Tommy of another regiment went into a public bar where men of the Black Watch were drinking, and felt brave enough to start a fight, he would ask the barmaid not for 'pig's ear', which is rhyming slang for beer, but for a pint of 'broken square'. Then belts would be unbuckled.[9]

Close to the frontline in Germany in March 1945, Martin Lindsay witnessed banter between men from his battalion of the Gordon Highlanders and others from the Black Watch. He recalled a savage feud between the two regiments that had continued for some time during the First World War, and hoped that this was not the prelude to a renewal of the conflict.[10]

[5] Marlantes, *What It Is Like to Go to War* (2012), xiii.

[6] Best, *Humanity in Warfare* (1980), chapter 3.

[7] WO 71/1048; WO 71/1061; and see in general, Ferguson, *Pity of War* (1998), 372–85 and 447–8; and Longden, *To the Victors the Spoils* (2004), chapter 14.

[8] IWM (S) 679, George Michael Clarkson, reel 32.

[9] Graves, *Goodbye to All That* (1960), 72.

[10] Lindsay, *So Few Got Through* (1946), 226.

Men also abused those from the other services, sometimes just because they wore a different uniform. In the summer of 1944, for example, a lieutenant of the RASC found himself on a series of charges following an incident in a Railway Transport Office. Extremely drunk, he had abused a sapper as a 'fat whore', and an RAF corporal as a 'fucking Air Force bastard [ . . . ] you stink.'[11] He was, perhaps, fortunate that he chose victims who did not retaliate. Sometimes the abuse and violence were in revenge for some earlier accident or incident. A fight in Newark between paratroops recently returned to England and RAF personnel early in 1944 was the result of the paras blaming the RAF for scattering them in a drop over Sicily the previous July.[12]

On occasions servicemen from Britain picked on and fought their supposed allies from other countries and from the Dominions. In the diary that he kept throughout the First World War, Father Achiel Van Walleghem, the parish priest of Dickebusch on the fringe of the Ypres Salient, recorded a Belgian soldier being stabbed in a fight with Tommies at the beginning of 1916. And there were other fights, often started, according to Van Walleghem, when the British hurled abuse that, to the priest's untutored ear, sounded like 'Fake Belgium'.[13] The higher rates of pay enjoyed by troops from the White Dominions fostered other conflicts. Tommies feared that more money gave their white, imperial comrades a head start in winning the favours of young women; and then there was the novelty and romance of the man from overseas with his different accent and, in the case of the ANZACs particularly, more attractively cut uniforms and flamboyant hats. Sometimes a fight was brought about by an individual boasting about the superiority of his personal unit or his country. Shortly before the Armistice in 1918, a drunken member of a US naval picket in Hull started a commotion involving both civilians and British servicemen by declaring that 'the Americans had come over to finish the war.' The picket's comrades aggravated the situation by coming to his aid, swinging their truncheons 'with that candour which is commonly reported to be the characteristic of the Police of New York City.' The US Navy commander in the district justified his men's actions by arguing that they were constantly interfered with in the execution of their duties and that the police in Hull had shown themselves unable, or unwilling, 'to control its citizen mobs'.[14] Similar trouble erupted a few months later in Inverness when an American naval picket demanded that one of their sailors, arrested by the local police, be handed over to them. Former soldiers were said to have joined in on the side of the burgh police and the American picket was forced back to its base with broken heads all round.[15]

During the Second World War there appears to have been considerable antipathy between allied troops and some Italians, including Italian soldiers after Italy acquired the strange status of 'co-belligerent' towards the end of 1943. Guns and

---

[11]  WO 84/71, f. 79.
[12]  Turnbull and Hamblett, *Pegasus Patrol* (1994), 52.
[13]  Van Walleghem, *De oorlog te Dickebusch* (1964–7), vol. 2, 8; see also, vol. 1, 161.
[14]  AIR 1/556/72346, Intelligence Summary, 1–30 November 1918.
[15]  *The Scotsman*, 28 April 1919, 4

knives were used and, on one occasion, a grenade was thrown following a drunken confrontation in a bar.[16] While Military Policemen and ordinary soldiers might not have seen eye to eye on many things, they wore the same uniform and claimed the same national loyalty. Military police dealt 'very violently' with gangs of young men in Rome who attacked British soldiers walking out with Italian girls, and who punished the girls by cutting their hair and pulling off their knickers.[17]

As in the first war, the soldiers from the White Dominions received higher pay, which led to annoyance and friction. But, as far as most British servicemen were concerned, it was their allies from the United States who were especially unpopular. Their pay was much better than that of the British soldier.[18] In addition, the Americans had smart walking out uniforms and shoes—very different from the all-purpose baggy British battledress with regulation hob-nailed boots. A Military Policeman serving with the 1st Parachute Brigade recalled that

> It was something of a local joke that the boys [ . . . ] could always find some excuse to have a go at the American troops, either because the Yanks didn't stand up quickly enough when the National Anthem was played in the local Dance Hall, or because of some imagined, or manufactured, insult to a local girl.[19]

The supposed allies fought back, and were no innocents when it came to beginning an affray. But if young men are trained in aggression, are put in a uniform that unites them with some young men and distinguishes them from others, and are encouraged to take pride in, and to support their new 'family', it is hardly surprising that rivalry occurs. They fought in dance halls, in pubs, in streets, often after considerable drink had been taken. The civilian police and military police came between them, often very violently; and occasionally injuries were serious, even fatal. One night towards the end of 1943 two young British soldiers, Thomas Donkin and Richard Smith, aged 18 years and 21 years respectively, got very drunk and saw a young GI walking down the road with two girls. As far as Donkin and Smith were concerned, Private Bernard Baxter probably looked typically overpaid, oversexed and over here. They set about their ally. Donkin was so drunk that he remembered nothing and Smith appears to have wielded the knife that struck the fatal blow. Donkin was acquitted; the jury at Stafford Assizes found Smith guilty of manslaughter and, in sentencing him to seven years' penal servitude, Mr Justice Singleton took his cue from the generous verdict of the jury.

> The jury have taken a merciful view of your case, and I am glad they have. It is another case that has come about through drink, and by your act a good soldier who had come

---

[16] CRMP Archive, SIB Crime Book, Sicily 1944, no. 368. See also nos. 28, 29, 364, and 369; and SIB Crime Book, Naples, 1945, nos. 53, 69, 129, 137, 188, and 297.

[17] IWM (D) 02/19/1, C.H. Butt, f. 45.

[18] Signaller Ken Beaufoy and a mate left camp at Ostend illicitly one night in 1945. They visited a few cafés and then in the dark—'we spotted a couple of girls along the street and whistled. They shouted back "You Americans?" We shouted "No." They shouted "You Canadians?" We shouted back "No." They shouted "You Tommies?" We shouted "Yes." They shouted "Go back to Front, you got no money." ' IWM (D) 99/46/1, J. Corbett, no folio numbers.

[19] Turnbull and Hamblett, *Pegasus Patrol* (1994), 56.

a long way to help has gone. You are very young, and for that reason the sentence is less than it otherwise would have been.[20]

There were men who needed neither a GI nor someone from another unit to provoke them to violence, especially when they had taken a few drinks. Aldershot was a military town that ought to have been used to rowdy behaviour by soldiers in drink but, early in 1940, the town's authorities were expressing concern. In January the local police superintendent told the town's magistrates that 'the conduct of some of these soldiers is getting very bad, and is giving us a lot of trouble.' A few weeks later the chairman of the bench warned: 'We are not accustomed to have this number of people drunk in the streets, and it must be known that if this sort of thing goes on we shall have to increase the penalties.'[21] Seaports were much the same. Early in 1943 Lavinia Holland-Hibberts, the respectable young gentlewoman who had been appointed the first training officer of the ATS Redcaps, found herself out, after dark, in Chatham with one of her sergeants. There was trouble with drunken sailors at a local dance hall. The ATS sergeant did not hesitate and plunged in to sort out the situation. Holland-Hibberts felt duty-bound to follow, and was shocked as drunken sailors manhandled her. 'How I should loathe to be a military policewoman and go out every night', she commented.[22]

Some drunken, violent sailors and soldiers, though not necessarily all, originated from the poor working-class communities where being a hard man was one way of making and maintaining a reputation. Sapper Thomas Mallon was notorious for resorting to his fists after a few drinks. One evening in December 1940, he and another soldier were drinking with two nurses. Mallon became violent and had to be dissuaded from punching a civilian. At the end of the evening he wanted to smuggle one of the nurses, also the worse for drink, into his billet. Sapper Roland Davison, a regimental policeman, had experienced Mallon's fists on a previous occasion and being ordered to ensure that the nurses left the premises, he decided to take his bayonet in his greatcoat pocket. In the inevitable fight that followed Davison's confrontation with Mallon, the latter died as a result of a wound inflicted with the bayonet. At an initial hearing before magistrates in Biggleswade, a lance corporal was asked if carrying a bayonet was usual in such instances. 'Well, I should use my own discretion,' he replied. 'If I was going on a police job I should do so— especially being a regimental police officer.' At the Bedfordshire Assizes in January 1941, Davison was prosecuted for murder. After the evidence had been presented, the prosecution agreed to drop the murder charge and then, with the judge's agreement, the jury found Davison not guilty on the charge of manslaughter. Six months later the magistrates at Biggleswade were asked to look at a case involving an airman who had run amok at a local airbase, attacking other airmen. When under arrest he produced a jack-knife and made for the sergeant commanding the guard. The sergeant drew his revolver and shot the man dead. The magistrates

---

[20] *Manchester Guardian*, 26 November 1943, 7. For an example of three sailors seriously assaulting and then robbing a GI see *Evening News (Portsmouth)*, 2 March 1945, 5, 3 March, 5, and 16 March, 5.
[21] *Aldershot News*, 19 January 1940, 7 and 9 February, 8.
[22] IWM (D) 96/34/1, Mrs L. Orde, f. 150.

decided that no jury would convict the sergeant on a manslaughter charge and the case went no further.[23]

## THE MORAL ECONOMY OF THE 20TH-CENTURY SERVICEMAN

Service personnel could be violent in their own interests, particularly when they considered that there was some legitimate reason for protest. In ones and twos they were to be spotted in the crowds that attacked German property at the beginning of the First World War; as the war progressed they became similarly involved in attacks on pacifists and pacifist meetings. Early in 1916, for example, under the headline 'Provost-Marshal Please Note', *Bystander* printed a photograph of 'two officers and gentlemen [ . . . ] holding the battered fragments of the bowler hat of a "peace-crank" orator in Trafalgar Square.' While the journal had little time for 'peace-cranks', it intensely disliked seeing Army officers engaged in what it con-sidered to be domestic politics. 'It was from such small beginnings that Prussian militarism—i.e. the military control of politics began. [ . . . ] England is, subject to war conditions, still a free country.'[24]

Army officers were never a requirement for directing such attacks. Other ranks were perfectly capable of organizing themselves in their platoon or company communities when there was an incident that appeared to require a group response. In September 1915 *John Bull* published an incendiary paragraph about a man of German origin, subsequently naturalized, who lived in the small Bedfordshire town of Flitwick and who, according to the journal, 'gloats over the reports of a German success, who celebrated the fall of Warsaw by a step-dance, and who greets a train-load of our noble wounded with the cruel, laughing taunt, "See what the Germans have done for you!"'[25] The day following publication of the paragraph, some twenty-five or thirty soldiers from Bedford barracks travelled down to Flitwick and gathered at the man's house. Most of the windows were smashed; the soldiers then broke in and, when they could not find the man they sought, they set about the furniture. A group of police arrived, some names were taken, and the situation was calmed; the soldiers then returned to their barracks. Two or three days later the police visited Bedford Barracks and the troops were paraded. The police were unable positively to identify any of the culprits and the rate-payers of Bedfordshire were left with a bill for £36 7s. for damage to the house in Flitwick.[26] Everyone agreed that the story in *John Bull* had no substance, but no action was taken; the journal itself made no apology and no mention of the disorder. But there

---

[23] *Bedfordshire Times and Citizen*, 20 December 1940, 3, 27 December, 6, 21 January 1941, 9 and 25 July 1941, 3.

[24] *Bystander*, 2 February 1916, 191.

[25] *John Bull*, 12 September 1915, 2.

[26] *Bedfordshire Times and Independent*, 17 September 1915, 2; Beds and Luton Record Office, SJC 13, meeting of 23 October 1915.

were other instances where violent attacks by soldiers were a response, if not a justifiable response, to real events.

British troops have been accused of committing several unofficial reprisals during the campaign in Ireland at the end of the First World War. A recent analysis, however, has suggested that these are often best understood as a clash of cultures: that of the enlisted men coming up against local street culture, and such clashes were periodically aggravated by the more violent context of conflict between the British Army and Sinn Fein. Just as soldiers of different nationalities stationed in Britain clashed over women, so some of the violence involving British soldiers in Ireland also arose over women. And, significantly, similar violence erupted in Cork when Sinn Fein supporters turned on girls and women who consorted with US sailors. One of the most notorious incidents involving British soldiers followed what has been dubbed 'the Wesleyan Raid' in September 1919. Thirteen men from the King's Shropshire Light Infantry were ambushed on their way to the Methodist Church at Fermoy; their weapons were taken and one of them, 20-year-old Private William Jones, due for discharge a week later, was killed. The other ranks of Jones's unit marched into Fermoy and attacked commercial and domestic property in the town. In particular, it was noted, they singled out the property of locals who had sat on the coroner's jury that had refused to deliver a verdict of murder on the body of Private Jones. It appears also that much of the subsequent looting of shops was the work not of soldiers but of local people who took goods out of the smashed shop windows. The officers were sympathetic to the soldiers' behaviour, but nevertheless regarded the reprisal as a threat to discipline. The lance corporal who was identified as an organizer of the reprisal was convicted by a court martial and punished.[27]

The attitude of the troops who attacked the property of the Fermoy jurors is reminiscent of the moral economy and the legitimizing notions that have been described as inspiring many of the riots in 18th-century England, particularly the food riots that occurred in years of dearth and high prices. Linked by bonds of kin and community, crowds demonstrated to bring their complaints to their social superiors who, it was believed, should be doing something to alleviate the problems, and to take action particularly against any profiteers. Occasionally the crowds took direct action by seizing and selling goods at what was considered a fair price; occasionally too they might adopt some of the more traditional forms of community shaming, turning the world—or at least the social hierarchy—upside down with what was known in England as rough music and more generally as charivari. This behaviour was, as one historian has labelled it, 'community politics', undertaken by communities that had no political voice. The law might have enabled such actions to be labelled 'riot', yet often there was little or no violence offered to persons by the demonstrators.[28]

Mutinies during and immediately after both world wars were similar to these manifestations of community politics and legitimizing notions. It is possible to

[27] Sheehan, *Hard Local War* (2011), especially 24–7, 31–5, and 40.
[28] See especially, Thompson, 'Moral Economy' (1991); Bohstedt, *Riots and Community Politics* (1983).

equate mutinies with modern labour disputes and strikes. Yet drawing too close a parallel with the strike distorts the hierarchical and disciplinary relationship between officers and men in the armed forces. It also has the potential to impose a more formal structure on a mutiny losing its ad hoc and sometimes bacchanalian aspects.

In service law 'mutiny' had no statutory definition but a definition was suggested in notes accompanying section 7 of the *Manual of Military Law*. Mutiny, accordingly, was an act of collective insubordination by persons subject to service law, or two or more such persons combining to resist, or to induce others to resist lawful authority.[29] But mutinies during the 20th century, and especially those involving conscripts or men who had enlisted as a patriotic duty in time of war, are often illustrative of men coming to terms with the demands of service life and the insistence that the soldier, sailor, or airman obey a superior without question. Mutinies were rarely political; they were commonly the only way in which service personnel could voice complaints and negotiate with superiors over what they saw as the rights and the respect that were owed to them to ensure their loyalty and obedience. Mutinies could be extremely threatening and potentially violent; they could equally be very minor and ribald, though this did not necessarily mean that they were dealt with any less harshly. A. E. Perriman volunteered for Kitchener's New Army, and early in 1915 his battalion was ordered to Larkhill. Shortly after their arrival there was a thunderstorm, which brought down all the marquees that had been erected; there were no rations and the quarters provided for the men resembled chicken pens. The men sought to make light of their situation by clucking like chickens. After a wet, hungry night, two companies were ordered to fall in, without breakfast, for shooting practice. But enough was enough. The anger of the previous night had been partly assuaged by the silly game of playing chickens. There was no more room for humour and they refused to fall in. Eight men were tried before a court martial; a sergeant and a corporal were reduced to the ranks and both they and the six privates tried at their side were given two years' detention. Refusals to parade such as this were a common form of protest by troops stationed in Britain during the First World War. But generally they appear to have been settled without recourse to charges of mutiny; such a charge usually required the threat of, or actual violence. The more sensible officers and NCOs listened to grievances and tried to do something about them; or simply allowed the men to let off steam. Other ranks were never blindly obedient cannon fodder, especially the citizen soldiers who volunteered in 1914, and leadership by listening and negotiation was always important.[30]

---

[29] Rubin, *Durban 1942* (1992), 106; for a good general survey of mutinies see James, *Mutiny in the British and Commonwealth Armies* (1987). 'Mutiny' was not a term applied solely to the armed forces in the late nineteenth and early twentieth centuries; police strikes were labelled as such and so too were prison disorders.

[30] IWM (D) 80/43/1, A. E. Perriman, f. 4. See also, Sheffield, *Leadership in the Trenches* (2000), especially chapter 8; and for a general account of First World War mutinies see Putkowski, *British Army Mutineers* (1998).

The men of the Australian Imperial Force (AIF) were all volunteers. They were immensely proud of this fact; equally, they appear to have had a disproportionate number of trade unionists in their ranks, who had a firm belief in their right to a working day of limited hours with time off in lieu for what they considered overtime. They were, as one of their number put it, 'an army of a new type'. Unpopular officers, especially those who were British and who made unpopular demands and ordered sudden inspections, could be greeted with the humiliation of being 'counted out' on parade; but while the men of the AIF might have been trade unionists, 'counting out' was closer to the tradition of rough music than the strike. Perriman, after being wounded on the Somme, was promoted to staff sergeant training instructor and posted to an Australian division. He found the Diggers very different from the Tommies and described being present at two counting out incidents caused by Friday afternoon inspections when the Diggers appear to have thought the weekend had already started. It did not matter that one inspecting officer was the Duke of Connaught, Queen Victoria's son, himself a soldier and the last royal prince to hold a significant command in action—the Guards Brigade during the Egyptian campaign of 1882. When the duke arrived he was greeted with a chant: '1, 2, 3, 4, 5, 6, 7, 8, 9, 10, out you Tommy Woodbine Bastard.' The Australians then relented and the initial chant was followed by: '10, 9, 8, 7, 6, 5, 4, 3, 2, 1, Your [sic] in, your [sic] a Bonza, your [sic] one of us.' The duke had experience of Dominion troops, having served as Governor General of Canada from 1911 to 1916, but quite what he made of the Australians' welcome is anyone's guess. Some weeks later a less distinguished British officer was greeted with the same chant when he demanded a parade. The Australians then sat down and began their popular gambling game of two up. The officer announced furiously: 'This is mutiny.' 'Call it what you will, Sir,' [Perriman] replied, adding, 'there's nothing we can do about it. No troops here will dare interfere.' At Perriman's suggestion the affair was reported to the brigade major who, very sensibly, took no action.[31]

Violence in mutinies could easily be engendered by NCOs and officers offering an aggressive response to complaints and protest. Perriman's warning to his officer was sensible and, while Perriman himself makes no mention of it, he might have had at the back of his mind the violent mutiny at Etaples in September 1917. Etaples, a few miles south of Boulogne and at the mouth of the River Canche, had become a massive base area for the British Army. There were port facilities and a railway and the Army had established an Infantry Base Depot, where drafts from Britain were trained alongside men recently discharged from hospital and were incorporated with others who had previously seen active service. Training largely consisted of marching and double marching across dunes known as the Bull Ring. It was harsh and directed by NCOs with a reputation for bullying; this was aggravated by poor accommodation, poor food, and difficulties in getting passes to leave camp for the town. The Etaples disorder began with troops in the camp protesting over the arrest of a New Zealander. A Military Policeman panicked and

---

[31] IWM (D) 80/43/1, Perriman, 14–15; see also, Stanley, *Bad Characters* (2010), 37–8, 59, 99, 149, and 209.

fired his revolver, mortally wounding a Scottish soldier and also wounding a French woman. Over the next few days there were repeated confrontations between troops and, particularly, the Military Police. There was violence, but the mutineers did not use their rifles and bayonets and, after a few days, the trouble subsided without further loss of life. Senior staff officers, perhaps inevitably, blamed the trouble on the ANZAC troops and the Scots—'the scum of the earth, from the slums of Glasgow', according to one general echoing and perhaps seeking to amplify the Duke of Wellington. The staff also saw a revolutionary tinge in the affair. Corporal Jesse Short of the Northumberland Fusiliers, who suggested to an Army picket that they put a rope round their officer's neck and throw him in the river, was the one mutineer tried by court martial. Witnesses said that he had been seen talking to men waving red flags. Short said he was drunk. The court decided that he was guilty of mutiny and he was shot.[32]

The end of the First World War witnessed a wave of unrest as men, who considered that they had volunteered, or been conscripted until the Germans were defeated, resented both the fact that they were not demobilized more rapidly and the decision to send some units to a new conflict in Russia. Some officers showed tact and common sense to ease difficult situations; but others did not. Some soldiers ran up red flags, probably to ensure a rapid and positive response to their demands rather than as a reflection of any political radicalism.[33] And the red flags added something of a traditional, carnivalesque element of the world turned upside down and a way of cocking a snoop at discipline and the hierarchy. But such incidents were not necessarily good-humoured and could be violent. The two most serious, the attack on Epsom Police Station and the rioting at Kinmel Camp, during both of which individuals were killed, involved Canadian troops angry and resentful about the time it was taking to ship them home. There were fatalities in both of these incidents; yet both also have echoes of the old moral economy of pre-industrial crowds. At Epsom the trouble was sparked by the arrest of two Canadian soldiers for being drunk and disorderly. Four hundred of their comrades marched on the police station where the two men were being held, and demanded their release. The inspector in charge of the station, with rather more courage than wisdom, ordered the fifteen men then present under his command to disperse the Canadians with a baton charge. Police Sergeant Thomas Green, a veteran of the Royal Horse Artillery, died of the injuries that he received in the ensuing mêlée.[34] The determination of crowds to rescue individuals from custody had a long pedigree; but so too did the friction between civilian police and soldiers though, in this case, the soldiers involved were not the British Regulars who had commonly tangled with Bobbies in the streets of Victorian garrison towns.

In the spring and early summer of 1919, Kinmel Camp, near Rhyl in North Wales, held thousands of Canadian troops eager to go home. Accommodation in

---

[32] Gill and Dallas, 'Mutiny at Etaples' (1975); Putkowski and Sykes, *Shot at Dawn* (1992), 200–2; Putkowski, *British Army Mutineers* (1998), 26 for quotation of General Asser.

[33] French, *Military Identities* (2005), 198–201; Rothstein, *Soldiers' Strikes* (1980).

[34] Knight, *'We Are Not Manslaughterers'* (2010).

the camp was poor and so was the food, but what increasingly exasperated the troops there were the constant postponements of their voyage home. The final straw was the news that men were to be demobilized by unit rather than by the amount of time that they had spent in the service; and this was aggravated by the report that the ocean liners originally allocated to the Canadian Army were being used to take home troops from the United States. In the resulting riots, and the clumsy acts of suppression, five men were killed and a dozen seriously wounded. While the events at Kinmel are understandable, if not excusable, in the light of the men wanting to go home now that the war was over, this did not prevent accusations of Bolshevism against them. 'ORGY OF DESTRUCTION', proclaimed a headline in the *News of the World*, 'BOLSHEVISTS RIOT AMONG CANADIANS IN CAMP'.[35] Similar, generally groundless accusations were levelled by the military authorities at the end of the Second World War against men involved in protests over slow demobilization and the reintroduction of what they saw as pointless spit and polish.[36] But when, over two nights in July 1945, several hundred Canadian troops, angry over poor food and late pay and anxious to go home, took the centre of Aldershot apart, the authorities had learned from Kinmel and Epsom. Both civilian and military police were told not to intervene and while the town was said to look 'as if it had been subjected to a heavy air raid or a tornado', and the damage was estimated to exceed £15,000, no one was injured. This policy, it was stated at the time, 'was based on past experience'.[37]

Mutinies during the Second World War never experienced the turbulence and violence of Etaples or Kinmel, but they often sprang from similar origins. Once again there were instances of leadership by listening and negotiation but, on a few occasions, the unrest was poorly handled and left a legacy of suspicion and discontent. In May 1940, in North Africa, eight troopers of the 7th Hussars were tried by court martial for mutiny. All of the men in this instance were Regulars, but they were infuriated by a spit-and-polish colonel who, in their eyes, never gave any praise or encouragement and who seemed unable to grasp the fact that in servicing armoured vehicles, the men might get oil on their clothing. Different witnesses gave different numbers, but it appears that at least 100 men joined in a rowdy demonstration one Sunday afternoon at Maadi Camp. The men were prepared to talk to other officers, but refused to wait to speak to the colonel. Trooper Francis Goodswen, a man with eight years' service and who had recently turned down promotion to lance corporal, became an unofficial spokesman. He was noted by all witnesses for his respectful behaviour and calming influence; this did not prevent him being sentenced to twenty-eight days' detention, but others among the mutineers, who had sworn at their officers, received two years' hard labour. Interestingly, the commanders in the theatre appear to have been aware of the problem in the Hussars. They removed the colonel before the court met, but

---

[35] *News of the World*, 9 March 1919, 3; for the events see Putkowski, *Kinmel Park Camp Riots* (1989).
[36] Rubin, *Murder, Mutiny and the Military* (2005), chapters 6 and 7.
[37] *Aldershot News*, 6 July 1945, 5, 13 July, 6, 3 August, 5, and 10 August, 7–8.

they appear to have felt that the court martial still had to take place for the sake of discipline in general.[38] Goodswen's sentence seems harsh; presumably it was felt that a spokesman from the ranks was, by definition, a challenge to authority, and eighteen months later the Army was even less generous towards another soldier's spokesman.

A popular doggerel of the day, invoking Harry Pollitt, the Secretary General of the British Communist Party, ran:

> Troopships more than Pollitt can
> Radicalize the working man.

The truth of this became apparent from events in Durban, South Africa, in January 1942. The troopship *City of Canterbury* was in an appalling state; it was filthy and infested with bugs. When it docked in Durban, the angry soldiers and airmen on board were allowed to disembark with little supervision and with little order. The Deputy Judge Advocate who came down from Southern Rhodesia to supervise the prosecution of the men who had refused to re-embark was also appalled by the state of the ship; and he was singularly unimpressed with the local APM who 'appeared to have little knowledge of matters connected with his appointment.' Ultimately 130 RAF personnel and thirty soldiers remained in Durban when the *City of Canterbury* sailed. Thirty airmen were prosecuted for mutiny and acquitted. A few days later, twenty-nine Army privates faced one court martial and Sergeant George Jackson faced another. All were found guilty; the privates were sentenced to eighteen months' imprisonment with hard labour and Jackson to two years with hard labour. The authorities then found themselves with the problem of the remaining hundred airmen, fearing that, to let them go as their comrades had been acquitted, would only aggravate interservice rivalry. It was resolved to prosecute them in one group on the lesser charge of being absent from their place of duty; they were found guilty and sentenced to twelve months with hard labour. The Air Ministry recommended suspension of the sentence and the Deputy JAG held discussions with the local Army commanders, who agreed to suspend the sentences on all of the soldiers, except for Sergeant Jackson. The evidence in court suggests that, like Trooper Goodswen, Jackson's behaviour had been respectful and reasoned to the officers; it showed also that he had endeavoured to persuade the men to re-embark. But he was an NCO and, since he acted as spokesman for the men, he appeared to the Deputy JAG as 'the worst offender'. The JAG explained further the general opinion among the military authorities that

had the sentence been suspended it would appear in spite of the seriousness of his case that no one who had been tried would have undergone immediate punishment. Further our view was that matters of this kind rarely arise without a leader. If it were known in any case that leaders were punished expeditiously, it would have a deterrent effect on producing other leaders.

[38] WO 71/694.

The military authorities may also have been aware of Jackson's politics. He had been a member of the radical Independent Labour Party, though he had quitted its ranks because of its pacifist stance. In the event, however, Jackson did not serve the full sentence. He was sent back to England and to prison in Liverpool, but he was released on 1 July 1942 and posted, reduced to a private, to a Royal Army Ordnance Corps base in Lancashire.[39]

The implication in the cases of both Goodswen and Jackson was that, even when there was an identifiable problem giving men just cause to complain, the spokesman for the men was likely to find himself charged with mutiny. Just over eighteen months after the trouble around the *City of Canterbury*, an incident that was described to the mutineers by a general as a serious 'military cock-up' resulted in the prosecution of 191 men. Yet, in spite of the faults of the Army command, it was the men who protested who were singled out for punishment and who continued to be stigmatized thereafter.

In September 1943, 1,500 men from the 50th Tyne Tees Division and the 51st Highland Division left North Africa to join, as they believed, their units. The majority of the men were replacements but others were veterans of the campaigns against the *Afrika Korps* and had only recently left hospital where they had been recovering from sickness or wounds; some of the latter had even volunteered for the draft before they were properly fit so as to be reunited with old comrades. But, rather than landing in Sicily, where their units were based, the men sailed on to mainland Italy and were landed at Salerno, where they were ordered to join units assisting the US 5th Army. When the men heard the news of their posting on the beach at Salerno they refused to march to the front. Threats and cajoling eventually persuaded most of the men to move, but 191 steadfastly refused. These men were returned to North Africa for court martial. The defence was given just six days to prepare the mutineers' cases; the prosecution had had as many weeks. In addition, the defence had no time to interview the mutineers and no opportunity to call witnesses who were elsewhere on active service. All of the defendants were found guilty; three sergeants were sentenced to death, though this was subsequently commuted to twelve years' forced labour. Sir Ronald Adam, the Adjutant General, who was in North Africa shortly after the verdicts, was appalled. He demanded that all the men be released; the sentences were suspended and the men were sent back to their units, though in many instances these were the units that they had refused to join on the Salerno beach. Thereafter there were stories of victimization of the mutineers and many deserted. The bitterness and feeling of injustice prompted questions in Parliament nearly sixty years after the events but, even though a 'cock-up' was acknowledged at the time, and even though Adam had made his feelings known about the proceedings, officially both the Army and Parliament found it difficult to admit the shameful extent of the episode.[40]

---

[39] WO 71/734; and see also, Rubin, *Durban 1942* (1992); and Rubin, *Murder, Mutiny and the Military* (2005), chapter 2.

[40] David, *Mutiny at Salerno* (1995); *Hansard*, 22 March 2000, cols 242–49.

Such naval mutinies as occurred during the two world wars appear to have had similar legitimizing notions and to have taken a largely non-violent course, at least on the part of the mutineers. Jack Chadwick recalled the men of *HMS Edgar* refusing to coal their ship during the Gallipoli Campaign. Some goods had been stolen from a canteen store and the captain stopped the lower deck's mess privileges. For some four hours the ratings sat in their mess, stubbornly refusing to do anything, while the colliers floated idly at the *Edgar*'s sides. Once the captain agreed to restore the privileges, the men set about the filthy and exhausting work of coaling.[41] The Invergordon Mutiny of 1931 generated reforms and made the Admiralty more aware of the changed circumstances of having to deal with a skilled industrial workforce. Good captains were expected to be aware of the morale and sentiments of their crews; they were expected to hear grievances and pre-empt problems.[42] Yet not all officers lived up to the ideal.

The mutiny on the landing ship *HMS Lothian*, or *Loathsome* or *Unsanitary* as the ratings on the lower deck named this converted merchant vessel, sprang from old notions of fairness and rights. There appears to have been poor leadership on the ship and a belief among the ratings—a mixed bunch including men drafted from both the Army and the RAF—that there was one law and a decent diet for the officers and something quite different for them. The British flotilla commander, Admiral A. G. Talbot, sailed on the *Lothian* as it journeyed to assist an American invasion force bound for the Philippines. According to Bill Glenton, a mutineer who subsequently chronicled the affair, the admiral insisted on regular inspections and smart uniforms. He was believed to have daily baths while the men had limited drinking water fouled by a fault in the evaporators that were designed to remove salt. The fresh vegetables and tinned fruit that had been carried on board never appeared on the ratings' mess decks. The ventilation system was in poor shape and this encouraged activity among the ship's cockroaches and rats. Glenton recalled the mutineers singing 'The Red Flag', probably for much the same reasons as soldiers had raised red flags in 1919. 'As much as it added a more rousing political dimension,' Glenton wrote, 'it also introduced a touch of black humour.' The Second Sea Lord concluded that the majority of the mutineers 'appear to have regarded the outbreak in the nature of a "strike".' Seventeen senior men were court-martialled and reduced in rank for their part in the protest; the others were dealt with summarily and were given six months' extra duties and punishment drill. Glenton himself, a 'hostilities only' seaman, remained disgusted with the way that the ship's executive officer, Lieutenant Commander Kenneth Buckwell, who had risen from the lower deck, appeared to have been made the scapegoat for the mutiny and to have had his career ruined.[43]

The behaviour of a martinet officer, unnecessarily appalling conditions, broken promises, legitimized protest in the eyes of a group. But the perception of behaviour

---

[41] IWM (S) 10918, Jack Chadwick, reel 2.
[42] Prysor, *Citizen Sailors* (2011), 413.
[43] Rubin, *Durban 1942* (1992), 110–13; Glenton, *Mutiny in Force X* (1986), quotation at 104; Prysor, *Citizen Sailors* (2011), 416–19, quotation from Second Sea Lord at 418.

or conditions could also be confined to an individual's eye, and possibly the eye of an individual who found it difficult to fit with the group of his new service family. In some instances men struck officers, NCOs or Military Policemen. Like the inter-unit fights in pubs, dance halls, and elsewhere, such violence was sometimes linked to the tough masculine culture of the services. But the occasions of the violence could be varied. Able Seaman Matthew Carr cut a petty officer's face with his jack-knife following an argument over his sick-bay card; above all, however, Carr seems to have resented Maurice Pascall's senior rank: 'there are Petty Officers *and* Petty Officers and men *and* men, and you ought to act like one, and I have had more time at sea.' Able Seaman Daniel McQuade behaved with contempt towards a sub-lieutenant: 'You've been in the Navy sixteen months and I've been in seven years and know more about it than you do. As far as I'm concerned you can go and get fucked.' On Captain's Report the following morning McQuade abused his commander: 'I didn't like the officer for a start and I don't like you either.' He raised his fists and had to be restrained by the master-at-arms.[44] In the early summer of 1942, Bombardier E. E. Leech was savagely beaten by six gunners from his AA battery. The assailants insisted that he had referred to one of them as 'an IRA bastard'; Leech claimed that the men were always trying to cause trouble and instanced an assault on a young civilian some six months earlier.[45]

## LETHAL VIOLENCE

Occasionally the violence inflicted on superiors by service personnel was lethal. Sometimes this involved men on active service and grew out of confrontations arising from other disciplinary offences. In such cases the charge for the violent behaviour was one in a series prepared for a court martial. A private in the RASC, for example, charged with attempting to shoot his sergeant major in September 1944, had this charge coupled with one for being absent without leave.[46] But, as was the case with Sapper Davison described earlier, shootings and stabbings at home generally resulted in charges before a civilian court. In May 1944, for example, 19-year-old Private William Naylor Smith had been on fatigues in an Army cookhouse in Ayrshire. He complained to the cook that he needed some assistance in peeling the number of potatoes set before him; the cook allegedly responded with a punch. Smith promptly rushed to his quarters and returned armed with a Sten gun. He admitted the intention of shooting the cook in the arm or leg, but the gun's mechanism was defective and, even though the catch was set to single shot, it fired a burst that sprayed and hit the cook in the abdomen. The Lord Justice Clerk, hearing the case at Edinburgh, told Smith that he could count himself lucky that, in place of murder, the authorities had accepted his plea of guilty to the less serious offence of culpable homicide. Even so, Smith was sentenced to ten years' penal servitude.[47]

---

[44] ADM 156/235 and ADM 156/261.   [45] WO 71/742
[46] WO 84/71, f. 127.   [47] *The Scotsman*, 10 May 1944, 3.

It is difficult to make any assessment of the number of unpopular officers and NCOs who were shot during battle when the enemy might be blamed and hence the killer, or killers, got away with it. Hostility to unpopular officers was sometimes shown anonymously and collectively during the First World War, and anecdotal evidence suggests the occasional killing.[48] Guardsman Len Waller commented that, during the Second World War:

> Many vendettas were provoked by sadistic N.C.O.s and Warrant Officers and the confusion of battle provided the opportunity for the perfect murder to be committed. I know of two N.C.O.s whose names are included in the Roll of Honour in their village church, each of whom met an inglorious end at the hands of a member of his own unit.[49]

Occasionally, too, soldiers fired guns indiscriminately when drunk, killing or wounding comrades. Shortly after the landing in Sicily, one of Arthur Bastone's comrades was seriously wounded by two very drunk Canadians who claimed to be shooting at the insulars on telegraph poles with their Sten guns.[50] Other shootings, however, smacked quite clearly of premeditated murder. One seaman of the First World War recalled a man being stabbed as he slept in his hammock on a battleship at anchor in Scapa Flow. The murdered man had just exchanged hammocks with a ship's corporal who was assumed to have been the intended victim; no one was ever charged with the offence.[51] Where suspects for such offences were found, and especially at the front, they were tried by courts martial.

On 4 May 1918, Sapper R. Bell paraded a little behind the trenches on the Western Front without his putties. He claimed that they hurt his legs. Lieutenant Wynell Lloyd ordered him to put them on. Bell left the parade but, as he climbed out of a trench returning with his putties, his rifle went off, killing the lieutenant. Bell insisted that he had slipped and that the gun had gone off accidentally; he also told the court martial that he had forgotten that he had left a bullet in chamber from hunting the previous day. This seemed an unlikely story as Bell was said to be a good marksman who had often shot game, especially rabbits. Just over two weeks after the incident, Bell faced a firing squad. Bell was one of seven men executed for killing officers or NCOs during the First World War. A driver in the AIF, however, was acquitted of shooting dead a British officer. The British High Command believed that the acquittal was against the evidence and was primarily the result of entrusting the court martial to a board made up entirely of Australian officers. A further five men were executed for killing comrades during the war—usually, like Private Charles Knight of the Royal Welsh Fusiliers, after firing their rifles while drunk. Knight was a volunteer who had answered Kitchener's call. His unit had only spent a short period in the front line at the end of 1915 when, after a heavy

---

[48] Sheffield, *Leadership in the Trenches* (2000), 150.
[49] IWM (D) 87/42/1, Len Waller, 'When Bugles Call', 7.
[50] IWM (D) 01/32/1, A. L. Bastone, 1943, 30.
[51] Brown and Meehan, *Scapa Flow* (2008), 68.

night's drinking in a rest area, he returned to his billet and began firing indiscriminately, killing Private Alfred Edwards.

These offences are similar to the large number of civilian homicides in which the victim and the perpetrator were known to each other. The major contrast with civilian cases is the lack of domestic murders but, given the situation in a theatre of war, the lack of such offences is hardly surprising and, as will be discussed below, there were many instances of domestic violence committed by men while home on leave or shortly after demobilization. The overall pattern of murders tried by courts martial does not appear to have been greatly different from the murders and manslaughters tried before civilian courts during the same period. The number of killings committed as a result of other crimes such as theft was, as in the civilian world, relatively small. Joseph Chandler of the Lincolnshire Regiment was involved with three comrades in a series of burglaries around Calais. One of the gang appears to have tried to keep more than his fair share of the booty and Chandler killed him, probably with the assistance of the other two. Chandler also tried, unsuccessfully, to avoid the firing squad by pleading mental illness. Gunner Frank Willis and Lieutenant John Paterson were executed for murdering Military Policemen while deserters. Paterson, a former trader in West Africa, was also passing false cheques and might have been involved in black-market trading. Lance Sergeant Wickens of the Rifle Brigade was shot for strangling a prostitute in Le Havre; he appears also to have searched her room for money. Three other men, one from the British West Indies Regiment and two from the Cape Colony Labour Company, were shot for murder linked with attacks on women.[52]

## SEXUAL VIOLENCE

The number of courts martial under the heading of offences against civilians in both world wars was relatively small. As noted earlier, there is no breakdown of the number of service personnel who were tried before civilian criminal courts. Civilians were among those punched in pubs and among those robbed in the streets by service personnel. Civilians also complained that their property was damaged by men staggering back from pubs and bars, by troops on manoeuvres or by units tramping through their district on the way to the front. Doubtless some complaints were exaggerated in the hopes of significant compensation, but it is unlikely that all fell into this category. Some such instances occurred on British soil and, early in 1916, the War Office urged commanding officers to ensure that British property was not damaged. In particular it instanced wilful damage to houses in which troops had been quartered, the breaking of hedges, cutting field drains, and disturbing of stock. Officers were also instructed not to ride or march through fields in unsuitable conditions or site latrines injudiciously. In Britain, the letter warned, such behaviour wasted resources and, as a consequence, had a prejudicial

[52] All of these cases, except for that involving the AIF driver, are discussed in Putkowski and Sykes, *Shot at Dawn* (1992); for the Australian case see Stanley, *Bad Characters* (2010), 129.

effect on the country's military potential.[53] Overseas, such behaviour created problems with the civilian populations of allies as soldiers damaged and even destroyed property to provide everything from roads to the trenches or bathhouses for men out of the line.[54] In the novels comprising *The Spanish Farm Trilogy*, R. H. Mottram described not only the tribulations of soldiers but also those of the French and Belgian civilians who found armies marching, countermarching, and fighting over their land between 1914 and 1918. Mottram's grasp of the French language meant that, after a year as an infantry officer, he found himself ordered to deal with complaints by French and Belgian landowners of depredations allegedly committed on their properties by British troops. The third book in the trilogy chronicles the frustrations of a British officer coping over a period of two years with the demands of a family of Flemish farmers for recompense after a driver from a mortar battery smashed his way into a building to find shelter for his mules, one wounded and the other sick. For the local community, and subsequently the French high command, the incident was aggravated by Tommies jeering at the elderly local mayor who turned up to protest. For British staff officers, with a rudimentary grasp of French, the initial reports of the incident led to considerable confusion and fears that the case involved rape. In the process of breaking in the driver also smashed a statue of the Virgin.

> *'Esquinté une vierge chez moi!*
> 'What's *Esquinté?* It's not in Cassell's Dictionary.'
> 'I should say—knocked asquint, sir! Spoiled, ruined; they often say it, if the troops go into the crops.'
> 'Well, how does that read, then? Knock asquint; no, that won't do; ruined, you say. Ruined a Virgin in my house. This sounds like a nice business, with the French in their present mood!'[55]

The label of interpersonal violence that is used by contemporary criminologists includes a variety of sexual offences. Sexual intercourse with a minor can result in a charge of rape, no matter whether the sex was consensual. Thus in September 1914 a 22-year-old sailor found himself before magistrates in Portsmouth for a relationship with a girl aged 15 years and 9 months. The sailor insisted that the girl had told him she was 16 years old when he had met her the year before. The couple intended to get married, and the girl had even arranged to have the banns read in a local church. The local newspaper noted that the girl 'looked older' than she was. It also steadfastly refused to name the crime, writing only of 'a grave offence'.[56] Such sensitivity was common to the press throughout both wars. Thirty years later, a 30-year-old artilleryman was sentenced to six months' imprisonment for 'carnal

---

[53] *Aldershot News*, 11 February 1916, 7. For an example of soldiers raiding gardens and stealing fruit in Winchester, and then throwing stones at pursuing police see, *Evening News (Portsmouth)*, 21 September 1914, 2; and for destruction in billets in Chelmsford by officers and men, see Clark, *Echoes of the Great War* (1988), 73 and 145.

[54] See, inter alia, WO 95/4042, the War Diary of the British 'town major' of Poperinge.

[55] Mottram, *Spanish Farm Trilogy* (1979), 391. The third book in the trilogy, *The Crime at Vanderlynden's*, was first published in 1926.

[56] *Evening News (Portsmouth)*, 22 September 1914, 3.

knowledge' of a 13-year-old. The soldier protested: 'She looks 17 and I don't think I was the first one.' However, in spite of the fact that the judge at the Kent Assizes 'knew how little girls got themselves up and pestered soldiers', he also reminded the soldier that it was 'one of his duties to protect children against themselves.'[57] Such protection required getting an offence to court—either civilian or military—in the first place. And this could be a problem especially, it seems, when the offence was committed overseas.[58]

Soldiers committed rape. Indeed, the argument is often advanced that it is inevitable in wartime since war unleashes the beast in man.[59] Wilfred Gallwey of the AIF recorded seeing a group from his battalion gang-rape a young woman in the village of Bouzincourt early in 1917. He, and others who witnessed the attack, did nothing; perhaps they thought it none of their business, feared reprisals by the rapists, or even believed that, since the woman worked in an *estaminet*, she was little more than a prostitute and therefore not worth their getting involved. When an Australian officer was accused of rape, his fellow officers allegedly sought to persuade the victim not to testify and, at the resulting court martial, she declined to identify the man.[60] In July 1915 the town major of Poperinge handed the case of the alleged rape of a 5-year-old girl over to his corps superiors, though what happened afterwards is unclear.[61] The prosecution and example made of Lieutenant Foxell's sapper in the following year, and described earlier, suggests that the Army was concerned about, and sensitive to complaints from their allies of rape, attempted rape, and assaults on women or girls.[62] Private Jonas Hart of the Essex Regiment recalled the manner in which a French village celebrated the Armistice in 1918 and feted him and his comrades. Their officers warned the men about assaulting the French women. 'One man', Hart recalled, 'was caught [in the act of rape], and he was taken back to the camp under escort, and the next morning at daybreak he was taken out and shot.'[63] The story may be true; or it may be that Hart's memory, or knowledge of the precise details, were at fault. No such case appears to exist in the official records.

Much was made of the German Army's 'rape' of Belgium and of the assaults and violence perpetrated by the invaders in 1914. The patriotic volunteers probably were generally well behaved towards French and Belgian women and, regardless of the temptations, some were determined to hang on to their innocence and save themselves for wives or future wives. The use of brothels was tolerated by the Army command on the Western Front and many young volunteers and conscripts seem to have been innocent and often surprised by the relaxed attitude towards human

---

[57] *Chatham, Rochester and Gillingham News*, 12 January 1945, 6, and 23 February, 8. A similar defence was made at the Old Bailey in 1940 by a soldier accused of a similar offence against a 14-year-old girl. *Aldershot News*, 12 January 1940, 7.

[58] For some of the problems in getting rape cases to court before the First World War see, Conley, *Unwritten Law* (1991), 81–95.

[59] For an important discussion see Bourke, *Rape* (2007), chapter 13.

[60] Stanley, *Bad Characters* (2010), 125–6.

[61] WO 95/4042, 27 July 1915.

[62] See pp. 53–4.

[63] Arthur, *The Road Home* (2010), 28.

bodies that was shown by the local peasant women. Reports of rape and sexual assault by British and Imperial soldiers both at home and overseas are rare in both the military records and the press. Such reports in the press would, however, have undermined the moral and ethical crusade against the Prussian militarists who had raped poor little Belgium. For the sake of a regiment's name, it is possible that some units concealed such offences, either by encouraging or pressurizing the victim not to complain or by punishing at company level.[64] The extent to which there were summary punishments, as Hart's story may suggest, as well as systematic ignoring of the offence, must remain an open question. Equally, there is the problem of assessing the extent to which the civilian populations were prepared to report sexual offences. Whatever their relaxed attitude shown towards the human body, in many of the areas, especially rural areas, through which British troops marched to and from the trenches on the Western Front, the population was staunchly Catholic and traditional in outlook. There does not appear to have been much discussion of sexual behaviour among this population, particularly deviant sexual behaviour. However, there are some suggestions of long-term changes. From the mid-19th century there appears to have been the beginning of a shift away from private arrangements, under the direction of a community leader, towards a greater preparedness to report sexual assaults to patrolling gendarmes. Moreover women appear to have taken a greater role in informing gendarmes and other representatives of the state about socially prominent seducers or aggressive paedophiles. Yet a sexual assault was still perceived as a source of shame for the victim and the victim's family.[65] The problem between 1914 and 1918 was that shameful issues could be less easy to keep within the local or district community when the alleged attacker came from an armed, alien force whose young men were fighting and dying on behalf of the national community.

During the Second World War, rape by members of the British armed forces appears again to have been relatively rare. It was certainly nothing like either the eleven-month rampage of the Moroccan Goumiers serving with the Free French in Italy from late 1943, or the systematic assault on German women by the Soviet Army. However, it appears that soldiers of the British Commonwealth Occupation Force in Japan, mainly troops from Australia, New Zealand, and India, engaged in a series of brutal rapes from the late summer of 1945. According to a post-war report, 904 US servicemen were accused of rape during the conflict; other assessments offer slightly different figures. Extrapolating from these, and from the suggestion of the eminent Cambridge criminologist, Sir Leon Radzinowicz, that only 5 per cent of sexual crimes were reported, has led Robert Lilly to conclude that US servicemen were responsible for raping just under 2,500 women in Britain, more than 3,600 in France and more than 11,000 in Germany.[66]

---

[64] Gibson, 'Sex and Soldiering' (2001); see also Bourke, *Dismembering the Male* (1996), 158–62.
[65] Le Clercq, 'Sexual Violence and Social Reactions' (2001).
[66] Bourke, *Rape* (2007), 357–9; Williams, *Crime and Disorder* (forthcoming 2013); Lilly, *Taken by Force* (2007), 11–12.

The Judicial Statistics show reported rape in England and Wales falling slightly over the first forty years of the 20th century, with a particularly noticeable drop in the last two years of the Great War. In contrast there was an upward blip in the last two years of the Second World War and then, much like the crime statistics in general, the figures began to move upwards through the 1950s. The figures for indecent assaults on women show a similar pattern to those for rape during the First World War, but thereafter reveal a steady increase that accelerates during the second conflict (see Figures 5.1 and 5.2). The reports of indecent assault may cover instances that were in fact rape; it was easier to get a conviction for indecent assault or common assault than for rape, and the lesser charge meant that the victim could avoid the trauma of a ferocious interrogation while in the witness box that sought to explore her previous sexual experience. There is a general consensus that rape was notoriously under-reported; for this reason alone, quite what the official statistics can be said to reveal or represent remains a problem. If it is suggested that the drop during the First World War reflects the large number of sexually active young men away at the battle fronts, then it might be expected that the Second World War upward blip would be between 1941 and 1943 when a large part of the Army, and from 1942 also American allies, were stationed in Britain, rather than in 1944 and 1945 when so many of these men were deployed in Northern Europe. And, of course, not every rape or indecent assault was committed by a serviceman.

As during the First World War, between 1939 and 1945, rape and sexual assault by service personnel and others were scarcely reported in the press, and several of

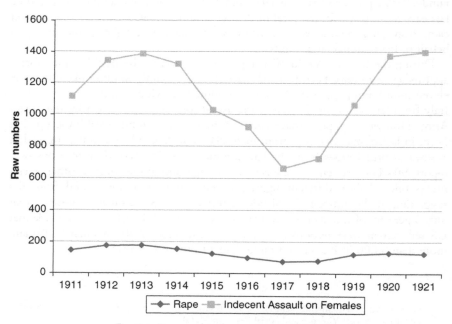

**Fig. 5.1** Rape and Indecent Assault 1911–21

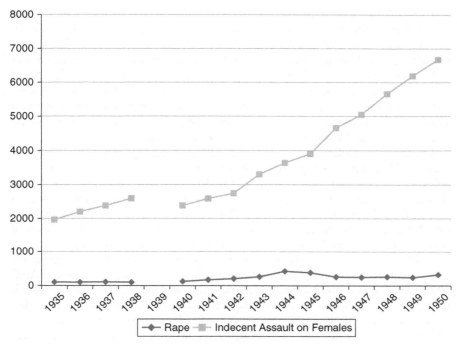

**Fig. 5.2** Rape and Indecent Assault 1935–50

the relevant documents for offences committed in the British Isles remain closed. In January 1942, for example, *The Times* reported that three Canadian soldiers were being sent for trial for seriously injuring a hospital sister who was dangerously ill in hospital and not likely to leave it for 'many months'. The Metropolitan Police and the Old Bailey papers, which remain closed, reveal that the offence with which the men were initially charged was rape.[67] *The Times* made no further mention of the case. In its report of the trial the *News of the World* explained that the sister was found naked, with a cloth covering her face, and that she had a fractured skull and jaw broken in three places. Two of the three soldiers pleaded guilty to criminal assault and committing grievous bodily harm, and they were sentenced to five years' penal servitude; the third pleaded guilty to criminal assault only, and was sentenced to three years.[68] It seems possible that the men entered a plea on a lesser charge, in the hope of a lesser penalty, and also that the plea was accepted to save the sister the embarrassment of appearing in the witness box. Although newspapers like the *News of the World*, and their readers, revelled in the frisson created by such cases, they remained squeamish about too much detail; and, at the same time, few victims were keen to have their ordeal and possibly also their former sexual behaviour exposed

---

[67] *The Times*, 13 January 1942, 8; MEPO 3/2205 and CRIM 1/1381.
[68] *News of the World*, 15 February 1942, 2.

and probed by defence counsel. The case of Guardsman Samuel Morgan was reported primarily, it would seem, because his 15-year-old victim was murdered; the details of the sexual assault, however, were scarcely mentioned in the press.[69] Gunner Harold Hill, sentenced to death for the murder of two girls aged six and eight years, was diagnosed as suffering from schizophrenia by a Harley Street specialist. The *News of the World* described him as 'a slightly bald, studious individual who might be a research worker.' But there were no allegations of sexual assault and it seems that, almost with relief, the judges hearing his appeal could dismiss it, noting that there were 'no signs of interference'.[70]

The Italian statistics record eight rapes and nineteen attempted rapes by white British soldiers between September 1943 and December 1945.[71] There are a few references to rape and sexual harassment by British servicemen in the SIB Crime Books that survive for the campaign in Sicily, as well as in a variety of Belgian sources from the period of liberation.[72] There were also rapes as the Army advanced into Nazi Germany. When British troops occupied the town of Soltau, midway between Hamburg and Hanover, in the closing weeks of the war, German civilians were robbed, sometimes at gunpoint, and several women were allegedly raped; one of the assailants was reported to have been an officer.[73] On a single day in mid-April 1945, three women in Neustadt were reported to have been raped by British soldiers.[74] A senior British Army chaplain following the troops reported that there was 'a good deal of rape going on'. Given the context of the paragraphs in which this was written, he was probably referring to attacks by former slave labourers of different nationalities who were seeking revenge, but he went on: 'those who suffer [rape] have probably deserved it.' He noted how smart and well-fed many of the Germans in the north of the country appeared, in contrast to the people of the British Isles. Moreover, he added, British troops, apparently including himself, were not 'inclined to feel sentimental about the Germans' after the discovery of Belsen and the revelations about the treatment of British PoWs in the closing months of the war.[75] Such attitudes may well have limited the extent to which accusations of rape were investigated and charges preferred. It is also possible that, particularly in rural areas with more traditional attitudes, such offences were not reported so as not to bring shame to a family, or else not pressed because of the fear of repercussions. In the summer of 1945, Reginald Crimp was acting as a

[69] *Manchester Guardian*, 20 November 1940, 7, 19 December, 2, 20 December, 10, 18 February 1941, 2, and 19 April, 6; *The Times*, 25 March 1941, 6, and 10 April, 9.

[70] *News of the World*, 8 March 1942, 3; *The Times*, 3 March 1942, 2, 4 March 2, 17 April, 2, and 2 May, 2.

[71] Williams, *Crime and Disorder* (forthcoming 2013). The Italians recorded offences by foreign troops according to their colour; thus there were another ten rapes and nine attempted rapes by *inglesi di colore*, twelve rapes and twenty-six attempted rapes by men of the British Indian Army, six rapes and six attempted rapes by Canadians. The same statistics record the Moroccan Goumiers as committing, respectively, 1,035 and 82.

[72] CRMP Archive, SIB Crime Book, Sicily, 1943–44 and SIB Crime Book, Sicily, 1944; Schrijvers, *Liberators* (2009), 226–8.

[73] Bessel, *Germany 1945* (2009), 161.

[74] Longden, *To the Victor the Spoils* (2004), p. 195.

[75] IWM (D) 90/6/1, Revd C. D. H. Cullingford.

translator for his unit stationed in Klagenfurt in Austria. A distraught peasant family reported the theft of an identity document from the young man of the family who was the principal breadwinner; without the document he would be unable to work. They explained that two drunken soldiers had broken into their farmhouse with a drawn revolver when there were just two women present. The older of the two women was forced to go upstairs while the other, an 18-year-old girl, was raped by one of the soldiers. Possibly for reasons of shame, like Belgian and French peasants in the previous war, the family did not want to press the matter of the rape and only mentioned it 'in case there [were] consequences'. The really pressing matter was to get a replacement identity card. Crimp's CO promised to do what he could.[76]

Unfortunately there were no separate headings for rape or sexual assaults on women and children in the court martial statistics. A bombardier who allegedly 'placed his penis in the mouth of [ . . . ] a child under the age of five years' was charged with 'Disgraceful Conduct of an Indecent Kind' under Section 18 of the Army Act.[77] Moreover in the case of such assaults on children there were concerns about the competence of the victims' evidence. Thus, when a corporal in the Catering Corps was prosecuted for indecently assaulting two girls under the age of 8 years the JAG thought it necessary to ensure that the girls were instructed on the nature and obligation of an oath.[78] A similar case arose at roughly the same time, the summer of 1944, concerning a private of the Royal Army Medical Corps, accused of indecently assaulting two French girls and then proposing sexual intercourse to a French woman. The adviser in the JAG's office believed that the story told by the girls was plausible; they were, he reasoned, hardly likely to have cried out if they had only received a gift of chocolate, as the private maintained. Moreover the proposal to the woman suggested that the man was in a state of sexual arousal which could have been occasioned by touching the girls and starting to get his penis out of his trousers. Yet the advising officer had to admit that not all of his colleagues shared his opinions on the case.[79]

Overall, however, there is very little reference to sexual offences in the records of courts martial preserved in the National Archives. This might have been because of the reluctance of victims to come forward, for similar reasons that they were reluctant to come forward in cases of rape in the civilian context; but when the offender was a member of an alien, and worse still an enemy army, the fear of making a complaint was potentially greater. Similarly, if the complainant appeared to be linked in any way with prostitution, her evidence appears to have been viewed with suspicion; while drink, linked with the belief that the victim was a prostitute, was also seen as an extenuating circumstance.[80]

---

[76] IWM (D) 96/50/1, R. L. Crimp, vol. 4, 26 July 1945.
[77] WO 84/53, 41–2.
[78] WO 84/71, f. 98.
[79] WO 81/177, f. 525.
[80] CRMP Archive, SIB Crime Book, Sicily, 1943–44, no. 71; Bourke, *Rape* (2007), 373.

There could be problems in as much as service personnel to whom offences were reported might not have been aware of how to conduct a rape investigation. ATS women were warned about the potential of rape and their officers were instructed on how to deal with accusations: they were to contact the local police and the medical officer, and they were to advise the complainant that she might ask for another woman to be present with her during an interrogation.[81] But male Military Policemen appear not always to have known how to proceed. Kenneth Ryland, serving as a Redcap in Düsseldorf at the end of the war, thought he had a watertight case against a soldier of the Royal Signals; the victim knew her attacker and she picked him out at an identification parade. Ryland was dumbfounded when, rather than going to a court martial, the case was dropped. His RSM subsequently told him that while he had handled the case extremely well, he had omitted the key element of having the woman medically examined. 'I was only a young soldier,' Ryland later explained, 'I didn't know about those things.'[82] Other soldiers or MPs, being complained to by a rape victim, might well have considered such matters as marginal to their immediate tasks. In May 1945, for example, an Italian woman told the Command Sergeant Major (CSM) of a Royal Engineers' construction and repair unit that she had been raped by one of his men. The CSM told her to come back later that afternoon, though he did at least arrange for an officer of the SIB to be present to hear her story. In the event this case was followed up; the SIB officer arranged an identification parade as well as a medical examination and the investigation of clothing. A soldier was identified but charged only with indecent assault.[83]

The identification of an assailant from the armed forces might have been rather more difficult than in the civilian context; clothing can play an important part in identification but one British battledress looked much like another British battledress.[84] Even when there were distinctive elements to the alleged assailant's uniform, identification of an individual soldier was not easy. At the close of 1945 the SIB in Belgium were investigating an assault with intent to rape that had left a woman with severe head injuries. The description implied a young soldier from, possibly, an armoured unit. The entry in the Crime Book for Brussels read: 'Description of wanted man 19–20 years 5' 10" slim build, fresh complexion, clean shaven, wearing black beret with shiny badge, wearing roll neck pullover and leather jerkin. Not identifiable.'[85] The problem of identification was a key issue in the court martial for rape of a paratroop officer in the summer of 1945. The victim, a 40-year-old German woman, described being woken by an airborne officer carrying a torch and a pistol, but without the distinctive red beret. When she resisted, he turned his attentions towards her 14-year-old daughter and, to protect her daughter, the woman went with him. Shortly after she reported the incident, a slightly dishevelled airborne officer, without any headgear, was apprehended by two

[81] IWM (S) 9598, Stella Priscilla Mary Fisher, reel 3.

[82] IWM (S) 27312, Kenneth Albert Ryland, reel 5.

[83] CRMP Archive, SIB Crime Book, Headquarters 64 Section, 1945, no. 126.

[84] This point was emphasized to me by a group of retired Military Policemen at a meeting on 3 June 2010.

[85] CRMP Archive, SIB Crime Book, Brussels, 1946, no. 57.

Military Police officers. The accused claimed that he had been at a mess party at the time of the rape and that, bicycling back to his billet, he had been set upon and roughly handled by three Soviet soldiers. A court martial found the officer guilty; he was cashiered and imprisoned. In 1946 his wife's solicitors sought a copy of the court martial record for her divorce proceedings. The following February, however, the officer received a royal pardon in respect of his prison sentence and cashiering.[86] It may be that this case went to trial because a suspect was identified immediately and virtually ran into the arms of two Military Police officers.

Finally, it seems probable that there were occasions when a unit closed ranks to protect one of their own from a charge of sexual assault or even rape. Two young soldiers were accused of raping two young women and stealing their bicycles at Lübeck in 1945. Their colonel denied that they could have been responsible, in spite of the fact that the bikes were there for all to see, and he insisted that he had seen the men throughout the afternoon of the alleged offences. Moreover, he had just signed the leave passes of the men and was intent that they were to go on their leave. The young women had their bikes returned, and were sent away in tears. A sergeant who witnessed the colonel's behaviour was disgusted.[87] There were other occasions when servicemen were shocked by such an assault and, however popular a man had been, his behaviour led to rejection by his comrades. At the end of the war, Eddie Clark was posted to Trieste as part of the force organized to patrol the border with Yugoslavia. He and his fellow Scots got on well with the locals, especially the owners of bars and restaurants. One of his comrades was a professional accordion player who had been a member of a well-known band. He was provided with free drinks all night for playing in the bars. But the accordionist raped a young woman farm worker and was sentenced to seven years' imprisonment.[88] Clark recalled that no one in the unit ever saw the man again, and that they did not want to. John Gray, a tank driver from Fulham with strong socialist principles, took an even tougher line. He did not believe that many of the British troops who entered Germany at the end of the war engaged in forcible rape, but in Gray's strict and humane manner of thinking, the giving of food or cigarettes in exchange for sex was tantamount to rape.[89]

## GROSS INDECENCY

Homosexual activity between consenting adults was a criminal offence in England and Wales until 1967, in Scotland until 1980, and in Northern Ireland until 1982. It was not until 2000 that the armed forces permitted openly practising homosexuals to serve in the ranks. The Judicial Statistics for what the law described as 'Gross Indecency Between Males' also shows a dip during the First World War (see Figure 5.3). In contrast to rape, however, and in common with most other offences,

---

[86] WO 71/1105.          [87] Bourke, *Rape* (2007), 368–9.
[88] IWM (S) 26579, Eddie Clark, reel 9.
[89] IWM (S) 20202, John Gray, reel 10.

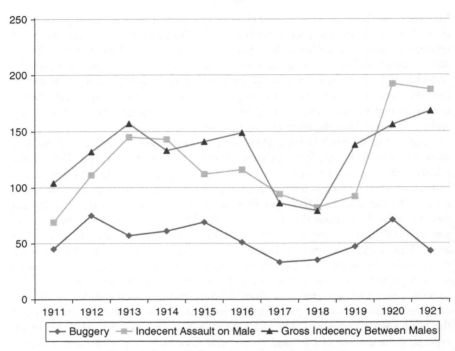

**Fig. 5.3** Sexual Offences between Males 1911–21

there is a very gradual rise in the figures during the interwar period. This increase was in spite of the problems of making arrests for the offence, which were highlighted in *The Police Review* in the summer of 1937. The *Review* feared that most of the arrests made for the offence were, technically, 'unlawful'. It suspected that a high-profile case would lead to clarification of the law but added that, when such an incident came before the judiciary, 'we would not [...] like to be the [arresting] constable.'[90] The number of reported offences increased significantly during and immediately following the second war (see Figure 5.4). Court martial trials for the offence of indecency were also significantly greater during the Second World War than during the First, yet they did not, as some sensationalist commentators have been tempted to suggest, amount to anything like the largest category tried by these courts.[91]

Jokes about homosexuality in the Royal Navy were common, and the lower deck joked about it singing:

> Backside rules the Navy.
> Backside rules the sea.

[90] *The Police Review*, 30 July 1937, 109.
[91] For this section in general I have drawn on the measured and thoughtful analysis by Vickers, '"The Good Fellow"' (2009).

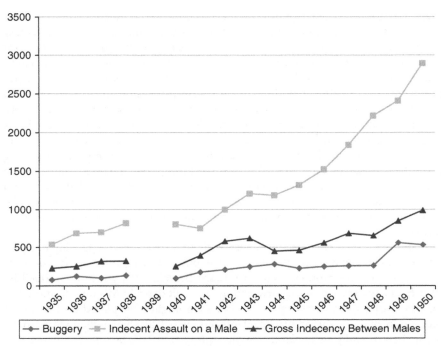

**Fig. 5.4** Sexual Offences between Males 1935–50

> If you want some bum,
> Better get it from your chum,
> 'cause you'll get no bum from me.

Long sea voyages and absence from home ports generated close personal friendships among seamen and occasionally a sexual relationship emerged. Only one official communiqué was issued on the subject of homosexuality by the Admiralty during the Second World War and, generally speaking, the matter seems to have been ignored, providing that an incident did not impact upon efficiency or morale. The aggressive pursuit of boy seamen, however, was always regarded differently. On board ships, boy sailors found mentors who took them under their wing, hence such boys became known as 'wingers'; they were also called 'raggies'. These relationships could also develop sexually, but such sexual relationships, and especially the coercion of boys by older ratings or petty officers was dealt with vigorously by the Navy. Moreover this behaviour was as strongly disapproved of by the lower deck as it was by the Admiralty.[92]

Private soldiers made advances to others in their barrack rooms and climbed into bed with them. Officers suggested liaisons with their men, and sometimes groped

[92] McKee, *Sober Men and True* (2002), 193–204; Prysor, *Citizen Sailors* (2011), 411.

them. Occasionally the relationships were consummated.[93] A lance corporal of the Seaforth Highlanders appeared to have stepped straight out of the popular fantasy image of the homosexual predator when, in the summer of 1944, he was brought before a court martial for soliciting indecent acts with boy soldiers.[94] The hierarchical structure of the armed forces, and the all-pervading class system could put junior ranks in a difficult position if they were propositioned by a superior. In November 1940, for example, a scion of the British nobility, a Regular soldier and a fine sportsman, was reported by five different RASC drivers for stroking their thighs and putting his hand on their crotches on separate occasions while they were driving him. The soldiers appear to have been reluctant to complain. Summing up at the subsequent court martial, Christmas Humphries, a barrister hired by the defence, deployed social class, education, and age on his client's behalf, but to no avail. The court chose to believe at least three of the young soldiers, found the officer guilty on three out of the five charges, and ordered that he be dismissed the service.[95]

Exposure in such circumstances, even without a trial, was an appalling prospect for any soldier, and it meant social ruin for an officer and a gentleman. It is possible that Vera Brittain's brother, Captain Edward Brittain MC, got himself killed by launching a suicidal counter-attack fearing the result of an APM's investigation into his relationships with other ranks.[96] Some men might have played on the fear of social ruin and sought to blackmail officers who had shown themselves to be particularly friendly or generous. In the spring of 1917, an officer invited two privates back to a London flat. It is unclear whether he was merely foolish or whether he hoped for some sexual gratification. He subsequently insisted at the soldiers' court martial that they demanded money or else 'they would make a row [ . . . ] and charge him with indecency.' According to one of the officer's witnesses, one of the soldiers, both of whom were absent without leave, also said: 'You go out to the front as we have been, and you would rather five years than go back again.'[97] In September 1941, Captain Sir Herbert Paul Latham, a former MP for Scarborough and Whitby, attempted suicide when he heard that he was to face a court martial for homosexual offences.[98]

The Army high command appears to have assumed that homosexuality was a sign of 'mental defect or temperamental instability', and that such men were more likely to break down in the front line.[99] The language deployed in official reports reflected the broad homophobia of the day. Thus when, in February 1945, Major St George Stedall raided pubs in Tottenham Court Road with his favoured mix of

---

[93] See, for example, WO 84/9, f. 384; WO 84/53, ff. 166–7, 171–5, and 248–51; WO 84/71, ff. 3, 5, and 70.
[94] WO 84/71 f. 122.
[95] WO 71/1049.
[96] Holmes, *Soldiers* (2011), 590.
[97] *The Times*, 24 April 1917, 3. For a general description of homosexual behaviour, for money or blackmail by guardsmen in London see, Houlbrook, 'Soldier Heroes and Rent Boys' (2003).
[98] *The Times*, 5, 6, and 24 September 1941.
[99] An Army memorandum of 1942, quoted in Vickers, '"The Good Fellow"' (2003), 127.

civilian and military police, they found only one soldier, a guardsman, but 'a great number of civilians being immoral perverts among whom were several discharged from the Services.'[100] There was generally a vigorous heterosexuality espoused by members of the armed forces which encouraged both men and women to pretend to be 'normal' and to avoid being branded, in the case of men, as 'queans', 'poufters', or 'pansies'. But others played to their homosexuality and became a joker bantering with their comrades. One soldier in Normandy after D-Day was alleged to have been wearing lipstick; he said that he wanted 'to look pretty for the Germans'.[101] There appears to have been considerable pragmatism where a man was noted as a good soldier or a good officer. Such a man would be shielded by his unit; such an officer would be backed by his men and also by his superiors. But an unpopular or lazy serviceman, whatever his rank, could expect no such protection. And it was probably the same in the Navy. Cases of homosexual rape and the coercion of boy seamen were severely punished, but discreet behaviour by consenting adults appears to have been viewed through a Nelsonian blind eye by officers and ratings, especially where the men involved were competent and dependable.

The support or the hostility of his immediate group could affect the serviceman whether or not he was homosexual, and it could impact on his behaviour towards others. Occasionally an outsider, or the man who felt himself victimized by the group, by an NCO, or by an officer might respond with violence. Interpersonal violence committed by service personnel might often have been more serious and more common than that in the civilian world. It was more serious when the assailant took the opportunity of access to the lethal weaponry that was readily available. It was more common because the immediate service community encouraged and developed what were seen as the kind of masculine traits that were deemed necessary for conflict, particularly aggressiveness and looking out for each other. When groups got drunk—another element of service bonding and masculinity— fights could easily start with other, similar groups. In some respects, and depending on the informal leadership within the group, a platoon, a ship's mess or an Air Force squadron might offer the fraternity, security, and ethos of a street gang. The use of the masculine form is deliberate here since men far outnumbered women in the armed services and, in the context of violent crime within the services, women are conspicuous by their absence from the records. Women, and children could be victims of service personnel in much the same way that they were victims of male violence or sexual assault in the civilian world. The separation engendered by military service, however, aggravated the kinds of fears and incidents that led to domestic violence, and encouraged civilian courts to lenience and to an acceptance of what was labelled the 'unwritten law'.

---

[100] Brotherton, Liddle Collection (GS 184) G. St George Stedall.
[101] Vickers, '"The Good Fellow"' (2003), 120.

# 6

## 'The Unwritten Law'
### Servicemen and Domestic Violence

T. A. Silver was born in Fulham, the son of a waggoner. He joined the Army as a Regular a few months before the outbreak of war in 1914. One day in the early summer of 1916, while waiting for the Somme offensive, he received a letter from his girlfriend in London.

> [T]he stamp was upside down and I said to my pal what do you think of that as I showed him the letter and he said don't let that upset you so when I opened it I got a shock she said that she was fed up with waiting for me and that she had found someone close too [sic] so I said to my pal wait till I get back to Blity [sic] she will have some explaining to do and he said how do you know you will be going home you might be pushing up the dasies [sic].

Silver got 'a Blighty wound' early in the offensive.

While recuperating in Burton-on-Trent, Silver found a new girlfriend and came to an agreement with the London girl. When posted back to his regiment, now quartered in Barrow-in-Furness, his love-life tempted him to go absent without leave. He slept on the sofa in his new girlfriend's parents' house, and she made nightly visits downstairs to see him, until the police picked him up. He was court-martialled and sentenced to fifty-six days with Field Punishment No 1, but after only two weeks in a military prison in Derby he was sent back to the front and attached to the Machine Gun Corps.

> While I was there I received a letter from my girl saying that she had not seen her periods for two months and she did not know what to do she was afraid to tell her mother so I thought I had better do something about it. I took the letter to our Paddry [sic] and he took it to the CO and while waiting for the result I got another letter saying she was allright [sic].

Nevertheless, when the CO offered Silver seven days' compassionate leave to get married, he took it, rushed back to Burton-on-Trent and got married. But the separation following his return to the front did not help the relationship. Silver was discharged at the end of the war; his frostbite and a missing finger (the result of his Somme wound) left him unfit for the service. Returning to his new Burton home he heard from wagging tongues that his wife 'had been going out with two Belgeins [sic] soldiers while [he] was away doing [his] bit.' Silver recalled that he and his wife often rowed about it, especially when one of the Belgians sent her a postcard signed 'from your loving Victor.' That, he declared, 'nearly busted up our marriage.'[1] Other marriages were broken up, often violently.

War upsets family life and puts relationships under enormous strain. Active service in a theatre of war means that service personnel are separated from civilian friends and any family that they might have. In some instances during both world wars this separation lasted for years, particularly when a man was taken prisoner or sent to a distant theatre such as Africa or the Far East. When men returned, there could be problems in picking up a relationship on both sides; there might have been a brief affair, or affairs, by either party; sometimes service personnel were mentally scarred by experiences of fear, violence, and brutality. Children might have little recollection of the father that returned; he was a stranger in the house, encroaching on their mother's affection and time. There was little official help or guidance provided for reunited families. The situation after the Second World War was marginally better than that following the first war but, generally speaking, families were expected to get on with it and, in the best British tradition, to keep their upper lips stiff. Thousands did cope, more or less. Some men accepted as their own the children born to an affair in their absence. Others sought separation or divorce.[2] But there were also those that failed to cope both during the wars and afterwards; a newspaper article, or something being dropped on the floor occasionally brought on a flash of anger or a strange, wild excitement.[3] In a few instances a serviceman's behaviour towards his wife or girlfriend led to cases in the criminal courts, but with verdicts not necessarily in keeping with the precise letter of the criminal law.

## 'MANSLAUGHTER UNDER GREAT PROVOCATION'

Henry Charles Martin had been married for thirteen years and had three children when, early in 1915, he answered Kitchener's call for volunteers. His wife Amy encouraged him to enlist. But when Martin left for Army life, his wife rapidly fell for another soldier whose unit was quartered in Luton, near the family home. When Gunner Martin returned on leave in October 1915, his wife taunted him and announced her determination to go away with her new soldier. On the last morning of his leave, Martin took his wife a cup of tea and a slice of buttered bread as she lay in bed. Again, allegedly, she taunted him, threw his spurs at him, and wished him dead. Martin lashed out in response; unfortunately he still held the jack-knife with which he had buttered her bread and the knife cut her neck. Martin promptly surrendered himself to a police constable. His wife was taken to hospital, where she died. Doctors testified that the knife blow appeared to have no serious force behind it and that it was the act of withdrawing the blade that had done the lethal damage. Tried for murder at the Bedfordshire Assizes, Martin was given a

---

[1] IWM (D) 74/108/1, T. A. Silver (no folio numbers).
[2] These issues are discussed in Summers, *Stranger in the House* (2008); and for the Australian experience see Damousi, *Living with the Aftermath* (2001), chapter 6.
[3] Leese, *Shell Shock* (2002), 135–6 and 155.

good character as a workman and a soldier. The judge warned the jury that they must remember to differentiate between a 'Court of Justice' and a 'Court of Revenge'. After a brief deliberation the jury returned the verdict of guilty of 'manslaughter under great provocation'. The judge felt this to be right and proper, but added that he could not let it be thought that people could do anything as a result of provocation; he therefore sentenced Martin to twelve months' imprisonment. Gunner Martin's case, and the court's response, was not an isolated instance.[4]

Henry Stephen Canham was another soldier given a good character by his officers. He was granted leave at Christmas 1917 after eighteen months at the front with the Machine Gun Corps. He returned home forewarned that his wife had been going out with Australian and Canadian soldiers, 'had contracted a certain disease', had neglected their child, and had sold their home. When they eventually met at Canham's parents' house on New Year's Eve 1917, his wife confessed to the 'disease' as they went to bed. Canham shot her with his service revolver, told his parents what he had done and, like Martin, promptly gave himself up to the police. At his trial at the Old Bailey, the jury found him guilty of manslaughter. 'In deciding what punishment shall be given', declared the judge, Mr Justice Aitken, and recognizing that he did not want people to believe that he regarded the taking of human life lightly,

> I have to inflict punishment such as a reasoned and instructed public opinion will believe is fitting in the case, and I believe no body of instructed and reasoned men would believe that punishment in a sense of imprisonment is fitting to this case. I shall order you to be bound over to come up for judgement if called upon.[5]

Private Canham had been given the benefit of the doubt and his act of manslaughter had been treated with even greater lenience than that of Gunner Martin. A third case reveals an even greater measure of lenience being given to a serving soldier. Class might have played a role in this case since the offender was an officer and a gentleman, while his victim was a Jew from Eastern Europe who claimed to be a count. Lieutenant Douglas Malcolm shot his wife's lover several times while the man lay naked in his own bed; against all the evidence, the Old Bailey jury that heard his trial for murder brought in the verdict of 'not guilty'.[6]

In the half-century or so before the First World War, the courts had begun increasingly to clamp down on domestic violence; judges were often more progressive than juries in denying that, for example, a husband had any right to chastise a wife for failing to provide a hot meal the moment he arrived home from work or the pub. And even when a wife did not live up to the expected marital codes, Victorian and Edwardian judges increasingly took a dim view of any violent punishment administered by the husband.[7] Infidelities, real and imagined, that occurred when a

---

[4] *Bedfordshire Times and Independent*, 22 October 1915, 5.
[5] *Manchester Guardian*, 1 February 1918, 8; see also *The Times*, 3, 7, and 24 January and 1 February 1918.
[6] Emsley, *Hard Men* (2005), 77–80.
[7] Wiener, *Men of Blood* (2004), especially chapters 5 and 6.

man was at the front led to a check in this judicial practice. Newspapers in particular tended to write of the 'unwritten law' that explained, and even justified the actions of men like Martin, Canham, and Malcolm. But concerns were also expressed about this 'unwritten law'. The *Manchester Guardian* described how, summing up for the jury in the Malcolm case, Justice McCardie 'rejected with powerful decisiveness what is known as the unwritten law, which, he declared was nothing but the law of the individuals as exemplified in lynch law, and the very negation of law as understood in any civilized community.'[8] He appears, however, to have made no comment following the acquittal.

Yet, while sympathetic to some of these offenders, judges and juries seem commonly to have weighed up the circumstances of the crime before them, together with the character and previous behaviour of the accused and his victim. The courts rejected appeals to the unwritten law by men who had ignored their wives or subjected them to abuse. Henry Gaskin, a Staffordshire miner, had lived apart from his wife for two years before he enlisted for wartime service. During the period that they were apart, Elizabeth Gaskin had three children by other men. On his return from the Army Gaskin beat her to death, savagely mutilated her body and cut off her head. The 'unwritten law' was raised in Gaskin's defence, primarily because his wife had had children by other men. The judge urged the jury to take no notice of what he considered to be 'unwritten folly', moreover the previous separation and the appalling violence used in the murder seem to have wiped out any sympathy that the jurors might have felt for Gaskin. He was found guilty, sentenced to death, and executed.[9] Lewis Massey's wife had obtained a separation order against him in 1917. When he returned from the Army in September 1919 they tried living together again, but Massey's wife obtained a second separation order during the following month. In November he beat her to death with a poker. Massey did not appeal to the unwritten law but his defence was that there was insanity in the family and he appears to have hoped that this would ensure a sentence of manslaughter rather than murder. Judge and jury were unconvinced and Massey also was sentenced to death and executed.[10]

The judicial protection of wives from husbands who believed themselves to have been wronged appears to have reasserted itself during the interwar period, but only to receive a new check during and immediately after the Second World War. In April 1946 the Court of Appeal dismissed Leonard Holmes's appeal following his conviction for murdering his wife on learning of her adultery during his absence in the army. Mr Justice Wrottesley explained:

It cannot be too widely known that a person who, after absence for some reason such as service, either suspects already or discovers on his return that his wife has been unfaithful during his absence is not, on that account, even if she confesses the adultery, a person who may use lethal weapons upon his wife and, if violence should result in her

---

[8] *Manchester Guardian*, 12 September 1917.
[9] *The Times*, 6 March 1919, 7 and 5 July, 9; *News of the World*, 9 March 1919, 3, 16 March, 4, and 6 July, 11.
[10] *The Times*, 20 December 1919, 4.

death, claim to have suffered such provocation as would reduce the crime to man-slaughter.[11]

Holmes was accordingly hanged for murder. But other men returning on leave or at the end of the Second World War and administering violent justice to wives and girlfriends did get away with convictions on less serious charges, with relatively light sentences and even acquittals.

Alexander Norval McWilliam, a 34-year-old house painter of Dunbar, had been happily married for ten years and had three children when he joined the Army in the spring of 1940. In August 1940 he was about to be sent overseas and, when he came home on embarkation leave, he found love letters addressed to his wife from an Army sergeant. The shocked, furious McWilliam set about his wife with a hatchet; she died from her injuries. McWilliam's defence counsel suggested that the jury might want to reduce his offence to one of assault. The Lord Justice Clerk judging the case considered this would be an improper verdict. 'The law of Scotland', he went on, 'had always made allowance for the natural human passion that such a situation would evoke.' He advised the jury that, if McWilliam had caught his wife and the sergeant in the act of adultery, his crime in killing her would have been culpable homicide rather than murder. He left it to the jury to decide whether there was sufficient provocation to reduce the charge in this way. After a 'few minutes' of deliberation the jury found McWilliam guilty of culpable homicide and the Lord Justice Clerk passed the 'least' sentence that he could—eight years' penal servitude.[12]

Scottish law and sentencing practice in such cases appears to have been tougher than the equivalent in England. Like McWilliam, William Needham had also joined the army in 1940; his wife took up with another man, who moved in as a lodger, and she began drinking heavily. When Needham came home on leave in the autumn of 1942 he took the precaution of leaving his rifle and bayonet at his mother's house. He also moved his small child to his mother's and then confronted his wife who was said to have been drunk and protesting that she wanted to be with Alby, the lodger. Needham stabbed her with a clasp knife. He was found guilty of attempted murder at the Old Bailey. The judge warned him that no one should ever take the law into their own hands, but sentenced him to two days' imprisonment—which meant immediate release.[13] A little under three years later Private Reginald Keymer was cheered as he walked free from a Nottingham Court, even though he had admitted strangling his adulterous wife in a maternity hospital.[14]

As during the First World War, in cases where there had been a history of domestic violence, the courts tended to be far less forgiving. Sapper Clifford Holmes had a history of domestic abuse. Towards the end of 1940, his wife was granted a separation order. Holmes had opposed the order and was given compassionate leave to try to sort matters out with his wife; but his senior officers were wary of his potential behaviour and ordered that he should not be allowed

[11] *The Times*, 6 April 1946, 8.     [12] *The Scotsman*, 6 November 1940, 5.
[13] *Daily Herald*, 15 October 1942, 3.     [14] Allport, *Demobbed* (2009), 95.

to carry live ammunition on his leave. Somehow Holmes avoided the order and, on his return home, he shot and then bayoneted his wife. At his trial at the Manchester Assizes he entered a plea of insanity, but to no avail as the jury found him guilty. He appealed on the grounds that he was 'abnormally obsessed sexually with regard to his wife' and that separation from her in the Army had disturbed his mind. This too was rejected and Holmes was hanged in Strangeways Prison in February 1941.[15]

The above cases received many column inches in the press, most probably because of the outcome of the violence. In many other, indeed probably in most instances, a returning serviceman's violence did not result in his wife's or girlfriend's death. It is also important to recognize that long absences in peacetime, most apparent perhaps among Royal Navy personnel, could lead to similar domestic suspicions and violence. At the beginning of the Second World War Leslie Darton, a naval stoker, returned home after an absence of two and a half years. There were stories that his wife had taken up with another man; these led to arguments that ended only when Darton struck his wife with a poker. He thought that he had killed her and promptly gave himself up to the police. At the Hampshire Assizes in November 1939, Darton pleaded guilty to a charge of unlawful wounding. The Navy gave him a good character adding that it wanted to keep him. The judge was sympathetic and thought it better in the present circumstances that Darton was at sea rather than in gaol. In consequence he bound the stoker over on the grounds that he return to his ship; and he requested that the police and the naval authorities arrange for him to see his children.[16]

But most cases are unlikely to have made it to court. As with Private Silver, long after the war husband and wife might argue about rumours, suspicions, and allegations. Blows might have been struck but, given the attitudes of the time, bruises might have been hidden and never reported. It was when weapons were used, and when neighbours became involved, that matters ended in the courts. Early in 1945, an RAF corporal returned on leave after several years in the Far East. A female neighbour noted in court how devoted the corporal seemed to his wife; but the corporal suspected that his wife had had an affair. His fragile emotional state broke when his 6-year-old daughter, one of five children, told him: 'Uncle Ted did not let me come into bed when he was sleeping with mummy.' The corporal produced a pistol. He suggested joint suicide to his wife. He pointed the gun at her. There was a struggle, the gun went off but then the couple made up. The magistrates at Gosport dismissed the shooting charge on the grounds that no jury would convict, but they fined the corporal ten shillings for having a firearm without a certificate.[17]

[15] *Manchester Guardian*, 1 November 1940, 10, 17 December, 2, 18 December, 10, and 28 January 1941, 2; *The Times*, 28 January 1941, 2 and 12 February, 2.
[16] *Evening News (Portsmouth)*, 2 October 1939, 5, and 29 November, 2.
[17] *Evening News (Portsmouth)*, 10 March 1945, 5.

## 'I FOUND HIM WITH MY WIFE AND
## DID WHAT I WAS ENTITLED TO'

Attacks by cuckolded soldiers were not just directed at a wife or girlfriend; the man involved could also be the target, as in the case of Lieutenant Malcolm's victim described above. Here again the unwritten law was evoked in courts and appeared in newspaper headlines; and here again, magistrates, judges, and juries could be lenient, but men of the law were also uncomfortable. Corporal Ernest Cray appeared before the magistrates' court at Dalston at the beginning of 1919. He had returned after three years in Salonika to hear allegations about his wife and a telephone engineer; his response was to beat the engineer severely. The presiding magistrate warned that 'the "unwritten law" did not prevail in this country, nor was it desirable that it should.' Nevertheless, given the circumstances, he considered it acceptable to reduce the charge against Cray to one of common assault and to require him merely to find two sureties for his behaviour for six months. In a similar case heard at the Marylebone Police Court the following April, the recently demobbed Alfred Swanson protested: 'I found him with my wife and did what I was entitled to.' Again the magistrate protested that such behaviour was not sanctioned by law but, given the circumstances, he was prepared to bind Swanson over for assault in the sum of £5.[18]

The case of Gunner Vivian Coryton became a *cause célèbre* in some quarters and one on which the judiciary determined to fight the notion of the unwritten law. Coryton had enlisted in 1916. The following year, coming home on leave, he caught Walter Davies, variously described as an egg merchant's traveller and an insurance agent, with his wife in their bedroom. Davies fled, without either his trousers or his boots. Coryton identified him the following day and pursued him, firing at him with a revolver. In May 1917 Coryton was tried for attempted murder at Manchester Assizes; the jury acquitted him and he returned to his unit.[19] Eighteen months later, at the end of the war, Coryton returned home to find that his wife was still involved with Davies; moreover, Davies appears to have moved in to his house and to have had the run of her bank book. Once again Coryton pursued Davies through the streets, firing his revolver, and on this occasion he wounded him in the side. And, once again, Coryton appeared before the Manchester Assizes where he protested:

> I have done nothing I am ashamed of. The law provides no real punishment for scoundrels like this. If one values the honour of one's home one has to take the law into one's own hands and put up with the consequences.

The judge made the usual criticisms of the unwritten law, and when the jury pronounced a verdict of guilty, he sentenced Coryton to seven years' penal servitude. His declared intention was to give Coryton the opportunity to repent

---

[18] *News of the World*, 5 January 1919, 3 and 20 April, 4.
[19] *Manchester Guardian*, 9 May 1917, 2.

and to discourage others from behaving similarly. The court of appeal upheld the sentence, but it provoked considerable anger among ex-soldiers and notably those organized in the Discharged and Demobilized Soldiers' Federation. The federation was a largely proletarian body of veterans determined to press for what they considered to be fair treatment from government and employers. Its meetings in Manchester, at which several hundred ex-soldiers were reported to have been present, took up Coryton's cause, and demanded his release and measures 'to deal with men who ruin the homes of others.' Some even suggested 'the cat' for such offenders in the mistaken belief that flogging had 'cured' the Victorian streets of the robbers known as 'garrotters'.[20]

During the Second World War once again servicemen on leave or returning from the war attacked the men that they believed had wronged them; and again the courts showed some sympathy. Early in 1945, Gunner Ambrose Carter was given twenty-eight days' leave from Italy to go home and get married. On his return he found that his fiancée had jilted him in preference to a lorry driver. Carter and the girl's brother, also an artilleryman, beat up the lorry driver. 'I have been overseas five years', Carter protested to the magistrates at Gosport, 'I got leave from Italy to get married. [ ... ] I had been receiving letters from her just the same, and was granted special leave for marriage.' In spite of the seriousness of the assault, the magistrates simply bound over both soldiers for six months.[21] Such judicial leniency also sometimes extended to greater violence.

Towards the end of 1941 a jury at the Manchester Assizes took just seven minutes to acquit Private David Walker of manslaughter. Like Gunner Coryton some twenty years earlier, Walker had come home on leave and, arriving at his house early in the morning, had found another man in bed with his wife. Walker claimed that he wanted to frighten the man with his rifle but, in the ensuing struggle, his gun went off and mortally wounded the other man.[22] A few months later Lieutenant William Hennant was found not guilty of murder, but guilty of manslaughter for shooting a Canadian soldier who was having an affair with his wife. 'It is in my view impossible, and I should be doing what is very wrong, if I passed over without any punishment the deliberate shooting of a man in these circumstances', declared the judge hearing the case. 'But I will make the sentence as light as I feel it is possible to make in such circumstances.' Hennant was sentenced to six months' imprisonment.[23] Gunner William Smith pleaded not guilty to attempted murder, but guilty to unlawfully wounding 'the other man', to use the popular, contemporary phrase that was employed in the *News of the World* headline. The judge at the Northamptonshire Assizes thought that Smith had been 'much wronged' and sentenced him to one day's imprisonment. Since Smith had been held for two months awaiting trial, this meant that he returned

---

[20] *Manchester Guardian*, 24 January 1919, 7, 31 January, 8, 20 February, 9, 21 February, 3, 26 February, 9, 1 April, 5, and 7 April, 9.
[21] *Evening News (Portsmouth)*, 9 March 1945, 4.
[22] *Manchester Guardian*, 1 December 1941, 2.
[23] *Daily Herald*, 2 July 1942, 3.

directly to his unit on leaving the court.[24] Driver Edward Jones of the RASC came home on leave from The Netherlands unannounced in January 1945; unexpectedly for him, he found that his wife had taken their two children and moved in with another man. Jones returned to the front but, after receiving a letter from his wife saying that she loved the other man, he was granted compassionate leave. He tracked down his rival to his workplace. He insisted that he did not go there with the intention of killing the man, but he subsequently admitted shooting him with a Sten gun. Kenneth Bush was hit by nineteen bullets and died instantly. The jury at the Bedfordshire Assizes took just twenty minutes to find Jones not guilty of murder, but guilty of manslaughter. The judge agreed with their decision and told Jones: 'In view of the good character you have borne, and the tragic circumstances of your own life, for which you are in no way to blame, I do not think it is necessary to inflict punishment in your case.' Jones was bound over for two years in the sum of £5.[25]

Private William Henry Lovelock shot and killed both his wife, Ethel, and Norman Whalley, her merchant seaman lover. Lovelock, serving in the Ox and Bucks Light Infantry had already warned Whalley never to enter his house again, but when he came home on leave at the end of 1941, he found his wife and Whalley together in his bedroom. There was an automatic pistol on the table by the bed; Ethel and her lover had allegedly acquired it to use on Lovelock, but he got to it first. He then went to the nearest police station and gave himself up. His plea of not guilty to murder but guilty of manslaughter in both instances was accepted by the prosecution; the judge hearing the case at the Oxford Assizes declared that, had the case gone before a jury, he would have directed that these crimes were manslaughter and not murder. Lovelock was sentenced to twelve months on each charge; the sentences were to run concurrently.[26]

Lieutenant Hennant's victim was a Canadian, but it was American soldiers who were most popularly branded as the real villains in seducing servicemen's wives. Beating up an American Casanova was an aspiration captured in the bitter 'Second Front Song' written by the celebrated playwright, folksinger, socialist, and, at one point during the Second World War, army deserter, Ewan MacColl.

> I let myself in quietly and tiptoed up the stairs,
> The thought of being home again had banished all my cares.
> In the bedroom then I murmured, 'Nell, your soldier boy has come!'
> When a voice replied, in sharp surprise, 'Say Nell, Who is this bum?'
>
> For a moment I stood speechless, and rooted in the ground
> And then I switched the light on, and what do you think I found
> My little Nell was lying there, exposing all her charms
> Like the famous Whore of Babylon—in a Yankee MP's arms!
>
> The geezer looked me over and then sat bold upright;
> He was wearing my pyjamas (the ones with the purple stripes)

---

[24] *News of the World*, 25 January 1942, 3.
[25] *Bedfordshire Times and Standard*, 23 February 1945, 6, and 18 May, 6.
[26] *News of the World*, 22 March 1942, 7.

He made a sudden movement and tried to grab his gun
When I landed him a good straight left and stopped his bleeding fun.

And then I waded in, me boys, and pasted him like hell
The bastard lost so many teeth he couldn't even yell
I kicked him down the stairs, me lads, and out into the street
The geezer must have thought it was the middle of next week.

My story's nearly over, there's little left to tell,
I wasn't wearing any overtures from little Nell,
And every time I think of her, with grief my body fills
But she will do all right as long as there's a Yank to pay the bills.[27]

MacColl's soldier might have lost his Little Nell, but he had scored a double success: the man he beat up was not just a Yank, he was also a Military Policeman.

## 'THE RISING TIDE OF BIGAMY'

Respectable Victorian society had another unwritten law, though it was never described as such either in the courts or in the press, namely that sexual activity should be confined to marriage. The Victorians recognized the sexual urges of young men and this fed into the double standard that reluctantly accepted young single men resorting to prostitutes while, at the same time, stigmatizing the prostitute and denying that normal women could enjoy sexual relations. Many disregarded these customary perceptions and the pressures of war accentuated and almost certainly increased this disregard. War fostered romances and hasty marriages; long absences brought about by war fostered affairs. Divorce had been limited to the aristocracy and, although legalized in England and Wales in 1857 and made more generally available, it remained difficult and expensive. Legal separation was allowed in 1878 and magistrates were empowered to require a bad, brutal, or drunken husband to pay maintenance for his wife and children. The resort to the magistrates' court for a legal separation was a much faster and much cheaper option than divorce, and hence it was much more common among the working classes. Unlike divorce, however, a legal separation did not give the right to remarry, and anyone who remarried without a divorce, while their first spouse was still alive, was guilty of the criminal offence of bigamy.[28]

It is possible that, during the First World War, some were unaware of the legal position when, perhaps because of loneliness and homesickness, they entered into a bigamous marriage. But there were other, more self-serving motives. Sometimes such a marriage was contracted simply as a means of seducing a member of the opposite sex. 'I might have been killed,' Lieutenant Reginald Pointer of the Royal

---

[27] Page, ed., *Kiss Me Goodnight Sergeant Major* (1982), 143–6 (chorus omitted).

[28] In Scotland the law on divorce was rather more liberal and, from the seventeenth century, allowed women the right to divorce on the same grounds as a man. Access to maintenance in Scotland, however, was at least as difficult as in England for divorced or separated women.

Engineers is alleged to have said when charged with bigamy, 'so I thought I would have a good time.'[29] And on at least one occasion, a serviceman contracted a bigamous marriage in order to get at someone's money. In September 1918 Edward James Humphrey, a 32-year-old sailor, was sentenced at the Old Bailey to twenty-two months with hard labour for bigamy and eighteen months with hard labour for theft; hearing that the widow of a soldier killed at the front was to receive £33 following her husband's death, Humphrey had wooed her, married her, stolen £31 while she slept, and left her.[30] Reported cases of bigamy were increasing slightly before the outbreak of war in 1914, but they remained well under 200 a year. They rose dramatically during the war, reaching a peak of more than 900 in 1919. *The News of the World* reported such cases with its customary mixture of outrage and prurience. A headline of July 1919 proclaimed 'RISING TIDE OF BIGAMY' over reports that more than one-third of the cases heard at the recent Liverpool Assizes involved bigamy and that at the Newcastle Assizes Justice McCardie had sentenced a soldier following his second conviction for the offence. Two weeks later McCardie heard another case in which an ex-Guardsman was acquitted of murdering his wife, whose body was found floating in a canal in Leeds, but was sentenced to fifteen months' hard labour for entering into a bigamous marriage with a woman who he had met while in hospital.[31]

The statistics for reported cases of bigamy fell back during the interwar years and, at the same time, the grounds for divorce were made more equal between the sexes. From 1923 a wife was put on an equal footing with a husband and had only to prove adultery rather than a string of other additional misdemeanours. In 1937 the grounds for divorce were extended to include cruelty, habitual drunkenness, insanity, and various sexual activities such as, for example, contracting venereal disease. The statistics for bigamy rose again during the Second World War. In a 'light calendar' of offences for trial three soldiers were charged with bigamy at the Bedfordshire Assizes in October 1941. What is noticeable in these three cases is the manner in which the judge used his discretion with respect to the different circumstances and previous behaviour of the offenders. Lance Corporal John Ledward of a bomb disposal unit had been married to his first wife for less than two years; the judge sentenced him to twelve months in prison. Private Albert Swan had an extensive criminal record including six separate convictions for theft. When he was found guilty of bigamy, the judge handed down a sentence of eighteen months. Private William Spencer, in contrast, entered a plea of guilty. He was forty-five years old and had been separated from his first wife for fourteen years; he had also told his new wife about his circumstances. 'I will not send you to prison', announced the judge. 'You will have the nominal sentence of one day.'[32] In March 1945, as the war drew to an end, the judge at the Hampshire Assizes expressed

[29] *News of the World*, 21 December 1919, 7.
[30] *The Times*, 11 September 1918, 6.
[31] *News of the World*, 6 July 1919, 2, and 20 July, 2; see also, 9 February, 6, 9 March, 8, 4 May, 3 and 5, and 11 May, 2.
[32] *Bedfordshire Times and Standard*, 24 October 1941, 5.

concern about the number of bigamy cases to be heard.[33] A few weeks earlier the *Daily Mirror* had picked up on the fact that fifteen bigamy cases had 'recently' been heard at the Old Bailey; ten of these cases involved service personnel—five soldiers, three sailors, and one member each of the ATS and the RAF. The paper believed that these offences were committed 'by ordinary people who have drifted apart through war conditions from their legal partners. Respectability is the keynote of their "crime"—however muddled and untrue the idea of respectability may be, marriage is respectable.'[34] Moreover there appears still to have been confusion about the law. In the case of a soldier tried for bigamy at the Bedfordshire Summer Assizes in 1943, the judge noted that, as a result of the Matrimonial Causes Act passed six years earlier, many people 'thought that if they had been absent from their spouses for three years it automatically occasioned a divorce.' The first wife of the particular soldier before him had obtained a decree nisi in June 1942; the soldier had remarried the following August, but the decree only became absolute in January 1943. The soldier had written to his first wife's solicitor requesting information, but the reply had not been clear. The judge considered that the soldier, who pleaded guilty to a bigamous marriage, 'had made a genuine mistake to which the solicitor had contributed.' The sentence was one day's imprisonment, and the soldier 'stepped out of the dock a free man.'[35]

Not everyone whose marriage or intended marriage suffered as a result of war resorted to violence or bigamy. William Marshall, an engraver of Barnsbury, had volunteered in 1916. He was wounded the following year but, when he returned home to recover, his wife told him that she would have preferred it if he had been killed. Marshall found that his wife had begun a relationship with a neighbour. He confronted his wife in the street as she left the neighbour's house and, during the ensuing argument, other neighbours joined in, urging Marshall to give his wife 'a good hiding' since she deserved it. But Marshall preferred to keep his hands to himself; at the end of the war he sued for divorce and was granted a decree nisi with his costs.[36] Again the *News of the World* produced a series of sensational headlines and stories. In October 1919, for example, a front-page headline declared: SWELLING TIDE OF DIVORCE. JUDGES OVERWHELMED WITH CASES. SHATTERED WAR ROMANCES.[37] But it was far more than wartime romances that were shattered when peace came. The divorce statistics for the first half of the 20th century reveal significant spikes at the end of both world wars.[38] Some of this was the result of hasty marriages, long absences, loneliness, and desires leading to affairs. The majority of marriages probably got by without violence, separation, or divorce; but many of the men who returned were profoundly affected, and sometimes seriously damaged by their experiences.

---

[33] *Evening News (Portsmouth)*, 1 March 1945, 4, and see also 3 March, 5.
[34] *Daily Mirror*, 31 January 1945, 2 and 7.
[35] *Bedfordshire Times and Standard*, 21 May 1943, 4.
[36] *News of the World*, 8 June 1919, 8.
[37] *News of the World*, 12 October 1919, 1; and for similar stories see 20 April, 1, 27 April, 1, and 21 September, 1.
[38] Rowntree and Carrier, 'The Resort to Divorce' (1958).

# 7

# The Shell-shock Defence

In some instances the criminal behaviour, especially the violent criminal behaviour of service personnel or veterans was attributed to the effects of what has been variously labelled shell shock, battlefield stress, and post-traumatic stress. On Christmas Day 1915 Private William Leach stabbed his uncle to death. Leach had been an early volunteer and had been wounded the previous June. The judge at Leach's trial was critical of the family for spending Christmas Day 'in a most discreditable manner.' Presumably considerable drink had been taken and, at some point, Leach's uncle broke Leach's mother's nose and the young soldier attacked him in revenge. Leach and his family sought a doctor and immediately notified the police. The officers who escorted Leach to the police station described him as talking in a rambling fashion about seeing Germans and the need to outflank them. No defence of shell shock following his wounds appears to have been considered, but then the term had only recently appeared in Britain. Nevertheless, the Old Bailey jury found Leach not guilty of murder, but guilty of manslaughter. The judge, in turn, praised Leach for his alacrity in volunteering for the Army and praised him as an example to other young men. He then sentenced him to eighteen months' hard labour.[1]

## 'MY MIND WAS BROUGHT BACK TO THE YEARS WHEN I WAS IN FRANCE'

The term shell shock had no precise medical definition. Dr Charles Myers, a medically qualified psychologist who had volunteered to work in a British military hospital in France shortly after the outbreak of war, was the first person to use the term in a British medical publication in February 1915.[2] By the end of the war, however, the use of shell shock as a defence was becoming a commonplace in British courts, and some individuals pushed it to the limit. Court reports in *The Times* show that it was used in cases of assault, bigamy, burglary, fraud, loitering with intent, theft, and obtaining money by false pretences. The most imaginative use was that by a farmer in Kent charged with selling adulterated milk. He insisted that his milk had been sold exactly as it came from his cows and suggested that,

---

[1] *The Times*, 28 December 1915, 3, and 13 January 1916.
[2] Myers, 'A Contribution to the Study of Shell-Shock' (1915); and see in general, Jones and Wessely, *Shell-Shock to PTSD* (2005a).

since the cows had been milked shortly after a German air raid, their milk was watery since they were suffering from shell shock.[3] In November 1919 it was implied during the General Court Martial at Aldershot of a decorated lieutenant colonel who pleaded guilty to 'acts of indecency' with a sergeant and six men of his battalion. The colonel's counsel explained that: 'Men of the finest character had done most extraordinary things foreign to their nature through the strain of war.' A nerve specialist from London was also called to give his opinion that the offences were the result of 'the strain of war'.[4]

Shell shock was usually introduced by the defence as an excuse or an explanation when the evidence for the prosecution was incontrovertible. A young man appeared before the Bedfordshire Assizes in October 1918 on two charges: the rape of a 13-year-old girl and, secondly, with an indecent assault upon her. The man had been discharged from the artillery the previous December with a good character; and the reason for his discharge was that he was considered to be suffering from shell shock. His shell shock was disclosed by the police but only after the jury had found him guilty on the first count. Throughout his trial he had relied on the alibi that he was fishing with his brother and a friend at the time of the attack. The judge felt that, in spite of his good character and the claim of shell shock, 'he had to protect little children and he could not pass a less sentence than twelve months' imprisonment with hard labour.'[5]

In the decades immediately before the First World War mental derangement was stigmatized largely as the result of heredity and this, in turn, was often linked with alcoholism, crime, and syphilis. Battlefront exposure to horrific sights, doing horrific things, the constant thudding of a bombardment, and attempts to manage fear affected the minds of most men, but led some to develop various kinds of mental or physical derangement. Research into American service personnel returning from Iraq and Afghanistan suggested that Post-Traumatic Stress Disorder (PTSD) and Traumatic Brain Injury (TBI) could increase an individual's anger and hostility and decrease their self-control. Those suffering the former tended to be hypervigilant, often depressed, and they avoided certain activities and environ-ments. They appeared more likely to be physically abusive to wives or girlfriends and to get into fist fights, but they did not show much potential for premeditated aggression. TBI, often caused by the thud of constant shellfire, could foster more dangerous behaviour, especially if it affected the orbifrontal cortex, that area of the brain just above the eyes.[6] There is debate about whether such battlefield stress has always existed; it does not, for example, seem to fit well with the code of the medieval knight. But the growing awareness from the late 18th century among military doctors, and others, of what was subsequently called shell shock or battlefield exhaustion, can be seen to fit well with the changing ideas towards

---

[3] Emsley, 'Violent Crime in England' (2008), 186–9.

[4] *News of the World*, 30 November 1919, 5.

[5] *Bedfordshire Times and Independent*, 15 September 1918, 8, and 25 October, 6.

[6] David Brown, 'The Link between PTSD and Violent Behaviour Is Weak', *Washington Post*, 31 March 2012, www.washingtonpost.com/national/health-science/link-between-ptsd-and-violent-behavior-is-weak/2012/03/31qIQApYFZnS story.html?hpid+z2, accessed 2 April 2012.

violence and masculinity. The full horrors of industrialized war might not have been fully appreciated by people on the home front, and many senior military men and military doctors remained sceptical of the idea of shell shock and battlefield trauma, yet there was much public sympathy for men who appeared to have been mentally damaged by war. The War Office sought to make a clear distinction between men who were shell-shocked and 'ordinary lunatics', and such a distinction continued in the post-war world among the public and in the debates involving professionals about lunacy reform. A few suggested that allowances might be made for shell-shocked veterans who committed moral or criminal lapses and whose disorder was the result of combat; such an injury, after all, suggested bravery and courage. In contrast there were to be no allowances for the shell-shocked man who simply broke under pressure; and certainly none for the 'ordinary lunatic'.[7] The traditional perspective on lunacy tended to reassert itself from the mid-1920s; but the memories of war continued while the national memory of the war became ritualized.

How individual men remembered the terrible, but often very different experiences of bombardment on sea and land, of going over the top, of sinking in Flanders mud, splashing through the bloody water at Gallipoli, or marching into captivity at Kut is difficult to assess. The different events, and incidents within those events, occasioned serious trauma in some; and memories affected men in different ways. Remembrance of the war became a national ritual in Britain on the anniversary of the Armistice in 1918. The ritual seems to have acquired very different meanings for different people. The bereaved appear to have taken it most seriously and were increasingly seen as the focus of the event. For some former servicemen it provided an opportunity for reliving the celebrations of the first Armistice, though with rather more decorum than the bacchanalia enjoyed by many on that occasion. Some former servicemen, unemployed in the bleak interwar period, used it as an occasion for protest. '1914 on the roll; 1932 on the dole' chanted some men in Stratford, East London on Remembrance Day 1932. In other places the unemployed assembled for the ritual with pawn tickets pinned to their lapels rather than their medals; and, as during several wartime mutinies, they were condemned as 'Bolsheviks' who had never wanted to fight for their country. The maroons or artillery fire that sometimes indicated the beginning of the two minutes' silence—the Silence, with an initial capital, as contemporaries expressed it—might have recalled the sound of battle, and a few men broke. The most celebrated instance occurred in 1937 when Stanley Storey, a 43-year-old former serviceman, ran out into the roadway during the Silence at the Cenotaph in Whitehall shouting: 'Hypocrisy!' and words that sounded like: 'You are preparing for war.' On the afternoon of the Cenotaph incident, the Home Secretary, Sir Samuel Hoare, told the Commons that 'the man was obviously suffering from delusions.' He went on to explain that the Metropolitan Police Special Branch had identified Storey as the same man who, in the preceding January, had interrupted

---

[7]  Reid, 'Distiguishing between Shell-Shocked Veterans and Pauper Lunatics' (2007); and see also Jones and Wessely, *Shell-Shock to PTSD* (2005a), chapters 1 and 2.

the proceedings of the Commons. As a result of this incident in Parliament, Storey had been committed to Cane Hill Asylum in February but he had escaped on 21 September and had been at large ever since. There was no question of criminal proceedings for the disturbance at the Cenotaph, and Storey was recommitted to an asylum. The doctors at Cane Hill did not regard him as dangerous.[8] But then it was convenient to label an awkward offender like Storey as an 'ordinary lunatic' and not to dwell on his war service and whether, in any way, this had prompted his behaviour.

One or two members of the crowd at the Cenotaph in 1937 called for Storey to be dealt with violently. Violence had been directed to a protestor on at least one other occasion and, unfortunately, other men were dangerous. Thomas Knight, a 29-year-old veteran who had been wounded and who had lost three brothers during the war, could not stand still during the Silence in Liverpool in 1927. A police officer asked him to preserve the Silence, but when he continued walking, the sound of his footsteps carried a considerable distance and annoyed a large number of people. Leonard Peacock, another ex-serviceman, hit him. Knight protested that he had no desire to make a protest; he was simply deep in thought. 'He added that he had no longer a pension, though he had made several appeals. He had been in several hospitals.' The magistrates dismissed the case of assault brought against Peacock on the grounds of provocation.[9]

During the Silence in Manchester in 1938, William Mason, a 43-year-old former soldier, slashed a young woman across the face with a razor. Mason had just come from a Salvation Army hostel. He did not know his victim and could offer no explanation. The young woman, apparently, was using a mirror as a periscope to watch the ceremony and this might have brought Mason back to the trenches where periscopes were commonly used for observation. 'It is evident', he said, 'that my mind was brought back to the years of 1914–18 when I was in France.' The incidence of flashback as a part of shell shock was not much apparent in the first two-thirds of the 20th century—an example, perhaps, of war trauma being culturally constructed. Nevertheless, the war seems to have changed Mason's life. Detective Inspector Pierpoint told the court that Mason had been twice wounded during the war but:

> Since 1921 he had been sentenced on fifteen occasions on charges of house-breaking and larceny. From October, 1927, to December, 1937, he had been at liberty only twelve months. In January 1932, while undergoing sentence at Dartmoor, he had engaged with others in mutinous and riotous demolition of prison property. He was sentenced to eight years' penal servitude.

Unlike Storey, Mason was not to be excused as a lunatic and provided with even the often tough treatment of an interwar asylum. Probably the extent of his post-war

---

[8] For the Stratford veterans see Connelly, *The Great War, Memory and Ritual* (2002), 177; for Storey see Gregory, *The Silence of Memory* (1994), 165–6; *Hansard*, 11 November 1937, col. 1843; *The Times*, 12 November 1937, 10 and 13 November, 9.

[9] *Manchester Guardian*, 17 November 1927.

criminal career counted against him and the medical officer at Strangeways Prison could find no indication of 'mental disease'. The judge at Manchester Assizes recognized the 'great emotion' of the two minutes' silence 'even after all the years', nevertheless he sentenced Mason to another three years' penal servitude.[10]

Mason and Storey represent two alternative, critical perceptions of those suffering shell shock that developed among sections of the public during the interwar period. The Ex-Servicemen's Welfare Society (ESWS) was a charity organized in 1919 to provide care for those mentally damaged by the war. The ESWS's committee acknowledged that some of this damage had the potential to lead a few of its victims into crime and devoted much of its effort to these men. Generally it sought to keep incidents out of the courts and to handle matters privately and informally. Thus, for example, when towards the end of 1925 a man for whom the society had found work stole £5 from his employer, absconded, but then handed himself in to the society, he was well received and medically examined. The ESWS's doctor concluded that the man had suffered a nervous breakdown and had not been responsible for his actions. The society repaid the £5 to the employer who, in response, agreed not to press criminal charges. Where cases could not be kept out of the courts, the society commonly provided funds and a solicitor. It developed good relations with magistrates, with judges, and with police court missionaries; but there were, of course, cases in which the good offices of the ESWS had little effect.[11]

## 'THE VERY MAN WHO MIGHT GO MAD AT ANY MOMENT'

Murder is the most extreme form of criminal violence and one for which, during the interwar period, the capital sanction still existed. There were several instances in which the shell-shock defence was deployed when the accused had seen military service. One of the earliest such cases occurred in February 1920, when Frederick Rothwell Holt, a former lieutenant in the infantry, stood trial for the murder of Kitty Breaks. Holt was described as nervous, quite excitable, and rather dull as a child; he had been invalided out of the Army in 1916 and the eminent barrister Sir Edward Marshall Hall argued that the defendant's military experience had combined with his previous mental state to drive him mad. 'A man like the prisoner', he told the court,

> who had been in France and was subjected to the nerve-racking experience of the Festubert bombardment—a man who was neurasthenic and had suffered from loss of memory and depression—was the very man who might at any moment go mad.

---

[10] *Manchester Guardian*, 19 November, 12 and 13 December 1938; *The Times*, 13 December 1938; for the incidence of flashback in war trauma see, Jones, Hodgins et al., 'Flashbacks and Post-traumatic Stress Disorder' (2003).

[11] Reid, *Broken Men* (2010), especially 147–9.

But this, of course, did not explain how Holt had been sane enough to take out an insurance policy on Kitty Breaks's life, with himself as beneficiary. Holt was found guilty, declared sane, and was hanged.[12] Others accused of murder were rather more sympathetic, and were viewed as such by juries.

John Breeze was said to have been 'the best and kindest of fathers' until his war experience which left him 'depressed and morose'. In February 1926 he appeared before the Monmouth Assizes charged with having shot his three daughters 'in a sudden frenzy'. Both his father-in-law and his family doctor testified to the changes that the war had wrought on Breeze. He was found guilty, but insane. A few weeks later George Thomas, a miner, was tried for stabbing a former sweetheart on the steps of the chapel in Pontlottyn. It was stressed in Thomas's defence that not only had his service in France affected his mind, but also he had witnessed the disaster at Senghenydd Colliery in 1913 in which there had been 439 fatalities. The jury found Thomas guilty, but recommended mercy; the recommendation was ignored and Thomas was hanged in Cardiff Gaol on 9 March 1926.[13]

Sidney Harle had been wounded on the Somme. At the end of the war he married a French woman and moved to France where he worked first as a carpenter and then as a telephonist for a British company. In the summer of 1929 he confessed to the murder of a 4-year-old girl. His wife remained supportive and told an English newspaper reporter that, while she had no idea why he had killed the child, 'he was always liable to fits of madness due to the after-effects of malaria and shell shock.' A Parisian crowd had almost lynched him but, as the reporter for the populist *World's Pictorial News* explained,

> On reflection people are now inclined to extend sympathy to him as a victim of war conditions, and the authorities are being asked how it came about that a man with such a medical history was at large and able to settle in France when superficial examination by a doctor suffices to show that he is not normal and at any time liable to become a menace to those around him.[14]

French doctors concluded that he was unfit to plead. Harle was kept in a psychiatric hospital in Paris for twenty-six years. In November 1955 he was released and returned to Britain, but the press reports of his return made no mention of any war injuries or trauma, preferring to concentrate on the fact that his French wife had never visited him while he was incarcerated and on his ill-treatment by the French authorities.[15]

It was the possibility of a new war that seriously disturbed Dr Leonard Phipps Lockhart. He had served in the First World War and was injured during a bombardment. He became obsessively fearful of his wife being mutilated by German bombs and, the day before Britain's declaration of war in 1939, he and his wife were found at their home in Beeston, on the floor of his study near a gas

---

[12] See, inter alia, *The Times*, 27 February 1920, 11, and *Manchester Guardian*, 28 February 1920, 8.
[13] *Thompson's Weekly News*, 13 February 1926, 13, *Manchester Guardian*, 17 February 1926, 7, and *World's Pictorial News*, 7 March 1926, 7.
[14] *World's Pictorial News*, 27 July 1929, 1 and 3; see also, *Manchester Guardian*, 19 July 1929, 13.
[15] *Daily Express*, 14 November 1955, 7 and 21 November, 5.

fire. Mrs Lockhart was already dead; the doctor was unconscious. It is unclear whether this was a suicide pact, but Lockhart had first injected his wife with an anaesthetic and carried her, unconscious, from their bedroom to the study where he turned on the gas. In this instance medical experts agreed that Lockhart was suffering from a 'disassociated personality'. After only twenty minutes the jury found him 'guilty but insane' and he was ordered to be detained during his majesty's pleasure.[16]

In less serious offences, even when the defendants did not claim, either person-ally or through counsel, that they had been damaged by wartime experiences, a few magistrates were inclined to dismiss them with a warning or to pass a reduced sentence. John David Rutt, for example, appeared on a charge of fraudulently changing a postal order so as to obtain an additional £1. Rutt pleaded guilty and said that he was drunk at the time; he was given an excellent character by the Army and it was pointed out that, while serving in Mesopotamia, he had received three gunshot wounds and been sick with dysentery and malaria. The magistrates considered the offence to have been serious but, in the light of his military character and career, they passed the lenient sentence of twelve months' probation, together with the requirement that he refund the £1 and pay £2 5s. costs.[17] Rather surprisingly John Casey, who had eight convictions for indecency before the war, had the sentence reduced for a similar post-war offence on the grounds, the judge declared, that he 'had been fighting for his country without a blot for 4½ years, and that ought to have been regarded as something towards wiping out the memory of his former misdeeds.'[18] But more often, a long criminal record counted against a man, regardless of his military service. In sentencing John Granville for three offences of house-breaking in July 1917, the Lord Justice Clerk explained that he did not know for how long Granville had served in the Army 'but he had had a chance by being put into decent company of recovering himself, but he took an opportunity of again embarking on his career of crime.' He was sentenced, accordingly, to seven years' penal servitude.[19] By the same token, any man who, in the eyes of a judge or magistrate, sought to play unjustly upon his military service could find the attempt backfiring. A former soldier, apparently a conscript, who was sued for rent arrears at the Manchester County Court in October 1922, admitted to giving his wife thirty-five shillings a week for household expenses and for bringing up their seven children, while he kept another two pounds for himself. The judge ordered the man to pay the rent arrears in weekly instalments adding:

> You are one of those men who, having been compelled to go into the army, go about trading on the fact that you have served. I have sympathy with the men who volunteered and were wounded in the service of their country, but I have no sympathy with fellows like you.[20]

[16] *The Times*, 17, 18, and 20 November 1939; *Manchester Guardian*, 17 November 1939.
[17] *Aldershot News*, 23 January 1920, 4.
[18] *News of the World*, 9 November 1919, 7.
[19] *The Scotsman*, 24 July 1917, 3; and for similar examples see, 3 October 1918, 4 and 12 August 1919, 4.
[20] *Manchester Guardian*, 26 October 1922, 16.

Similarly the judge at Glasgow High Court had little sympathy for John Traquair when sentencing him to four years' penal servitude for assault in April 1934; and it was the same with the judges who rejected Traquair's appeal against the severity of his sentence. Traquair had served for twenty-one months with the Cameron Highlanders during the First World War and had seen action; this, together with the fact of his being unemployed and living with his seventy-five-year-old father 'without the assistance of any female in the house', was raised by his defence in a plea for mitigation. But Traquair had also acquired eleven previous convictions for violence and was known as a leading figure of the Protestant Billy Boys, one of interwar Glasgow's notorious sectarian street gangs.[21]

The shell-shock defence reappeared during the Second World War. It was used as a way for the police and individuals to explain problems that were not necessarily criminal but which took up police time and required a report. Once again the Occurrence Book of Wellington Arch Police Station provides examples. A man who collapsed in a gentlemen's toilet in Hyde Park in November 1942 was taken by a constable to St George's Hospital. The man had been discharged from the Army following some kind of accident. The doctor diagnosed hysteria; the police labelled it shell shock. A week later another man approached a constable saying that he felt unwell. He too was taken to St George's where the doctor concluded that he was suffering from a fit occasioned by shell shock. There was a third incident in August 1944 involving a man suffering from amnesia.

> I was in the army until this last month but I was in an air raid at Deal and received injuries, since then I have suffered with my nerves and I was discharged from the army on account of it.

Again the doctor diagnosed shell shock.[22]

In general shell shock appears to have been conceived culturally in a rather different fashion during the Second World War as one of a variety of functional somatic disorders affecting service personnel. The term 'shell shock' was replaced by others, such as 'battle neurosis'.[23] In general the evidence suggests that the disorder was not raised often as a defence though, from time to time, a man's exposure to conflict was suggested as a mitigating factor in a crime. In December 1941, for example, 21-year-old Sydney Stoney was found guilty of murdering a woman, but doctors who gave evidence thought him mentally damaged by German bombing when he was at Dunkirk. While awaiting trial Stoney had attacked another prisoner for no apparent cause.[24] A little over three years later, a lance corporal in the Marines appeared before the Quarter Sessions in Kent on a charge of indecently assaulting a woman in a railway carriage. He explained to the police:

---

[21] Davies, 'Football and Sectarianism in Glasgow' (2006). Significantly, while the judges had little time for Traquair, there was a large petitioning campaign on his behalf involving the Protestant working class of Belfast and Glasgow mobilized by the militant Scottish Protestant League.

[22] MPHC, Occurrence Book Wellington Arch Police Station, 15 and 21 November 1942 and 29 August 1944 (available at www.open.ac.uk/Arts/history-from-police-archives).

[23] Jones and Wessely, 'War Syndromes' (2005b).

[24] *Manchester Guardian*, 5 December 1941.

I had a sudden kind of sinking or blackout feeling and I had to do something to pull myself out of it. I asked the lady for a kiss and she refused. [ . . . ] I think the sinking feeling that came over me was due to my service on landing craft, having been in each landing since Sicily. Since Sicily I have suffered from bad attacks of nerves, especially since November 3 [1944] when I was survivor of a landing craft which was sunk at Walcheren.

A naval medical officer spoke in the marine's defence. He believed him to be suffering from 'high nervous tension attributable to long strain through military service in many parts of the world.' Moreover, the man had not reported sick for fear of jeopardizing the promotion he was due. The magistrates broadly accepted this defence and bound the marine over for two years.[25] But the problem for the courts, as for the historian, was assessing the part that war actually played in fostering this kind of behaviour.

Many service personnel, indeed the majority who appeared as defendants in criminal trials, made no attempt to plead any form of shell shock. Indeed, before the summer of 1944, the majority of those stationed in Britain had not seen any kind of action or been anywhere near a front line. George Frederick Cummins, the so-called 'blackout ripper', was executed for two murders in 1942; he was still training to be a pilot. Gunner Ernest Kemp, executed two years later for the murder of a woman from the Women's Auxiliary Air Force, was a deserter on the run from the Military Police but had only enlisted in 1942, aged 19 years, and had never been out of the country. The French-Canadian/First Nations infantryman August Sangret, executed for the murder of his English girlfriend, probably had a good case regarding his fitness to plead—among other things he was illiterate—and there remains some doubt about the evidence, the cause of death, and whether the victim was pregnant. But Sangret had never experienced battle or bombardment.[26]

## BARBED-WIRE DISEASE

Lancer Ernest Suckling was wounded and taken prisoner during the first winter of the Great War. When he returned home in January 1919, he was emaciated, sick, and described as 'in a terribly nervous state [ . . . ] on the jump the whole time, constantly looking round expecting people behind him.' But ill or not, within a month Suckling won a fight with a German PoW at Braintree.[27] There were no repercussions following the fight. In contrast, in May 1946 John Howarth, who had been captured at Dunkirk and held as a prisoner for the rest of the war, was tried at the Manchester Magistrates' Court for assaulting a German PoW in Withington. 'I learned about German methods when I was a prisoner of war', he told the court, 'and I suffered terribly [ . . . ] I saw the swastika on Becker's face and I hit him.' The stipendiary feared that Howarth had 'an obsession' about his time as

[25] *Chatham, Rochester and Gillingham News*, 9 February 1945, 7 and 2 March, 5.
[26] Thomas, *An Underworld at War* (2003), 101–5; Trow, *Wigwam Murder* (1994).
[27] Clark, *Echoes of the Great War* (1988), 65, 271, 274, and 278.

a prisoner, bound him over, and warned him that another offence would lead to a prison sentence.[28]

In addition to the awareness of the possible psychological impact of the battle-field in the first half of the 20th century, there was also a shift in the understanding of war trauma, particularly when former prisoners of the Japanese returned from the Far East after 1945. Shortly after the Japanese surrender, Nigel Balchin published a novel, *Mine Own Executioner*, and two years later his screenplay was turned into a critically acclaimed film. A central character in the story is an RAF veteran, shot down over Burma, captured and brutally treated by the Japanese. On his repatriation the airman is schizophrenic and homicidal. He murders his wife and then commits suicide.

In the aftermath of the First World War it was assumed that being a prisoner protected men against war neurosis, and that if they behaved oddly on release or escape, this was because of some hereditary problem or mental weakness already present before the war. 'Barbed-wire disease', resulting from the monotony, the lack of privacy, and of sexual gratification, as well as from the confinement itself, was noted as a problem by a few service doctors at the end of the war, but it had little impact and was rapidly forgotten. It began to be recognized as a problem in men who were repatriated and those who got away from PoW cages in some numbers during the chaos of the Italian political upheaval of 1943. Some such men were often found to be difficult and, in spite of excellent previous records, were found to go absent without leave. It is impossible to say whether they became disproportionately more likely to commit criminal offences, but for many with the trauma of capture and imprisonment, assimilating once again into family and social life was extremely difficult.[29]

Yet, even though 'barbed-wire disease' was recognized as a problem more in the aftermath of the Second World War, it appears from press accounts of trials that the defence of being mentally damaged as a result of being a prisoner was more often deployed in cases heard after 1918 rather than after 1945. This was probably because of the very negative and anti-German perception of the treatment of British PoWs that swept through Britain in the immediate aftermath of the first war and which, like shell shock, appeared a potential way of mitigating a man's offence.[30] At the beginning of 1920 Lieutenant Francis Harkin appeared before a court martial charged with going absent without leave, with passing a fraudulent cheque to a fellow officer, and thus, on a third count, of acting in a manner prejudicial to military discipline. Harkin was a Regular who had served for six years in the ranks with a clean record before being commissioned. 'I served as an officer two and a half years', he told the court. 'Since I was taken prisoner of war, however, I have not been a sane man. My disposition has entirely altered and my moral

---

[28] *Manchester Guardian*, 23 May 1946, 3.
[29] Jones and Wessely, 'British Prisoners-of-War' (2010).
[30] For the attitudes, generally misplaced, towards the German treatment of PoWs, see Jones, *Violence against Prisoners of War* (2010), 259–96.

temperament has changed. I was a prisoner of war eight and a half months.'[31] Such claims appear to have been made less in military courts than civilian ones where, it might have been hoped, a magistrate or jury would be sympathetic to a man who had served his country in its hour of need. George Henry Beyer, a man with a good record from his employer, a telephone company, and a good military character for his wartime service, was tried for demanding money with menaces in January 1920. His defence counsel made much of his 'very severe hardships' as a PoW in Germany. 'He was in a salt mine, where he was prodded with bayonets. [ . . . ] When captured he had a broken leg, and was put into a so-called German hospital camp, which was full of English soldiers dying of typhus and starvation.' Mr Justice Darling, however, sitting in judgement at the Central Criminal Court, was un-moved. 'If I am to pass over serious crimes committed by people against their fellow countrymen, because the Germans did wrong to our prisoners, there would be no justice left in England.' Beyer was sentenced to five years' penal servitude. Edward Godfrey Addington was rather more fortunate, or perhaps the fact that he came from a long-established business family influenced the magistrate at Marylebone Police Court. Addington had taken a white silk golf jumper for his wife from Debenham's in Vere Street. His solicitor employed the same defence as Beyer's barrister. Addington was wounded and half starved as a German prisoner. More-over, he now suffered from insomnia and was 'a nervous wreck'. A civilian doctor, who had examined him together with a prison doctor, considered that Addington had symptoms of neurasthenia. 'It was a well-known fact that people so suffering when they went into crowds did extraordinary things.' The magistrate agreed to reduce the charge to one of 'unlawful possession' and fined Addington £3 with £5 costs.[32] Class might also have played a role in the acknowledgement of the 'insanity' of Lieutenant Sidney Stuart of the RAF, found guilty of shooting a soldier early in 1919. It was stated at Stuart's trial that he had given up 'a lucrative position to fight for his country, and that it was owing to his treatment in a German prisoner-of-war camp that he became insane.'[33]

There were instances where the defence appears to have deployed the fact of an accused having been a prisoner of war as a last resort. Henry Perry, alias Beckett, for example, charged with the robbery and murder of Mr and Mrs Cornish and their two daughters, had little else to fall back on. His defence called several medical men to prove that Perry was insane at the time of the murder, including Sir Robert Armstrong-Jones, the resident physician and superintendent of an asylum and a consultant on military diseases for the Army. Perry claimed to have been wounded in the head by shrapnel and caught in an explosion; in addition, 'when he was a prisoner the Turks flogged him on his feet, struck him on the head with the butt end of a rifle, and [ . . . ] then put [him] into a dungeon.' But, as in the case of Beyer, the judge and jury were unmoved; Perry was found guilty and sentenced

[31] *Aldershot News*, 23 January 1920, 10.
[32] *The Times*, 20 January 1920, 7; 7 July 1921, 4.
[33] *The Times*, 3 March 1919, 2.

to death.[34] Towards the close of 1924, Arthur Simms, a 25-year-old miner, was charged at the Nottinghamshire Assizes with murdering his 9-year-old sister-in-law. 'It was suggested in defence that he was not responsible for his action, having been knocked on the head with a rifle by a German guard whilst a prisoner of war.' Again, the judge and the jury would have none of it, and Simms, who had admitted the crime, was sentenced to death.[35]

Not every serviceman, or ex-serviceman brought before the courts on a criminal charge attempted either the shell-shock defence or one based on brutal treatment and suffering as a prisoner of war. As with appeals to the unwritten law, war was used by the defence to explain or to mitigate the commission of illegal acts. Sometimes the appeals were successful, and sometimes remarkably so. However, in order to qualify as a recipient of mercy on either ground, the accused had to meet other criteria such as character or circumstance. A piece of versifying included in an anthology of ballads and songs from the Second World War describes a graduate of 'the school of war' and echoes the idea of the unwritten law. The poem speaks to both the popularity and the complexities of the mitigating factors but, on this occasion, with a tragic ending. The protagonist had been 'taught how to use a knife, and kill without a sound.' His killing abilities earn him a medal in Normandy; he returns home looking forward to the future, but finds his wife in the arms of another.

> The hate he'd learned in days of war
> Came running through his head.
> Swiftly the knife he raised on high
> And struck her lover dead.
>
> They pinned no medal on his breast,
> But friendless and forlorn,
> They found him guilty of his crime
> He'll hang tomorrow morn.[36]

The fear of a crime wave carried on by men educated in 'the school of war' was a serious concern at the end of both world wars.

---

[34] *The Times*, 28 May 1919, 7.
[35] *The Observer*, 2 November 1924, 15; *Manchester Guardian*, 3 November 1924, 9.
[36] R. F. Palmer, 'The School of War', in Page, ed. *Kiss Me Goodnight Sergeant Major* (1982), 128.

# 8

## Post-war Crime Waves?

At around 11.00 p.m. on Saturday 6 May 1927 there was a disturbance in one of the respectable houses on the delightfully named Content Avenue in Ayr. Raised voices were heard but, initially, none of the neighbours appears to have heard any shots. A boy ran to the local police station, while his shaken mother sought support from the neighbours. Her husband, Major William Ludgate, lay dying with a bullet wound in his abdomen. It was a sordid story.

Major Ludgate, a native of Belfast, was a veteran of the Indian Army. He had met and married his English wife in India in 1905. They had five children: three boys and two girls. Rosamund, the eldest girl was 19 years old. At the outbreak of war Major Ludgate had gone to France, where he won the Distinguished Service Order and was three times mentioned in dispatches. The family returned to India at the end of the war, but Mrs Ludgate was invalided at home in 1925 and Major Ludgate returned the following year. The major, now retired, was reported as drinking heavily and becoming violent towards his wife and children. On the evening of 6 May 1927 he had reached home very drunk and attempted to assault Rosamund sexually. She defended herself with a walking stick which the major wrenched away, striking her. Mrs Ludgate came to her daughter's defence with a brush. In the ensuing mayhem the major was reported to have threatened to kill the women. He stormed into his youngest daughter's room, the girl screamed, and Mrs Ludgate fired in his direction with a pistol.

Ellen Ludgate was charged first with murder; but when she stood trial at the High Court of Ayr in July this had been reduced to culpable homicide. Her defence counsel stressed that he did not appeal to any 'unwritten law' but to the law of Scotland, which allowed a person to act if they were in genuine fear for themselves and their children. It took the jury less than ten minutes to find Mrs Ludgate not guilty.[1]

Less than two weeks after Mrs Ludgate's acquittal, Annie Maxfield wrote her 'Homely Talks in Prison with John Robinson' for the *World's Pictorial News*. Maxfield had lived with Robinson for four years and considered herself to be his 'lawful wife.' He was now in Pentonville awaiting execution for murdering Millie Alice Bonati; Robinson had denied murder, but he had admitted to dismembering her body and putting it in a trunk which he left in Charing Cross Station. Maxfield accepted his story, and looked back to the trial of Mrs Ludgate, though with some fancies of her own.

---

[1] *The Scotsman*, 9 May 1927, 7; 10 May, 5; 27 July, 11; *The Times*, 27 July 1927, 11.

In that case the husband had in a mad fit attacked his daughter. The mother had taken a revolver to go to her assistance, and in the excitement, while the frenzied man was attempting to attack another daughter whom he threatened to kill, the fatal bullet was fired.

It is not those facts to which I refer, however. It is to the statement of the mother of the dead man who, by way of explanation—but not excuse—said, 'The war must have hurt his mind.'

I wonder how many grim tragedies can be laid at the door of that struggle for freedom? I wonder how many actual murderers of recent times were manufactured by the vile and senseless training to kill, which they received in the Army? In my opinion, no man who served during the war and who suffered the unspeakable tortures which every man suffered over in France, and on other fighting fronts, should ever hang.

I'm not excusing their killing, for nothing can excuse the taking of life, but at the same time nothing can ever undo the ghastly effects the warfare had on the minds of the young men who were, during the most impressionable years of their life, hardened to horrors such as the mind can scarcely contemplate under ordinary circumstances.

'I've picked them up in handfuls and shoved them in sandbags, poor devils,' Jack has told over and over again when describing some of his experiences during a big strafe. 'I've had bits of my best pal blown over me.'

He was not a callous and brutal murderer then; he was a hero. Acclaimed by the very people who now condemn him because in the sudden terror which came over him when he discovered a woman lifeless in his room, he took what he thought would be the best way out and hacked her poor body to pieces.

I am not trying to excuse his act. Nothing could do that, and we know now that it was the most foolish thing as well as the most wicked thing to do, but is there nothing in his war sufferings, nothing in the tortures he has suffered as the result of his war experiences since he came out of the Army—discharged, understand, with rheumatism—that might account for his mad and terrible act?[2]

Robinson was hanged five days after the 'homely talk' appeared.


## DESERTERS, BAD SOLDIERS, BAD CITIZENS

As noted in the introduction, the fear of the brutalized veteran, trained in violence and inured to it by battlefield experience, returning at the end of a war and ready for a career of rapine and murder has a long pedigree. The Judicial Statistics of serious criminal offences do not substantiate the belief that large numbers of veterans returned from the two world wars and engaged in violence (see Figures 8.1 and 8.2). There was a slight increase in the figures for homicide and wounding at the end of the First World War. But, as with the figures for indecent assault on women noted earlier, the figures had fallen during the war itself and the slight post-war blip did not differ greatly from the overall pre-war trajectory. The statistics running through the period of the Second World War are rather different. The figures for 1939, which are unavailable in this form, are unlikely to have made any significant

---

[2] *World's Pictorial News*, 7 August 1927, 1.

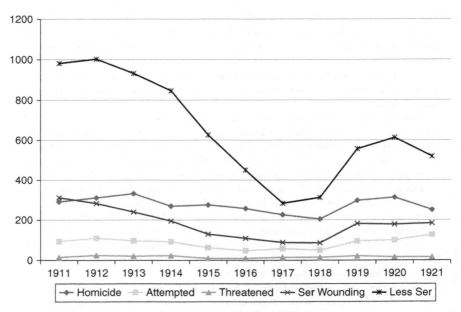

**Fig. 8.1** Interpersonal Violence 1911–21

change to the pattern, which does not reveal any significant wartime decline. There was a slight dip in wounding at the end of the war, but the figures began to rise again at the end of the 1940s. Once again, the pattern of the figures for wounding resembles that for indecent assaults on women, although these indecent assaults show no brief dip at the end of the war.

Crime figures of this sort have been much criticized. Long-term statistical patterns figured little in the assertions about crime at the end of both 20th-century world wars. As in previous generations, however, the British press and a variety of other commentators warned about the return of violent veterans or simply 'criminals' now trained to use weapons. At the beginning of 1918, for example, a committee established to report on the control of firearms feared that the war had increased enormously the world's stock of weapons. But more seriously:

> It must also be borne in mind that we can hardly hope to escape on demobilization an increase in crime. Large numbers of the criminal classes have entered the Army voluntarily and under Military service acts; and however effective may be the measures taken to facilitate the return of discharged soldiers to civil life and peaceful occupations, it would be unreasonable to expect that all these men will be ready to settle down at once to agricultural or industrial employment.[3]

---

[3] RECO 1/342, *Report of the Committee on the Control of Firearms*, 2.

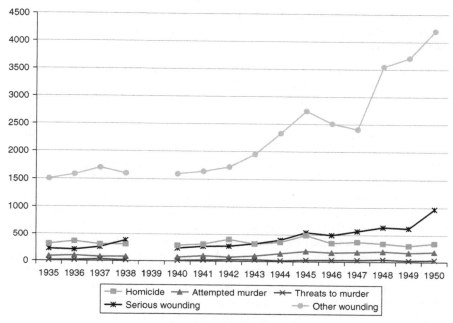

**Fig. 8.2** Interpersonal Violence 1935–50

A stringent Firearms Act followed. In May 1919 Sir Nevil Macready, the commissioner of the Metropolitan Police, warned about the appearance of criminals 'grown callous after four years of fighting.' 'In pre-war days,' he explained, 'if a burglar were met on the stairs by a householder in his pyjamas, his first thought was to escape, but today the thief would probably resort to violence, and, if necessary, to murder.'[4] The fact that Macready had served as Adjutant General to the Forces from 1916 to the end of the war and was, as such, responsible for the discipline of the whole of the British Army, gave this an added authority. A few years later one of the stipendiary magistrates in the London Police Courts wrote that men had returned from the war with violence as 'second nature' and some seemed to think that fighting for their country had given them licence to be disorderly. He recalled one defendant protesting: 'I fought for you in France.'[5] At the end of the Second World War women were advised of their duty to help their menfolk to readjust after their wartime experiences as 'mechanised men trained to do only one thing—kill the enemy.'[6] In September 1945, under the headline 'Ready for big crime wave', the *Daily Mirror* warned that 'a crime wave usually follows a war'. Two months later

[4] *The Times*, 5 May 1919, 7.
[5] Waddy, *The Police Court* (1925), 150.
[6] Noakes, *Women in the British Army* (2006), 140–1; the quotation is from an article in *Good Housekeeping*.

the *Daily Express* was writing of London suffering 'the worst crime wave since the lawless period after the 1914–18 war'. It described the offenders as 'deserters, bad soldiers, bad citizens'.

> Often they have been taught while still in the forces how to enter buildings, crack safes, use small explosives, and live as fugitives. But many more are the criminal-minded who evaded war service and are now organising bands from among the deserters and bad soldiers.[7]

Some deserters were 'bad citizens' in the sense that they made the best part of their living from illegal activities both before and after their military service. George Mooney, for example, had several convictions and prison sentences for violence when he volunteered for military service in 1914. He was promoted to corporal but in 1916 he deserted for the first time; he spent much of the next two years on the run from the Military Police. After the war, back in his native Sheffield, he became the leader of one of the gangs running the profitable betting rings in the city.[8] Some members of the notorious racecourse gangs of the early 1920s had begun their criminal activities before war service and picked them up again when peace returned. A few of these had deserted during the war; others did not and, if prosecuted for gang violence, they used good war service as part of their defence.[9] There was a continuity of such behaviour among such groups across the two wars. Alfred White was an associate of the Sabini gang who fell out with his old comrades over bookmaking on the London greyhound tracks in the interwar period. Two of Alfred's sons enlisted in 1940 and deserted in 1941. For the next two or three years, Harry White lived openly in Holloway, and there was a widely held belief that he had been listed as Grade IV in his Army medical and therefore unfit for service. Even some of the local police appear to have believed this, but when Detective Sergeant Stanley Taylor sought to recruit Harry as an informant, the story emerged of him having acquired a false identity card from another police officer, PC Sidney Nicholas. Since September 1942, Nicholas had been working in plain clothes making enquiries into absentees and deserters. Nicholas and William Llewellyn Johns, the Registrar for the Borough of Finsbury, were each sentenced to twelve months' imprisonment for providing Harry White with his false identity card. White appeared alongside them and was given a similar sentence; further charges against him, of larceny, receiving, and conspiracy relating to clothing coupons, were dropped. On his release White went back to the racetracks, where he became one of the principal rivals to the notorious Jack Spot.[10]

It would be wrong, however, to see Mooney and White as typical and to write off all deserters simply as bad soldiers or sailors, and bad citizens. In March 1942 the

---

[7] *Daily Mirror*, 24 September 1945, 5; *Daily Express*, 5 November, 1, and 17 November 1945, 1; and for the fear of violent veterans see, Emsley, 'Violent Crime in England' (2008), 175–6; Allport, *Demobbed* (2009), 172–85.

[8] Bean, *Sheffield Gang Wars* (1981), 11.

[9] Shore, 'Criminality and Englishness' (2011).

[10] MEPO 3/2353, PC Sidney William Nicholas—alleged theft of identity card; for the Whites and Harry's later career see Morton, *East End Gangland* (2000), 208 and 210–12.

*News of the World* carried an article on 'absenteeism [ . . . ] the Army's commonest "crime"'. It quoted a War Office inquiry, which showed that most cases stemmed from 'worry and anxiety about domestic problems'.[11] A brief glance through the wartime press lends weight to this. In March 1945, for example, the *Aldershot News* reported two courts martial involving soldiers charged with desertion: the first had gone home after hearing that his eldest daughter was 'associating with American soldiers' and was pregnant; the second had gone after hearing that his wife was 'entertaining soldiers' and he was worried about his four children. Another soldier, charged in the following month, claimed to have gone absent merely to see his brother, who had returned home after being wounded in Sicily and whom he had not seen for four years. He then became too scared to give himself up.[12] The Army itself noted that only about one in every ten deserters during the Second World War had any known criminal record.[13] Bill Wood's experience as a bored, poorly treated, and badly supervised young soldier who went absent without leave was described above. Tom Gore's experience early in 1945 was probably typical of many young men on the front line in both world wars who went absent. Gore was serving with the Cameronians fighting their way towards Cleves when his company, entering Moyland Woods, walked into a large German counter-attack. The Cameronians suffered heavy casualties; a corporal was killed at Gore's side. After a day of fierce fighting, Gore was ordered to take some prisoners to the rear. He delivered the prisoners, but then stopped to eat a meal with another unit, and when he set off to rejoin his unit he found that he could not face walking back through Moyland Woods. Gore turned away from the guns; he wandered into a town and met a few others like himself. His new associates decided to try to get to Brussels though, as Gore confessed in his memoir, it was not clear what they would do when they got there. The group thumbed a lift to Eindhoven on an empty tank transporter, but when they were back on the road on foot, they were stopped by an MP on a motorbike. They told the MP the truth and were held with some thirty others in a Dutch school, before being returned to their units. Gore was charged with seven days' absence without leave. His battalion commander, newly appointed in his absence, asked if Gore would accept his punishment or prefer a court martial. Gore opted for the former and, given glowing assessments for his previous behaviour by his company and platoon commanders, he was sentenced to twenty-eight days' field punishment, which consisted of working in the cookhouse and which, in the event, lasted for only seven days since, at the end of a week, the battalion was moved back into the front line. Gore fought on with his unit until the German surrender.[14] Had he and the other soldiers with whom he had linked up after Moyland Woods made it to Brussels, they would probably have slipped into the

---

[11] *News of the World*, 15 March 1942, 5.
[12] *Aldershot News*, 23 March 1945, 7, and 20 April, 7.
[13] WO 277/7.
[14] IWM (D) 99/85/1, T. A. Gore, 'Reluctant Hero: Reluctant Coward', 33–7, and 'In Order to Kill the Enemy', 105–9.

army of deserters in the city that had little means of support other than different kinds of criminal offending.

The problem of deserters was said to be less severe following the Second World War than the First, but even after periodic police round-ups, there were still reported to be about 21,000 of them in the summer of 1947.[15] The difficulties of survival for a deserter overseas, and how this might have led him into criminal activity was described earlier. The fact that at home, both during and after the war, a deserter was still a wanted man with no identity card or legal ration card meant that here too, for many, crime appeared the only option. One of the deserters arrested by Major Stedall's provost company in London over a year after the end of the war had a cache of stolen papers, such as leave passes, in his lodgings; more seriously he also had weapons that he had stolen.[16] But as one young soldier put it to magistrates when admitting to a string of petty thefts in October 1941: 'I could not go home as I was a deserter. Having no money I was driven into this.'[17]

## BEGGARS AND FRAUDSTERS

Most deserters tried not to be visible and quickly removed their uniforms. Other men played upon their military service, or their claims of military service, to solicit money and other forms of assistance. Such activities were apparent in wartime. In August 1916, for example, court-martial proceedings were initiated against two soldiers who had gone absent and then sought to obtain money by claiming to have lost an arm at the front; both men appear to have been in full possession of all their limbs.[18] Such behaviour was more apparent in the aftermath of the war and the men involved were not necessarily former servicemen, let alone deserters. In September 1921 Thomas Hague was given three months' hard labour for begging in Merthyr Tydfil. Hague had been arrested wearing a khaki tunic with three medals; his right arm was missing, until the police discovered it concealed under the tunic.[19]

The annual Judicial Statistics reveal a significant drop in the number of begging offences that were proceeded against after the First World War.[20] Nevertheless, concerns were expressed in London about what seemed to be an increase in poor traders and, particularly, musicians soliciting alms by playing in the streets. Often these men wore bits of uniform and medals, and they attracted crowds. The police were reluctant to interfere and to attempt to enforce laws against obstructions and begging, as the crowds were often sympathetic, especially if the man appeared to have old war wounds. But the police also suspected that some of the musicians were

[15] *Manchester Guardian*, 17 December 1945, 11 July and 11 August 1947.
[16] Brotherton, Liddle Collection, (ARMY 184) G. St George Stedall, Report 11 November 1946.
[17] *Bedfordshire Times and Standard*, 24 October 1941, 3.
[18] WO 84/12, to GOC London Division, 15 and 16 August 1916.
[19] *The Times*, 14 September 1921, p. 4.
[20] Godfrey, Cox and Farrall (2010) *Serious Offenders*, p. 54.

fraudsters. Their concerns about one former officer were passed to the Home Office by the Metropolitan Police solicitors. The man had, it appeared,

> received a War Gratuity of £1,500, which he had, according to his own admission, got through in three months while living with a woman who was formerly a prostitute. [ . . . ] [H]e is nothing more nor less than a fraudulent imposter preying upon the public, and seeking to enlist sympathy and alms on the ground that he is an ex-officer and had lost a [leg] in the war. As to his record before the war, we are extremely suspicious, though he was undoubtedly an officer in the regular Army for some time; his war record in itself seems to have been certainly distinguished as he won the DMC [sic] and the MC, but his record since the war is as contemptible as it could be, and he is obviously a very fair sample of those ex-officers who grind barrels [sic] organs in west end streets in order to enlist sympathy to which they have no sort or kind of right.

The man was charged with obstruction and soliciting alms at Marlborough Street Police Court. He was found guilty and sentenced to a month in prison.[21] There does not appear to have been quite the same concern in the aftermath of the Second World War, when the labour market was much healthier, yet it is interesting to note that one of the central characters played by Arthur Haynes, an immensely popular television comedian of the 1950s and 1960s, was an opinionated tramp with a string of medals who never lost an opportunity to tell his social superiors and those in authority how he had fought for the country 'up to his neck in mud and bullets'.

Begging and petty fraud on the streets by ex-servicemen, or at least by those claiming to be ex-servicemen, hardly constitute a crime wave, and the reality of post-war crime waves is difficult to prove. Those responsible for writing the introductions to the annual criminal statistics in the aftermath of the First World War appear to have believed that the war had some effects. But the need to write a new introduction every year suggests that, at times, they were clutching at straws to find reasons behind an annual increase in a type of offence. Thus the fact that more people were tried for indictable offences in 1920 than in 1919 was suggested 'as a reversion to normal figures consequent upon the return to civil life of the large portion of the population which, during the war, was serving with His Majesty's Forces.'[22] It was felt that an increase in fraud and commercial dishonesty noted for 1923 might 'reasonably [ . . . ] in many cases [be] assignable to the long continued debasing effects of the war upon conduct and character.'[23] The following year it was suggested that 'the getting rich quickly [opportunities] afforded in certain quarters by the Great War' had contributed to a decline in commercial probity; and also that 'reckless attempts to live more or less luxuriously without rendering any service in return [ . . . ] may also be traceable to experiences during the War.'[24] The prison commissioners also picked up on a large number of ex-service, first offenders sentenced to gaol terms after the war and saw in this the loss of 'the

---

[21] MEPO 3/2439, Begging by Ex-servicemen, 1918–24.
[22] *Criminal Statistics, 1922*, Cmd. 2265, 5.
[23] *Criminal Statistics, 1923*, Cmd. 2385, 10.
[24] *Criminal Statistics, 1924*, Cmd. 2602, 6.

normal restraints of conduct [ . . . ] banished by the stress of war.' The criminologist Hermann Mannheim quoted the prison commissioners with some approval, but felt that the deterioration in people's economic position at the end of the war was crucial. Moreover he believed, and in this he echoed the Home Office comments on the crime statistics, that the war had fostered a 'gradual diminution of the individual's respect for property of the state.' During wartime the serviceman had found everything provided by the state; when the state failed in such provision in peacetime, those same individuals, without considering their actions criminal, considered that they had the right to help themselves.[25] Yet when Mannheim's doctoral student, John C. Spencer, pressed his interviewees about the extent to which war training, bombardment, and battlefield experiences had led them to commit the crimes which put them in prison and Borstal after the Second World War, 'the suggestion was never accepted'. Equally interesting, he found that many of those sentenced for the most violent offences had never received aggressive, tough commando training, but generally had been given 'dull routine tasks in barracks or holding units'.[26] This raises the key issue about the extent to which men, who had been brutalized by tough training and battlefield experiences, returned home inured to violence and brutality and prepared to employ their new attitudes at home.

## VIOLENT VETERANS

By early 1942 the British Army was using new techniques of 'hate training' in preparing men for the battlefield. These involved much screaming, shouting, and abuse; men were even encouraged to gouge out their enemies' eyes. Sheep's blood was splashed around, supposedly to give extra realism. The violence of the training led to questions in Parliament and anxieties expressed by many. General Sir Bernard Paget, the commander-in-chief of Home Forces, eventually issued an order banning such training as 'foreign to the British temperament'. British Army psychologists had criticized it as 'so crude and inefficient that it could only be the product of an abnormal and infantile mind.' But more seriously they believed that it depressed some keen soldiers and did not improve combat efficiency.[27] Psychological studies, largely concerned with the armed forces of the United States during the Second World War, highlighted major problems resulting from combat and combat stress, but did not suggest that men would go on to make a career out of killing. Writing in 1946 R. L. Swank and W. E. Marchant estimated that 98 per cent of all men who survived sixty days of continuous fighting would become some kind of psychiatric casualty; the remaining 2 per cent were most likely to have a predisposition towards being 'aggressive psychopathic personalities'.

---

[25] Mannheim, *Social Aspects of Crime* (1940), 108–15.
[26] Spencer, *Crime and the Services* (1954), 119.
[27] Bourke, *Intimate History of Killing* (1998), 140–3; see also, *Manchester Guardian*, 25 May 1942, 3, and *The Times*, 25 May 1942, 2.

In the following year Brigadier General Samuel L. A. Marshall published his celebrated *Men against Fire*, which argued that only between 15 and 20 in 100 men in the firing line would engage seriously, or even fire their weapons in action. Large numbers fired high to avoid killing. Marshall appears to have been extremely cavalier in the way that he collected his evidence. But, drawing on Marshall as well as a range of other material, Lieutenant Colonel Dave Grossman, a former US Army ranger and paratrooper who subsequently taught psychology at West Point and Arkansas State University, suggested that much behaviour on battlefields involved posturing and that noise could often swing an outcome. He stressed how men in battle were invariably tired, often exhausted and aching from lack of sleep and marching with heavy kit, dirty, hungry, exposed to the elements, and afraid. But most importantly his experience of soldiers and soldiering, and his training as a psychologist, led him to conclude that even on the battlefield, killing often caused 'deep wounds of pain and guilt' among those that killed.[28] For the Vietnam veteran Karl Marlantes, killing on the battlefield and its effects were even more complex; there could be elation at the moment of battle and immediately afterwards, with sadness and nightmares coming later. For years Marlantes was haunted by a teenaged Vietnamese soldier with whom he locked eyes before he killed him: 'This time I had killed a human.'[29]

All of this would seem to suggest that the overwhelming majority of men who volunteered or who were conscripted to fight in the two world wars and who had become involved in killing at rifle range or closer, were unlikely to have become inured to violence and killing and unlikely to have carried on with similar violence once returned to civilian life. Ikey Bogard and Joseph Sabini were East End gangsters before the First World War, they were apparently good infantrymen during the war, and after their military service they went back to their gangs, their illicit guns, and their business of violence and extortion. Ronald John Chesney did not require the terrifying experience of having his ship blasted from under him to become a killer and fraudster. The notion of the brutalized, violent veteran created by war and at the centre of a post-war crime wave was largely a fantasy based on assumptions about military training and the battlefield. Possibly it was given an aura of substance by the slight upward blip in assault and homicide occasioned by men returning to find that their wives were changed—older, more independent, and perhaps with someone else as the focus of their affections. There were men who returned seriously damaged with what is currently called Post-Traumatic Stress Disorder or Traumatic Brain Injury. Some of these men were probably among those who assaulted wives or girlfriends they suspected of being unfaithful, or who attacked the men with whom their womenfolk were suspected of being unfaithful. But the application of modern medical understanding to individuals about whom little is known other than their names and offences, is fraught with danger. Some

---

[28] Swank and Marchand, 'Combat Neuroses' (1946); Marshall, *Men against Fire* (1947); Grossman, *On Killing* (1996). For a telling critique of Marshall see Spiller, 'S. L. A. Marshall and the Ratio of Fire' (1988).

[29] Marlantes, *What It Is Like to Go to War* (2012), 27–30 and 49.

men inflicted violence on themselves rather than on the woman that they blamed for their misfortune. Richard Gibbs, a driver in the Royal Engineers, shot himself on his return from Egypt in 1919; in his judgement on the case the Wandsworth Coroner declared: 'A woman who can be unfaithful to her man fighting for his country is not worthy of the name of woman.' Shortly afterwards a stoker from HMS *Essex* threw himself under a train when his fiancée broke off their engagement. The coroner's jury found that 'after the strain which naval men had been subjected to during the war, the man's mind became unhinged on being rejected by the girl.' Rejection by his wife led a sergeant major of the Tank Corps to shoot himself on the Embankment by Cleopatra's Needle. He had married in 1917 and spent just over a week with his wife, who moved back to her parents while he was away. Once again, the coroner criticized the woman involved, in this case the soldier's wife.[30] But self-harm was not just brought on by a woman's rejection. J. A. Dugdale had suffered dysentery and sunstroke marching to the relief of Kut; on his return home he found himself unable to concentrate on his undergraduate studies and shot himself. Major Sydney Douglas also shot himself. His wife spoke of his 'bad time' during the war and how, on his return, he was 'morose, depressed, and would sit for hours and stare at nothing'. Another suicide, Lieutenant Colonel Buxton Smith, was gassed and was ill with malaria during the war. At the war's end he joined the Royal Irish Constabulary and appears to have blamed himself for the death of sixteen of his men, and his own survival, during a skirmish in Ireland in June 1920. In the case of Thomas Fraser of Aberdeen, who killed himself in a New York garage in December 1921, his friends put his 'melancholia' down to shell shock.[31] The press did not contain such stories to the same degree following the Second World War and the statistics for suicide and the criminal offence of attempted suicide do not help to assess the extent to which damaged servicemen harmed themselves in this fashion.[32] Moreover, it is always possible that police officers who had themselves served at the front, or who had friends and workmates who had served, chose to avoid charges of attempted suicide in order to shield a distressed veteran and his family from embarrassment, gossip, and the shame of a criminal trial.

[30]   *News of the World*, 6 July 1919, 5, 10 August, 8, 26 October, 5.

[31]   *The Times*, 25 September 1919, 4, 3 December 9, 5 December 1921, 9 and 8 February 1922, 7.

[32]   The Judicial Statistics show reported attempted suicides averaging around 2,300 to 2,500 annually in the decade before the First World War. Like other reported crime statistics they fell during the war, reaching their lowest points in 1917 (964) and 1918 (845). They increased very slowly during the 1920s, exceeding the pre-war figures for the first time only in 1927 (2,742). In the 1930s they averaged around 3,100 to 3,300 a year, dropping once again during the war. They began to exceed the pre-war figures in 1946 (3,406) and climbed gradually from 1948 (4,553) to 1957 (5,436). They declined thereafter and disappeared from the statistics when suicide ceased to be a criminal offence in 1961. The Registrar General's reports on births, marriages, and deaths include a gender and age breakdown for the period of the First World War. These figures note that civilian males of roughly military age (i.e. 15–45) accounted for about 144 suicides annually in the period 1901–1910, but for only 115 in 1919. The further problem with these statistics is that they specifically ignore men in the armed services for the period 1915–1918. *Eightieth Annual Report of the Registrar General of Births, Deaths and Marriages in England and Wales*, Cmd. 40, 89; *Eighty-Second Annual Report...*

There were many more former servicemen who sought solace in drink rather than in suicide and, with or without the experience of war, heavy drinking could contribute to domestic violence. The point that requires emphasis however, is that whereas the imagined, brutalized veteran was assumed to be at the heart of a potential crime wave affecting property as well as life and limb, the actual man who returned from war seriously disturbed by what he had seen and done, if he became violent either as a result of post-traumatic stress or drink, or both, seems more likely to have committed domestic offences and perhaps too to have self-harmed.

Domestic situations could also be the prompt to nonviolent forms of offending. Alfred Biggs was a good soldier. At the beginning of the Second World War he was commissioned from the ranks and, at the same time, he married the daughter of the owner of a hardware shop in Reading. Biggs had a good war; he was mentioned in dispatches, slightly wounded, and reached the rank of captain; but he hardly saw his wife, other than during brief leaves when he sired two children. When the war ended, Biggs found family life strained; in an effort to please his wife he took a short-service commission and, when his unit was moved to Trieste, his wife and children accompanied him. Biggs appears to have been determined to put on a good show for his wife and they were known for entertaining other officers and their wives. But Biggs financed this generosity, and his wife's good clothes, by misappropriating public funds—specifically, the money for new band instruments. Biggs pleaded guilty at his court martial; he was given a good character by his commanding officer but was, nevertheless, cashiered and sentenced to six months' imprisonment.[33]

## THE VETERAN AS SPIV

For a few other offenders, criminal behaviour seems to have been an attempt to find some of the excitement and camaraderie of wartime. This was something picked up in the years immediately following the war by films like *They Made Me a Fugitive* (1947). Initially such films portrayed the criminal veteran as a fundamentally decent man who turned to crime largely because of the difficulties of readjusting to peace, what seemed to be a loss of status, and the dullness of life after the war. But within a few years such characters were increasingly less sympathetic, such as the thoroughly unpleasant but seductive former wing commander in *Cage of Gold* (1950), who treated badly the woman who loved him and who engaged in large-scale currency fraud.[34] Both of these fictional types resembled a few real-life characters.

Having left school towards the end of the 1930s, Colin Hodgkinson opted for Army life, but then transferred to, in his eyes, the more glamorous Fleet Air Arm.

---

[33] Bisset, *Trial at Arms* (1957), chapter 8 passim. Biggs was reconciled with his wife and, after serving his sentence, he managed his father-in-law's shop.
[34] Spicer, *Typical Men* (2001), 171–5.

An accident while training as a midshipman cost him his legs but, reading about Douglas Bader's achievements in a newspaper, he was able to pull strings to get back in the cockpit and serve as a fighter pilot. At the end of the war he was posted to a unit ferrying aircraft to wherever they were needed. Like hundreds of others he found that the opportunities for profiting from contraband were too good to miss. Hodgkinson and his fellow pilots developed their own, very profitable, triangle trade. They flew from their West Country bases, first Filton near Bristol and then Dunkeswell near Honiton, with lengths of utility cloth wrapped around their waists, and others stuffed into their parachute bags; Hodgkinson was able also to fill his tin legs with cigarettes and tea. Dodging, or lying to British and French customs, they stopped overnight in Paris where their contraband was sold netting up to £70 or £80. The money that was not spent on a good night out, with wine, women and song, was then used to purchase cognac, scent, and silk stockings. On the following day their aircraft were delivered to, for example, the French Naval Flying School near La Rochelle, and the pilots climbed into an Anson aircraft for their return trip, making sure to take cases of brandy with them. Again customs were dodged, as were the RAF's police. There seems to have been little difficulty in subsequently transferring the goods to London where they were sold to a fence, or else individual deals were done with restaurants or private individuals. On one occasion fifteen cases of cognac were sold for 100 guineas a case.[35]

But Hodgkinson had a conscience: smuggling 'bibelots and finery' was one thing and, in spite of the profit to be made, he drew the line at smuggling penicillin. He did, however, make two trips in which he believed he was carrying packages of drugs; and on the second occasion he returned with a consignment of gold fillings in his legs. Following these two trips he was given a warning by the RAF police, who suggested that he 'watch [himself] more closely in future'. But, once de-mobbed, Hodgkinson found himself in a boring job in advertising at £5 a week. Seeking some kind of exciting outlet, he decided to try his hand at 'spivvery'.

> It all seemed so easy in the beery euphoria of a Shepherd's Market pub. Chevrolet lorries; ball bearings; surplus overcoats; oil in drums; sheet iron; rubber dinghies. The war's great carcass was expelling its useless juices and the unparticular flies were swarming. Resourceful men in demobilization suits whispered hotly in your ear, took you for long dreary drives to ordnance parks and scrapyards, or windy, deserted docks. There was the stuff, old boy; all you had to do now was sell it and draw your fat commission. And now it was your turn to do the whispering and the running round the suburbs.

Hodgkinson made £25 on selling paper and £10 on some drums of liquid soap; but he failed miserably in selling a consignment of jeeps. The fact that the jeeps were at the bottom of the Adriatic, courtesy of a German U-boat, did not deter others, who sold them at £200 each. In addition to being a failure as a spiv, Hodgkinson also felt that he was 'growing loud, overbearing, glib and cynical, and—frighteningly—less aware of that shadowy boundary which separates sharp practice from crime.' He

---

[35] Hodgkinson, *Best Foot Forward* (1957), 219–22.

was no Ronald Chesney. He stepped back, stuck to the day job, and returned to flying in the RAF voluntary reserve.[36]

Most of the men who returned from the two world wars after serving as patriotic volunteers or conscripts appear to have seen their war service largely in terms of an interruption to their normal, civilian lives. They tried to pick up their lives where they had left them and got on with things—often, the consensus has it, with little help from the authorities. A few might have been tempted into criminal activity. A few continued with practices and opportunities such as the black market that they had come across during their service. A few stole or defrauded to make ends meet. A few assaulted a wife or girlfriend who had been unfaithful, or the man with whom she had been unfaithful. The 'crime waves' reported and warned about in the media were relatively small blips in the broad sweep of the crime statistics for the 20th century. Brutalized, violent veterans who created crime waves made good stories for the press but, in the surviving evidence, they are hard to find.

[36] Hodgkinson, *Best Foot Forward* (1957), 227–8.

# 9

## Conscripts and Professionals
### Beyond the World Wars

Number 14219761, Pte Low, J. had been called up in July 1942. Four years later, aged just 23 years, he was still serving in the Highland Light Infantry, now in Germany with the British Army of Occupation. Low developed an infatuation for a married woman, who claimed that her one-legged husband had been threatening her. Together with another soldier he attacked the husband and beat him severely. The second soldier was tried separately and acquitted; but Low was found guilty of wounding with intent to murder and sentenced to ten years' penal servitude. The defending officer argued that 'a temporary sexual infatuation had thrown the accused off his balance and made him anxious to pose as a ruthless hero to the object of his affections.' He also stressed Low's youth, previous good character and clean record. This appears to have carried some weight with the panel that met to confirm the sentence, and they reduced it by three years.[1] Low's offence was not a crime that was in any way typical of those committed by conscripts, but Low himself can be taken as typical of some of the young men who found themselves in uniform and far from home as a result of the two world wars of the 20th century.

During these wars Britain's armed forces reached unprecedented numbers and drew in enormous numbers of young men who, in the normal run of events, would never have worn military uniform or been subject to military discipline. Some of these men saw things and did things that they would never have dreamt of seeing or doing in their civilian lives. Among their deeds were acts of violence; there were also acts of despoiling or taking the property of others. Many of these actions were encouraged—sometimes purposely, sometimes unwittingly—by the service context in which the young men found themselves. Peace brought an end to the mass armed forces after the Armistice in 1918 but not in 1945; and in neither instance did it bring an end to criminal behaviour by service personnel.

At the end of the First World War the people in Britain seem generally to have assumed that the *status quo ante bellum* would be restored. A small Army of Occupation was posted to a bridgehead on the east side of the Rhine with a 30-kilometre radius centred on the west bank city of Cologne. A much larger part of the Army and the bulk of the Navy went back to imperial duties. Initially there was concern among some that, having defeated 'Prussianism', the Army was

---

[1] WO 71/1013.

behaving like its recent European enemy in Ireland and India. But the violence of small wars and imperial police actions soon slipped from people's awareness and interest, and the old prejudices, particularly about soldiers being recruited from unsavoury and deviant groups, began to reappear.[2] At the end of the Second World War conscription was maintained and, from 1948, was termed 'National Service'. The final intake of national servicemen was made in 1960. There were a few exceptions but the National Service Act of 1948 ensured that, following their 18th birthday, young men would be liable for military service for a period of initially eighteen months and later two years. The majority of these served in the Army; indeed, in the early 1950s they made up half of the strength of the Army. Some of the conscripts were sent to conflict zones and fought in the Malayan emergency, the Korean War, the Suez campaign, and a scattering of counter-insurgency operations that coincided with the end of empire. The majority of the national servicemen who went abroad, however, served in the British Army of the Rhine, which was originally deployed as an Army of Occupation but which soon became part of a force intended to impede any Soviet move westwards.

## THE BEST YEARS OF THEIR LIVES?

It is not always possible to identify conscripts and Regulars in such criminal records as exist, and certainly not in any statistics. Some offenders were men of seniority; early in 1950, for example, a staff sergeant of the RASC, a Regular with sixteen years' service, faced a court martial for selling around twenty tons of coke to German merchants from a Solid Fuel Depot in Immendorf.[3] Some young military offenders had signed on as Regulars. In January 1957, for example, two 18-year olds who had signed on as such appeared before courts martial at Kitchener Barracks, Chatham. The first, who was reported to be 'unsettled in life and restless in the Army', was sentenced to 112 days' detention for forging entries in his post office book. The second was sentenced to two years' imprisonment and to be discharged with ignominy. He was found guilty of offences ranging from fraud to theft and it was revealed that, before engaging for twenty-two years' service, he had committed a string of similar offences, which had led to a period in Approved School. 'Are there no other ways,' lamented his defending officer, 'in which he could be helped by special treatment, psychiatric or otherwise?' There were a few conscripts as prone to criminal activity as these offenders and as other young men who never left the civilian environment. Some six weeks after the two courts martial in Kitchener Barracks described above, a 22-year-old national serviceman appeared before the Surrey quarter sessions at Kingston. He had been released from Borstal on 28 December 1956, had been called up on 3 January and had absconded from barracks on 5 January. He pleaded guilty to two charges of house-breaking, one of shop-breaking, and requested that another twenty-three be taken into

---

[2] French, 'Big Wars and Small Wars' (2006), p. 47.
[3] WO 71/1023.

consideration. He apologized and insisted that he wanted work but had been unable to get it once he had deserted; he got three years' imprisonment.[4]

There were men who resented being compelled to leave their civilian environment for National Service and this contributed to the problems of absenteeism and desertion. Equally important here was the emotional upset at the end of a leave or the receipt of what became known as a 'Dear John letter', informing the recipient that his wife or girlfriend had found another.[5] But the reasons behind absenteeism and desertion were invariably complex. Early in 1959 it was reported that two junior NCOs had deserted in West Berlin, crossed the border and claimed political asylum. But the story that eventually emerged was of behaviour far more confused and complicated than a simple political statement. Corporal Allan Brooks of the King's Own Border Regiment had received a letter from his wife telling him that she was pregnant by another man. When his request for compassionate leave was refused, Brooks went out and got drunk. He was arrested by the West German Police and handed over to the military. Together with a lance corporal he escaped from military custody and crossed into East Berlin, where both men were arrested. It was at this point that they claimed political asylum. Brooks claimed that he believed that they could get East German identity and works cards and then get back across Germany and back to Britain where he could sort matters out with his wife. After trying to get out of the Soviet Zone he was arrested and sentenced to seven years' hard labour in East Germany. Rather than keep him, however, the East Germans decided to hand him over to the British Red Cross, after which Brooks surrendered to the British Military Police. Lance Corporal Alderson, meanwhile, thought that his best chance of getting back to Britain was to play along with the East Germans and the Soviets. He was right, and several months later he got back to Britain where, like Brooks, he faced a court martial.[6]

Some desertion cases were even more odd. Dennis George Earle hated the Navy. He stole a ten-ton ocean-going yacht from Cowes in the hopes of sailing to France and getting out of the service. In the event, he was not charged with desertion but appeared before magistrates on the Isle of Wight charged with theft of the yacht. Signalman Derek Kirby was charged with desertion but, at his court martial, it was revealed that, apart from two weeks at the beginning of his six-months' absence, he had never left Catterick Camp. He hid in toilets, a drying room, and a disused shower block, and he helped himself to Army food—mainly bread and butter. 'I was a soldier living within my own unit', he told the court, 'and as it seemed no attempt had been made to stop me from taking food, I assumed I had the right to do so.' The desertion charge was dropped; he was sentenced to six months' detention, subsequently commuted to 156 days. Kirby admitted to being fed up with Army life and the uncertainty of whether or not he would get a posting

---

[4] *Chatham, Rochester and Gillingham News*, 18 January 1957, 1 and 8 March, 1.
[5] Royle, *Best Years of their Lives* (1997), 119–20.
[6] *Manchester Guardian*, 6 April 1960, 9; 5 October, 1; *The Times*, 7 April 1960, 10; 31 May, 7; 11 November, 17. Brooks was sentenced to six months partly, it seems, because he had also lost equipment to the value of £2 5s. 7d. Alderson was sentenced to fifty-six days.

overseas. Kirby was harmless, but other bored young soldiers who went absent or deserted could be extremely dangerous. Early in 1958, for example, two young soldiers from the Oxfordshire and Buckinghamshire Light Infantry based in Cyprus armed themselves and hitched a lift from their camp to a village where they stole fruit, bread, and bedding. They forced a local man to drive them to Nicosia where they took his car and set off on their own. For three days they avoided the search for them; when they were eventually surrounded, while one man went quietly, the other opened fire on two British police officers who approached him. When the court queried what had prompted the soldiers' behaviour, two officers from their regiment responded that conditions in their camp were 'not at all pleasant', that the soldiers lacked entertainment of any kind and 'felt frustrated'.[7]

Absenteeism and desertion were military offences; so too was verbally abusing or striking a superior officer. In one instance from the summer of 1948 an officer in the JAG's office warned that some NCOs brought this on themselves by their own aggressive behaviour.

> It seems that the NCO was struck by the accused after the NCO had proposed to make a buttonhole in the accused's tunic with a bayonet. I am not at all sure that a court martial might not consider that this was a reasonable provocation and that if NCO's insist on carrying out repairs to soldiers' clothes with bayonets the subsequent striking of the NCO by the soldier, if not justified, will be considerably mitigated.[8]

Rough behaviour by NCOs continued to be regarded by some officers of the post-war Army as the only way to deal with roughs in the ranks.[9] But sometimes insubordination appears to have been the result of a seasoned soldier taking exception to the orders of a new, seemingly inexperienced superior—perhaps a National Service officer. 'Sergeant Grey is running this cook-house and not you', protested one exasperated NCO, 'and if you send all the men on weekend leave you can come and do their work yourself.'[10] On other occasions such incidents were the product of sheer bloody-mindedness, drink and/or boredom. When a Catering Corps corporal told an RASC private that he should consider himself on a charge, the private responded with a punch and the alleged words: 'If I am charged, I will be the last fucking man you will charge.' Similarly, when ordered to fall in by a major, a private of the Highland Light Infantry announced: 'I am not going to be ordered about by any fucking officer.'[11]

As ever, however, there were also plenty of the more conventional cases of drunkenness, violence, trafficking on the black market, theft, robbery, and sexual assaults among service personnel, both Regulars and conscripts. Sailors went ashore, got drunk, caused mayhem, and even created international incidents when arrested

---

[7] *Manchester Guardian*, 10 July 1954, 8; 5 February 1955, 10; 19 February, 2; 19 April 1958, 5.
[8] WO 84/92 f. 18.
[9] French, *Military Identities* (2005), 191.
[10] WO 84/94 f. 14.
[11] WO 84/76 f. 74; and WO84/92 f. 65.

by the police of foreign powers.[12] Goods were taken from cook-houses and NAAFIs, sometimes for personal consumption, and sometimes to be sold on to the civilian world where rationing and shortages continued. In December 1945, for example, a Welsh Guardsman stationed at home was charged with stealing around 9,000 cigarettes, together with chocolate, tea, sugar, soap powder, razor blades, and stationary from his local NAAFI.[13] In 1946 the SIB based in Brussels investigated the theft and resale of woollen vests, petrol and even two three-ton lorries; and across the next decade similar offences were pursued in Austria, Belgium, and Germany.[14]

Some soldiers in Germany behaved as might be expected from a victorious Army of Occupation. They assaulted and fought civilians. They accosted and sometimes assaulted women.[15] Andrey Kodin, an Austrian Jew who had escaped to England in 1938, served with the SIB in Germany from 1948 to 1952 where he reckoned that scarcely a week went by without a rape investigation.[16] And soldiers vandalized property. In May 1958, for example, the SIB were engaged in correspondence with the German Police in the Mohne See area following damage to young trees, traffic and other road and street signs allegedly committed by men from an anti-aircraft battery which had been camping in the area.[17] Yet such offences were not unique to the forces in Germany or the situation of an Army of Occupation. Units fought among themselves, as they had done in the war years; and if a man was seriously injured in a fight, what better than to accuse German civilians of being the assailants.[18] Similarly, young soldiers could be accused anywhere of assaulting women, of vandalism, and of any variety of offences. In January 1960, for example, a 19-year-old guardsman was found guilty at the Old Bailey of the manslaughter of a prostitute. Doctors called as witnesses regarded the man as a psychopath who was extremely dangerous when he had been drinking; and the judge expressed concern about the fact that no one had attempted to prevent the young man from drinking a pint of gin at his birthday party, after which he had to be carried out by his comrades.[19] In the following November 1960, the Press Council considered a complaint from the mayor and Corporation of Honiton about a story in the *Evening Chronicle* of Newcastle-upon-Tyne that officials of the Devon town were objecting to the presence of a battalion of the Durham Light Infantry following its behaviour. The Press Council agreed that the newspaper story was exaggerated,

---

[12] IWM (S) 32399, Peter White, reel 4; *Manchester Guardian*, 6 August 1952, 5, 7 August, 5, and 3 September, 7.

[13] WO 84/76, f. 31.

[14] CRMP Archive, SIB Crime Book, Brussels, 1946, nos. 22, 33, 97, 103; SIB Crime Book, BAOR, 1956–57, nos. 70, 80, 92, 156, 203. See also, Royle, *Best Years of Their Lives* (1997), 143.

[15] CRMP Archive, SIB Crime Book, BAOR, 1947–48, nos. 85, 179 (assaults on women); SIB Crime Book, BAOR, 1956–57, nos. 21, 46, 63, 72, 101, 104, 109 (assaults on/fights with civilians); nos. 77, 95, 102, 123, 132, 162, 175, 195 (importuning women); SIB Crime Book, BAOR, 1958, nos. 11/1, 1/2, 14/2 (assaults on civilians), no. 24/7 (accusation of rape/admission of assault).

[16] IWM (Sound) 30403, Andrey Kodin, reel 10.

[17] CRMP Archive, SIB Crime Book, BAOR, 1958, no. 20/7.

[18] CRMP Archive, SIB Crime Book, BAOR, 1947–48, no. 14; SIB Crime Book, BAOR, 1958, no. 9/4.

[19] *The Times*, 22 January 1960, 17.

though there had been some hooliganism and an alleged assault case that was now the subject of court proceedings. It quoted the battalion commander to the effect that the behaviour of his men 'had not been abnormal. In 800 men there were bound to be a few who behaved badly and these had tarnished the reputation of the whole body.'[20]

Alongside the petty theft, the black marketeering, the fights, the assaults, and the vandalism, men of the post-war conscript forces also continued to commit various forms of theft and fraud. Registered letters and packets containing money, cigarettes, and other goods were sometimes too much of a temptation for a few of those detailed to work in their regimental post office. At the beginning of 1957, for example, three teenage soldiers were brought before a court martial in Aldershot for such offences. The 19-year-old lance corporal in charge of the post office appears to have been the instigator.[21] This was a small group offence, but the bigger criminal packs were also active. In the late spring of 1956 a scandal broke over the theft of goods at the Military Forwarding Depot at Kirby near Liverpool. The depot collected and forwarded soldiers' kit and it dealt with just under 100,000 pieces of baggage in twelve months. It was staffed by both civilians and soldiers; normally there were twenty-five of the former and forty of the latter. There was also a squad of six Military Police on duty to supervise the unloading and the storing of baggage and, at night, to patrol the storage sheds. The problem was that both soldiers and civilians began to help themselves to property in the baggage. According to one of the defence solicitors, the thefts were known throughout the Army and the appropriated property was referred to as 'Kirby issue'. The SIB began an investigation after receiving over fifty complaints, but there was criticism that the sergeant entrusted with the bulk of the investigation was a 19-year-old national serviceman. The sergeant was praised for his assiduousness, but it was suspected that his youth led him to miss the biggest offenders who were more adept at covering their tracks and denying everything. The suggestion was made in court that young soldiers posted to Kirby were pressurized into joining the gang on the grounds that it was safer to have them involved. Many of those who appeared before the ensuing court martial had confessed and expressed remorse. In all, twenty-three soldiers were tried; fourteen were found guilty, of whom eleven were MPs.[22]

Ration cards, leave passes, and railway warrants continued to be taken and filled in illicitly, and men converted funds entrusted to them to their own use.[23] Men claimed benefits to which they, or more often their wives, were not entitled. At the end of 1945, for example, it was discovered that a regimental quartermaster sergeant had, two years previously, omitted to inform his commanding officer that he was separated from his wife. The omission appears to have been deliberate, thus enabling her to continue receiving her marriage allowance. A more complex

[20] *The Guardian*, 24 November 1960, 6.

[21] *Aldershot News*, 4 January 1957, 8.

[22] *Manchester Guardian*, 24 April 1956, 3, 26 April, 8, 27 April, 3, 28 April, 2, 1 May, 4, and 2 May, 3 and 14.

[23] CRMP Archive, SIB Crime Book, BAOR, 1947–48, no. 70 and no. 271; WO 84/76 ff. 36, 58, and 150; WO 84/92, ff. 15, 25–6, and 41.

case concerned a corporal of the RASC who had served a sentence for bigamy but
had arranged for his second, bigamous wife to collect the family allowance even
though, legally, this was not permitted. The office of the JAG saw considerable
difficulties in this affair.

> I am not at all sure that in these days when it is a well-known thing for 'unmarried
> wives' to receive marriage allowance and so on that it would be necessarily a simple
> matter to prove that this soldier, when claiming an allowance for his bigamous wife,
> was actuated by fraudulent motives. He would probably reply that he could see little
> difference in the Army paying an allowance to one 'wife' or to another 'wife'. He would
> probably agree that to try to get two allowances, one in respect of each wife, would be
> improper and probably fraudulent; but as long as only one was receiving an allowance a
> simple soldier might persuade a court that he honestly did not see that it mattered very
> much to the Army which one of them drew the allowance.

There was also the problem that the Army could be seen as complicit in authorizing
the payments having earlier permitted the 'real' wife to apply and draw an
allowance.[24]

In addition to the sexual assaults and offences involving coercion, men could still
be prosecuted for homosexual activity. A homosexual conscript could hope to be
excluded from National Service by declaring his sexual inclination, but Army
medical men took a dim view of this and many appear to have subscribed to the
belief that the shock of military training would 'cure' such a preference.[25] Many
young conscripts appear to have been shocked and frightened by homosexual
behaviour, and it was by no means behaviour confined to national servicemen.
The investigation of a major in a tank regiment in May 1945 led the SIB to the
arrest of eleven German civilians in what appears to have been a homosexual
group.[26] Six years later a brigadier, with an impressive wartime career, was court-
martialled and driven from the Army for gross indecency.[27] The aggressive homophobia present in many young men, and hence in many servicemen, also fostered
violent behaviour towards homosexuals. In the summer of 1955, Norman Struther,
a Glaswegian, an amateur actor and homosexual, invited two young naval ratings
back to his flat; they killed him.[28] At the same time consensual heterosexual activity
could lead men into trouble when, for example, the consenting female was underage. Following a letter from the Birmingham police in the summer of 1958, the SIB
arrested a young soldier from the Royal Army Ordnance Corps for unlawful sex
with a 14-year-old. The soldier promptly admitted the offence adding, with an
innocent honesty, that he also had just received a letter from Birmingham telling
him that his girlfriend was pregnant and that he was the father.[29]

There were probably feelings of triumphal superiority among the men serving in
Germany during the years immediately following the war and these might have

---

[24] WO 84/92, f. 87.          [25] Royle, *Best Years of Their Lives* (1997), 120.
[26] CRMP Archive, SIB Crime Book, BAOR, 1947–48, no. 204.
[27] Holmes, *Soldiers* (2011), 176.
[28] *The Times*, 12 July 1955, 11 and 21 July, 4.
[29] CRMP Archive, SIB Crime Book, BAOR, 1958, no. 6/8.

been the prompts to some of the aggression and violence towards German citizens. There were also more traditional inter-regiment and interservice fights, as well as opportunities to confront servicemen from other nations. T. W. Wood and his mates did not much like the Germans but, posted to Berlin after the war, they seem to have disliked Soviet troops even more, and were appalled by their behaviour. Wood's unit used to frequent the same café as a group of Red Army soldiers and they believed that the Soviets, resplendent in their medals and wearing side-arms, looked down on them. One night Wood got his revenge by following one of the Russians, whom he took to be a ringleader, into the café's toilet and beating him up. The toilet attendant, a German ex-serviceman, shook Wood's hand and let him out by a private door. At roughly the same time an airman shot dead a Red Army sergeant in a Berlin brothel and a private of the Argyle and Sutherland Highlanders went before a court martial in Vienna for killing a Russian in a fight.[30] American service personnel also remained favourite opponents. A fight involving a large number of men on both sides spilled from the pubs to the streets of the small county town of Bedford in August 1956. The town, or more particularly the smaller, adjoining town of Kempston, had a barracks which, at the beginning of the Suez emergency was extended to house a massive tented encampment for recalled reservists. The recall was unpopular with many of those ordered back to the colours and, later in the year, following serious trouble among soldiers and sailors in several bases in Britain, as well as overseas, the government stopped the dispatch of reservists to the Mediterranean which could have had operational implications had the war in Egypt been prolonged. In Bedford, however, on Sunday 12 August, the reservists chose to pick fights with men from the American Air Base at Chicksands. Neither the military nor the civilian authorities took any action against those involved. The report in the local newspaper was muted and took up only about one-tenth of the column inches of a story about the smooth running of the tented camp at Kempston where, it was said, the quartermaster's stores were processing 120 men every hour. Tucked away in the small print about the fighting was the advice subsequently issued to American servicemen that they should avoid Bedford's pubs during the call-up of the reservists.[31]

## WAR CRIMES AND OTHER CRIMES

Sergeant George Hadfield MM was estimated to have paid over £900 into his English bank account between March and June 1953 after having sold everything from batteries to bales of goods offloaded at Port Said and from vehicle parts to the parts of Sten guns. Not unlike the military dockworkers and the pioneers and

---

[30] IWM (D) 99/31/1, T. W. Wood, '"On Tracks" with the Armoured Engineers 1943–1946', f. 28; *The Times*, 13 August 1946, 3, and 3 September, 3.
[31] *Bedfordshire Times and Standard*, 17 August 1956, 7 and 12; *The Times*, 18 August 1956, 4. My thanks to David Taylor for alerting me to the trouble with reservists and the Bedford fight. For the subsequent disorder and protests by reservists see French, *Army, Empire, and Cold War* (2012), 145–6.

engineers who profited as groups from their wartime duties, members of Hadfield's RASC unit were involved and received their cuts. But Hadfield was seen as the ringleader and his men were required only to give testimony—an issue that was raised as part of his unsuccessful appeal against his ten-year prison sentence.[32] A year later, in Malaya, six soldiers were sentenced by court martial for stealing Army vehicles and selling them on to a scrap-metal dealer. The men were based on the docks in Singapore and succeeded in stealing vehicles and equipment, including two bulldozers, a tractor and a three-ton truck, to the value of £29,000.[33] Crime, as the above incidents reveal, had no respect for zones of conflict.

Before the First World War and during the interwar period, British soldiers had taken livestock, burned villages, smashed property, and struck and killed civilians from South Africa to the Middle East and on to the North West Frontier. In the twenty or so years following the Second World War, British service personnel, both Regulars and conscripts, found themselves engaged against the insurgencies that heralded the end of empire, and in police actions and small wars often linked to larger geopolitical struggles. The original narrative, at least of the conflicts surrounding decolonization, claimed that the British developed a successful system of minimum force in these struggles. More recent research, however, has suggested that, while there was a veneer of legality and a smoke screen that insisted on the winning of hearts and minds, coercion and intimidation were widespread. Some of this behaviour, such as the death and destruction inflicted on the Palestinian village of al-Bassa towards the end of 1938 and the massacre of plantation workers in the Malayan village of Batang Kali ten years later, could be classified as war crimes. But much of the behaviour was more conventionally criminal, sometimes prompted, or even officially sanctioned by the supposed requirements of counter-insurgency.[34]

There was little common pattern to the insurgencies and little common pattern to the territories in which they were fought. Feelings of racial superiority were present among some of those sent to outposts of the fading empire, though there were others, especially it seems among the conscripts, who expressed sympathy for the indigenous peoples and were critical of their treatment.[35] The critics, of course, are most likely to have been drawn from articulate, liberal, and left-wing young men keen to write about their National Service experience.

Palestine and the Canal Zone were territories in close proximity to each other and, while they both experienced insurgency in the decade following 1945, they had come under British control in very different ways and their insurgencies were dissimilar. Palestine was mandated to the British by the League of Nations in 1922.

[32]  WO 71/1217.

[33]  *Manchester Guardian*, 12 August 1954, 5 and 8 September, 7.

[34]  See in general, French, *British Way in Counter-Insurgency* (2011); and for al-Bassa and Batang Kali see, respectively: Hughes, 'Banality of Brutality' (2009); and Mark Townsend, 'New documents reveal cover-up of 1948 British "massacre" of villagers in Malaya', *The Guardian*, 9 April 2011.

[35]  Peter Burns, a national serviceman who was commissioned in the Ox and Bucks Light Infantry, noted prejudice and complete separation between the British (especially the officers) and the Egyptians. Bill Holdsworth felt that national servicemen like himself were rather more sympathetic to the locals than the Regulars. See Johnson, ed. *All Bull* (1973), 87 and 98.

The mandate was never going to be easy, given promises made to both Arabs and Jews in the territory. The Jewish population had increased considerably during the 1930s, and this had been a contributory factor to the Arab Revolt of 1936. In the aftermath of the Second World War, the Jewish community demanded that survivors of the Holocaust be permitted to enter the territory and set out to establish their own state, Israel. There were charges of assault and violence levelled against the British troops deployed in counter-insurgency, but at least one tactic was used unofficially for more conventional criminal activity. While off duty, a group of paratroops followed the practice of cordoning off and searching a block of flats in Tel Aviv but, rather than looking for weapons and suspects, they chose to line their pockets.[36]

As in Ireland in 1920, the demand for weapons by those seeking independence provided opportunities for profit. Lieutenant Colonel Thomas Gore DSO, in charge of 614 Ammunition Depot, was instructed to dispose of a number of surplus Browning machine guns and other weapons by throwing them in the sea. He preferred to sell them to the Haganah, the largest of the Jewish military groups; a major and two sergeants who were also involved admitted their offences at Gore's court martial and gave evidence against him.[37] The fighting in Palestine also led some men to desert, with a few stealing equipment in the process. More than fifty British deserters joined the Arab forces; four, for example, fought in the battle for Jerusalem in 1948, joining the Palestinian Djany family and calling themselves the Djanees. Rather fewer deserters appear to have joined the Israeli side, but notable among these were two tank crews that deserted with their tanks.[38] It is unclear what led Sergeant William John Spriggs to desert with a Humber Scout Car, a Bren gun, and a box of twelve magazines less than a month before the final British withdrawal and the declaration of the state of Israel. Almost exactly one year later he was apprehended by the civilian police in St Helens and a court martial was prepared on charges of desertion and theft. Spriggs's court martial echoed some of the problems noted earlier in the collection of material from overseas theatres. When he was arrested his unit was still abroad in the Middle East, so he was posted there for his trial. However, since one of the principal witnesses for the prosecution had now left the Army, and since there was no provision to subpoena a civilian witness for a court martial to be held abroad, everything had to be sent back and the trial rescheduled for a British setting. Some documents were lost in the toing and froing, some enquiries had to be repeated and, as a result, Spriggs spent 245 days under arrest before his trial.[39]

British presence in the Canal Zone went back to the 19th century but the Anglo-Egyptian Treaty of 1936 allowed a British garrison of 10,000 troops to be maintained along the Suez Canal for a period of twenty years. The garrison had

---

[36] French, *British Way in Counter-Insurgency* (2011), 146.

[37] Bisset, *Trial at Arms* (1957), chapter 2. Gore was found guilty, cashiered, and sentenced to two years' imprisonment.

[38] My thanks to Dr Anat Stern of the Hebrew University of Jerusalem for this information. A key text on this is Yoav Gelber, *Komemiyut Ve-Nakba* (2004).

[39] WO 71/1189; *Daily Mirror*, 7 December 1949, 7.

increased significantly during the Second World War and was not reduced to the agreed size at the war's end. Tensions between the Egyptians and the garrison ran high. In June 1949, six Military Policemen were tried by court martial for the murder of a young man arrested for taking jewellery from an army wife; the MPs admitted hitting him, but only because he tried to escape. The following year, in 'the case of the human torch', nine soldiers were convicted of grievous bodily harm after throwing a tin of petrol over another civilian; they claimed that they thought the tin contained water.[40] In 1951 the Egyptian government unilaterally abrogated the treaty and determined to make life difficult for the garrison. Egyptian labourers ceased working for the British; there were anti-British riots and troops were fired upon. British troops responded, both under orders and unofficially. Early in 1953, the Egyptian authorities complained that, in less than four months, there had been twenty-one incidents, including six alleged murders and two attempted murders, in which British soldiers had made serious attacks on the lives and property of civilians. They also complained of less serious acts of trespass and the destruction of crops. Throughout the remainder of the year and into 1954 there were further acts of violence on both sides, including the abduction of a British airman.[41] One night in March 1954, a very drunk, 20-year-old LAC Anthony Morgan, in company with several soldiers and a WAAC, took an RAF vehicle and was alleged to have said: 'We're going to kill some Wogs tonight!' Morgan and Fusilier Edward McKinney beat up two Egyptians, and when an Egyptian police car stopped to investigate the commotion, an Egyptian police lieutenant was shot dead. There had to be two separate courts martial since Morgan was in the RAF and McKinney in the Army. McKinney's trial was the first; he was found guilty and sentenced to death. The verdict in Morgan's case was the same. When the news reached Britain, however, there was an outcry. A petition for mercy with 28,000 signatures was handed to the government on the announcement of McKinney's sentence. Both sentences were commuted: McKinney's to twelve years' imprisonment and Morgan's to eight years. Both men were released before the end of their sentences.[42]

Racial hostility might have had a part in Morgan's and McKinney's offence; drink unquestionably did. And drunkenness contributed to other lethal, or potentially lethal incidents. In 1966, as the Aden emergency drew to its conclusion, a Welsh Guardsman killed a local taxi-driver in circumstances not greatly dissimilar from those of Morgan and McKinney.[43] But it was not just hostility to men of a different colour and whose fellow countrymen were engaged in an insurgency that led to drunken soldiers behaving murderously. According to their defending officer, it was drink and boredom that, in spite of the EOKA emergency early in 1956, encouraged four Glaswegians from the Highland Light Infantry 'to make their officers run' by throwing grenades at them in their camp in north-east Cyprus. It

---

[40]  *Manchester Guardian*, 3 June 1949, 10 and 20 July 1950, 7.
[41]  See, for example, *The Times*, 16 May 1953, 6; 13 July, 6; 22 January 1954, 6; 17 March, 8.
[42]  *The Times*, 5 April 1954, 8; 5 June, 5; 10 June, 5; 12 June, 6; 15 June, 2; 7 July, 4; 24, July, 3; *Daily Mirror*, 9 June 1954, 1; *Daily Express*, 15 June, 2. See also, Rubin, *Murder, Mutiny and the Military* (2005), chapters 13 and 14.
[43]  Rubin, *Murder, Mutiny and the Military* (2005), chapter 21.

was fortunate that no one was killed, but two officers were wounded and the four soldiers received prison sentences ranging from three to ten years for their 'practical joke'.[44] Elsewhere, and particularly when men who were seriously drunk had ready access to guns and ammunition, the violence could be lethal. In Aden, during the late summer of 1960 Lance Bombardier Harry Whiteside shot dead Captain David Dewsbury Evans when the captain did not respond immediately to Whiteside's request for a record player. The Director of Army Psychiatry examined Whiteside and found a 'violent antisocial history'. He concluded that the soldier's mental state 'could lead to schizophrenia under stress and complete lack of normal emotions and remorse.' Nevertheless, at his court martial, Whiteside was found guilty of murder, sentenced to be discharged with ignominy and imprisoned for life.[45]

Yet even during a counter-insurgency campaign, lethal violence could also take the more traditional form of domestic violence. Early in 1951, Bombardier John Stewart returned from a jungle patrol in Malaya and met his Chinese-Indian girlfriend in an amusement park. She began to tease him by waving photographs of another soldier. Stewart claimed not to remember what happened next; he shot her with his Sten gun. At the Malacca Assizes the jury found him guilty but recommended mercy. The judge sentenced Stewart to death, but he agreed with the jury's recommendation:

> I hope you will be shown mercy. I am aware that there are many young men like you in this country who must suffer terribly from the strain of jungle warfare. I think that you would not have done this if you had not been suffering from this strain.

The High Commissioner of Malaya reprieved Stewart and sentenced him to life imprisonment.[46] The comments of the judge echoed the notions of both the unwritten law and the impact of shell shock and, some years later at the turn of the century, they were to be expressed again in similar forms with reference to the stresses and strains of men's experiences in subsequent conflicts.


## CHANGES IN THE MILITARY JUSTICE SYSTEM

In the case of Bombardier Stewart, the civilian British Court in Malacca was given primacy; he had been off duty at the time of the offence and murder was a major crime punishable under civilian law; moreover the victim was a civilian. There could still be tensions between the civilian and the military law, though most apparent in less serious cases. In January 1946, for example, a magistrate at the West London Police Court, hearing the case of a drunken sailor who had wilfully damaged a Belisha beacon, expressed his concerns that the man was also to be tried by the Navy. He pointed out that 'it was a fundamental law of this country that a man could not be charged twice with the same offence.' When a Navy officer

---

[44] WO 71/1233; *Manchester Guardian*, 22 March 1956, 9.
[45] *The Times*, 29 September 1960, 8.
[46] *The Times*, 14 February 1951, 3, and 26 April, 4; *Manchester Guardian*, 28 April, 6.

insisted that the man was being charged with conduct prejudicial to naval discipline, the magistrate responded that this was 'simply altering the wording of the
charge'.[47] A few years later an Assize Court judge queried what an officer meant
when he gave a man a 'fair' character. The soldier had pleaded guilty to house-
breaking and asked for another twenty-eight offences to be taken into consideration. 'Is a soldier's military character "fair" when he gets nine months for what
must have been very substantial offences?' asked the judge as he sent the soldier to
Borstal. 'This rascal has been breaking into houses and stealing merely because he
could not get a ration book and had no money.'[48] But in the half-century following
the Second World War, the justice systems of the services continued to grow closer
to their civilian counterparts, partly through external pressure and partly because of
the broader changes within British society.

In the immediate aftermath of the Second World War many, probably the
majority of most minor offences committed by service personnel, went no further
than the summary jurisdiction of the Orderly Room or of the ship's captain. Such
cases rarely leave any trace in the historical record, unless there is mention in a
memoir or unless an incident was sufficiently notable to receive some public
attention. One such incident made the front page of the *Daily Mirror* in 1947,
when a Grenadier Guardsman wrote to the paper about an order issued to the
Welsh Guards that they were each to contribute one shilling towards a wedding
present for Princess Elizabeth. The *Mirror* contacted the War Office without
mentioning the informant's name. The War Office agreed that the 'compulsory'
element was wrong and that the order had been unfortunately phrased. But the
Guards were not prepared to let the matter drop. When the Welsh Guards were
paraded at Caterham, the informant was asked to identify himself. Grenadier
J. Wright, who was serving as a clerk in the Orderly Room, stepped forward.
According to the *Mirror* he was promptly 'crimed' and, accused of 'improperly
discussing the contents of the order well-knowing he should not do so', he was
severely reprimanded. Unfortunately for the Guards, the *Mirror* picked up on, and
made much of the fact that the officer who passed judgement on Wright was Major
F. J. C. Bowes-Lyon, second cousin to the Queen and thus related to the princess.[49]

Major Bowes-Lyon's actions might not have equated with bullying, but bullying
by NCOs and violent responses by other ranks continued to generate service
offences such as insubordination and striking. Some bullying and some assaults
were the result of unofficial punishments within the barracks. Two young signallers
in Catterick Camp were 'scrubbed' for bringing their unit into disrepute; they had
disobeyed an order about changing into civilian clothes to go out, a lance corporal
had almost throttled one of them by pulling on his collar and tie, and six other
young soldiers took this as a cue to beat up the offenders. The lance corporal then
threatened the victims not to say anything.[50] Bullying and 'beasting' as punishment

[47] *The Times*, 22 January 1946, 2.
[48] *Manchester Guardian*, 18 January 1950, 2.
[49] *Daily Mirror*, 11 October 1947, 1.
[50] *Manchester Guardian*, 11 January 1952, 8, 12 January, 2, 16 January, 3, and 23 January, 4.

or as a form of initiation, however, had long been a part of military life, and continued long after the end of National Service.[51]

The continuing presence of conscripts, often reluctant, in the peacetime services provided much of the impetus for changes in the criminal justice systems of the armed services. But public concerns followed hard on the end of the Second World War over the courts martial following a wave of protests and mutinies by disgruntled conscripts demanding demobilization and objecting to the reimposition of peacetime spit and polish and 'bull'. The new Labour government was sympathetic and appointed a committee to look into Army and RAF courts martial. The committee itself stressed the changed circumstances of National Service in the armed forces in peacetime. This was something which

> emphasizes the importance of the principle which we think no one would dispute, namely, that in the matter of legal safeguards, citizens should be no worse off when they are in the Forces than in civil life unless considerations of discipline or other circumstances make such a disadvantage inevitable.[52]

In consequence the committee recommended the establishment of an appeals court for courts martial cases in which the accused had originally entered a plea of not guilty. The new court was established in 1951. Equally significant, the committee recommended changes to the office of the Judge Advocate General and, in consequence, in 1948 the office was reorganized. Henceforth, the formal responsibility of the JAG was to the Lord Chancellor rather than to the ministers responsible for service departments.

There were further changes through the 1950s as the military justice system was brought more closely in line with that of the civilian world. Courts martial were instructed to take careful account of the age of a soldier before them, his previous behaviour, and the circumstances of the incident with which he was charged. Summary punishment was diminished and the behaviour of commanding officers was brought under more careful scrutiny.[53] But the changes to the prosecution system and the creation of a means of appeal did not resolve all of the problems. There could be delays in the new appeals system. In 1953 a corporal was tried by court martial and sentenced to nine months' imprisonment and a dishonourable discharge for indecent assault and causing bodily harm. The appeal judges overturned the sentence, but were concerned that the case only came to them after the sentence had been served.[54]

Difficulties could still occur when men were posted or left the services and documentation had to follow them around the world, as was evidenced in the case

---

[51] Holmes, *Soldiers* (2011), chapter 25.

[52] *Report of the Army and Air Force Court Martial Committee*, Cmd 7608, 30. See in general, Rubin, 'The Status of the Judge Advocate General' (1994).

[53] French, *Military Identities* (2005), 313–14. The most significant change in the organization of cases for courts martial, however, occurred with the creation of the Service Prosecuting Authority (SPA) under the Armed Forces Act of 2006. From its creation the SPA, headed by an eminent civilian QC, has dealt with cases for all of the three armed services.

[54] *Daily Mirror*, 23 March 1954, 1.

of William Spriggs's desertion in Palestine. Concerns about the documentation of courts martial and about the accuracy of returns of the numbers conducted were expressed at the highest levels towards the end of the Korean War. In March 1953 Brigadier H. C. W. Eking DSO, the deputy director of Personal Services, wrote to Sir Frederick W. Gentle, QC, the Vice Judge Advocate General, lamenting that the returns submitted by different commands were incomplete and that, even if these improved, his department would still have no efficient means of cross-checking for accuracy. Figures submitted for Korea reported 1,103 courts martial held during the conflict, of which 1,002 resulted in convictions. Once again, desertion was the major offence, with 128 trials and 106 convictions; more detailed typed tables accompanying these figures suggest that desertion, and the less serious absenteeism, were often accompanied by another offence, such as theft.[55] But in the absence of more details of the cases, it is difficult to know whether men deserted after having committed the theft, being fearful of the consequences, or stole to provide food and a vehicle to assist their escape. Either way, Korea was a long way and a difficult journey from home.

The pursuit of deserters and of other offenders against military law was still the task of Service Police and attitudes to these remained largely the same. As far as the soldiers were concerned, the Redcaps were still 'monkeys', and the term was given an added boost by the tune 'Little Red Monkey' which had originated as the theme for a television thriller serial and which was then turned into a popular, gently comic song sung by the cast of the radio comedy series *Take It from Here*. David Taylor, who finished his career as a superintendent in the Essex Police, recalled how, in February 1955, during his National Service as a Military Policeman, he was doing his first duty, alone, smartly spit and polished with his bright red cap, standing on Düsseldorf Railway Station. A troop train slowed down as it pulled through the station and a squaddie began to sing:

> Look at the monkey, funny monkey,
> Little red monkey, acting so fidgety.
> Look at the monkey, funny monkey,
> Little red monkey, cute as can be.[56]

Soon the entire train joined in. Taylor was not the only MP who recalled being serenaded by the song. And, after the end of National Service, with the appearance of the television series pop-group The Monkees, soldiers were given a new song with which to annoy MPs.

> Hey, hey we're the Monkees
> And people say we monkey around,
> But we're too busy singing
> To put anybody down.[57]

---

[55] WO 93/59, Korea, Courts martial, 1952–54.
[56] My thanks to David Taylor for this information. The song can be found at http://www/hjo3.net/lyrics/little_red_monkey.htm, accessed 25 February 2011.
[57] *RMP Old Comrades Link Up Newsletter*, 52 (October 2011).

In his description of the professional Army, published twenty-five years after Taylor's experience, Anthony Beevor noted how Scottish regiments and paratroops in particular regularly abused MPs as 'monkeys', even to their faces, and even when the MPs were providing assistance. The paras, allegedly, only had respect for 160 Provost Company, paratroops like themselves and attached to the 5th Airborne Brigade. Even gender was no bar to the paras' abuse, as one woman corporal from the Redcaps explained:

> Quite a lot of us have had to pick up the pieces after they've been on the rampage and, to put it mildly, it's always ended in tears. I have great respect for the paras as soldiers. It's their social habits I can't stand. As a woman you'll be told to get down on the floor with your legs apart because that's where you belong.[58]

Steve Roberts, who retired from the Military Police shortly before Beevor's book was published, recalled how the unpopularity of the 'monkeys' reached the ears of East German border guards. The guards waved nooses and whistles at the MPs from their side of the Berlin Wall and declared that they would hang all Military Police when war brought them into the west. Roberts's account of his military career is not unlike that of ordinary civilian police officers. He dealt with domestic incidents in married quarters; he checked that there were no problems in bars and, since they were often licensed overseas, in brothels; and both bars and brothels were good places for an unauthorized sit-down and a coffee on cold nights. Breaking up fights between rival units he likened to dealing with a confrontation between football hooligans. Most trouble occurred when men had taken too much drink, especially if they could not hold it; and at the time of Roberts's service, there was an emerging drugs problem—he describes a ferocious fight with a sailor who, one night in Belize, took, or was given, an unknown drug that appeared to make him immensely strong and insensitive to pain. Yet in spite of the hostility and other problems, Roberts showed a soft spot even for the men that abused him. Most soldiers meant well, he thought, and had the interests of their unit at heart; and they were most troublesome when they were not kept busy.[59]

The implication from Roberts's testimony, as from other evidence, is that the behaviour of most young servicemen in the years following the Second World War was little different from the behaviour of young people not in uniform. Some got into trouble, some did not. Some had committed offences before joining the services, some had not; and probably most of those who got into various forms of trouble did not continue with such behaviour when they left the services, grew older and more mature and, especially, when they settled down with a job, a partner, and a family. When National Service came to an end the armed forces began to be recruited from volunteers often drawn from social classes similar to those that had provided the backbone of the Victorian and Edwardian Army and

[58] Beevor, *Inside the British Army* (1990), 316–17.
[59] IWM (S) 31452, Steve Roberts, especially reel 5, reel 7, and reel 10.

Navy. But the experience of mass armed forces during the two world wars had had an important effect and by the turn of the millennium, as Britain was mired in a number of small wars and as awareness grew of the psychological impact of modern warfare on those who fought it, the popular attitudes towards service personnel had shifted significantly, and continued to shift.

# 10

## 'I Could Have Done Other Stuff'
### The Return to Professional Services

Harry Roberts was a career criminal. He recalled that, during and immediately after the Second World War, his mother's café in north London was a centre for black marketeers and receivers who employed him as their delivery boy. From here he progressed to armed robbery, and a Borstal sentence in his late teens. In August 1966 he was one of three men involved in the murder of three plainclothes police officers in Shepherd's Bush. Roberts's accomplices were quickly arrested, but he evaded capture until mid-November. For most of the period between the murders and his arrest, Roberts lived rough in woods near Bishop's Stortford. He slept by day and at night he raided a poultry farm, allotments, and greenhouses for food, and various buildings for money. His hideout was a camouflaged tent; his food was stored in a cabinet of cardboard and plywood; his cooking utensils, clothing, and boots were clean and tidy. Roberts had been a good soldier.

Roberts's call-up for National Service had arrived shortly after his release from Borstal. 'I loved the Army,' he told one biographer.

> I didn't find it too difficult. On the contrary, after Borstal, I found the army quite easy! So did many of the Borstal boys. We seemed to get on a lot better than the ordinary civilians who were called up. Army life agreed with me. I loved the discipline.

There is probably exaggeration here but Roberts was promoted to lance corporal and, as a national serviceman, he fought Mau Mau in Kenya and communists in Malaya. After his two years he returned to civvy street needing money. 'I felt strong and confident because now I was always armed', recalled Roberts, who enjoyed carrying a handgun.[1] The police, he told a *Guardian* reporter in 1993, were the enemy of professional criminals like him: 'it's like the people I killed in Malaya when I was in the Army. You don't feel any remorse.' Roberts was an exceptional case, not least because successive home secretaries kept him in prison after he had served his thirty-year sentence. But while correspondents to the *Guardian*, normally noted for their liberalism, showed little sympathy for him, towards the end of the century, and long after National Service had gone, Roberts became one of several examples used to illustrate the possibility of military training having a deleterious and dangerous effect on an individual.[2]

---

[1] Kray, *Killers* (2003), 122–3.
[2] *The Guardian*, 2 February 1993, A2; for letters to the editor critical of Roberts's lack of remorse over the police that he had killed, see 5 February, 20.

## DRINKING, VIOLENCE, AND POST-TRAUMATIC STRESS

Aly Renwick was a soldier radicalized by the deployment of British troops in Northern Ireland. He bought himself out of the Army and was a founder member of the Troops Out Movement, established in 1973 to campaign for a withdrawal from Northern Ireland. In 1999 Renwick spearheaded a new campaign with the publication of *Hidden Wounds*. Renwick's book mentioned Harry Roberts, together with the dangerous behaviour of a few other national servicemen, but his main concern was the damage inflicted on some of the volunteers to the Regular forces after 1960. These were commonly young men, encouraged to develop their physical fitness, trained for the battlefield where they could see horrible sights and do dreadful things, but then often thrown into peace-keeping operations with little awareness of what they were supposed to do, and where battlefield violence was the last thing that was needed. Renwick argued that, unlike the authorities in the United States who had been galvanized by the experience of the war in Vietnam, the British Ministry of Defence and successive British governments had largely ignored the potential for post-traumatic stress on service personnel. He stressed the problems of heavy drinking, violence, and homelessness among veterans. There were also problems of crime and, in consequence, while there were no official statistics, there appeared to be a disproportionate number of ex-service personnel in prison.[3]

Many of the criminal offences described by Renwick were committed by men while they were still serving and included the gamut of violent crime from armed robbery, to assaults on women or on gay men. Drink invariably played a significant role here also. But there were other instances more reminiscent of the concerns that had followed the two world wars and earlier conflicts about brutalized veterans, trained to kill and now on the streets. Notable among these was the case of Jimmy Johnson, a former corporal in the Royal Tank Regiment. Johnson, who from his prison cell became a campaigner alongside Renwick, had done two tours of duty in Northern Ireland during the early 1970s. He was mentioned in dispatches for rescuing a woman in the aftermath of a terrorist bombing but, after losing control and severely beating a rioter who he had chased into a house, Johnson bought himself out of the Army. Johnson found difficulty in readjusting to civilian life; he drank heavily and his marriage disintegrated. In what appears to have been some kind of flashback to his experiences in Northern Ireland, he killed a workmate. He served nine years in prison and, eighteen months later, he killed again while doing some building work on his victim's home. He was sentenced to life imprisonment.[4]

Nor was it only the other ranks who noted these problems, and nor was this recognition entirely new. Gordon Corrigan, who retired as a senior officer in the Gurkhas, began his career in the early 1960s with the Gloucestershire Regiment where there were veterans from Korea, many of whom had been taken prisoner

---

[3] Renwick, *Hidden Wounds* (1999).
[4] Renwick, *Hidden Wounds* (1999), 75–84.

following their heroic battle on the Imjin River in April 1951. Corrigan recalled that several of these men had serious mental problems and had ceased to function; they were overweight and often drunk, but no one would do anything about it. Indeed, no one appeared prepared to acknowledge it.[5] Patrick Hennessy was a graduate in English Literature from Oxford who, in 2007, served as a platoon commander in the Grenadier Guards in Afghanistan. Hennessy's highly praised memoir described how men like himself, returning from ferocious infantry fighting, could find difficulty in settling back with family and friends. There was heavy drinking with those who had shared the exhilaration of danger and the tragedy of losing mates. There was irrational anger that 'frightened kids and confused wives'; and there was the desire 'to slam someone into the wall of a club and be able to say with utter calm and terrifying confidence in your eyes that he had picked the wrong fight because you were a fucking killer.'[6]

Even before Renwick's and Johnson's campaigning energies began to highlight the problems of service personnel with PTSD, the media were finding grim stories to report about veterans from the small conflicts that had begun to stretch the armed services from the mid-1990s. As ever, it was violence and murder that particularly excited the media. 'How Gulf War drugs "turned ex-SAS hero into a killer"' was the headline chosen by the *Daily Express* to introduce its report of a former soldier who used a Kalashnikov assault rifle, smuggled back from the first Gulf War, to shoot his girlfriend. Like other men sent to the Gulf in 1991, Thomas Shanks, who had become an anaesthetist after leaving the Army, had been given a cocktail of drugs to protect him should the Iraqi Army deploy chemical weapons. The controversial and unproven 'Gulf War Syndrome' was hinted at by his defence.[7] Shanks's case was echoed in other stories. Charles 'Nish' Bruce, another SAS soldier, had experienced a breakdown a dozen years after his involvement in the Falklands, and had stabbed his girlfriend with a pair of scissors. On his release he committed suicide. Bruce was a friend and former comrade of Frank Collins. Collins had become an Anglican priest on leaving the Army; he also committed suicide. The depression and suicides noted among former soldiers prompted questions in Parliament in the summer of 2009, when it was estimated that 264 veterans of the Falklands War and 169 veterans of the Gulf War had committed suicide since the end of the conflicts: battle casualties in those wars had resulted in 255 and 24 deaths respectively.[8]

In reporting illegal behaviour or tragic incidents involving active or former service personnel, the media did not restrict itself to incidents involving serious criminal violence, homelessness or self-harm, but it was more generally away from the front pages of national dailies or in the local press that the less lurid, though often striking stories were mentioned. In February 2011, for example, four RAF personnel were reported as pleading guilty to a fraud similar to those perpetrated by

---

[5] IWM (S) 27718, Gordon Corrigan, reel 8.
[6] Hennessy, *Junior Officers' Reading Club* (2010), 307.
[7] *Daily Express*, 29 April 1999, 27.
[8] <http://www.guardian.co.uk/g2/story/0,3604,630819,00>, accessed 4 February 2011.

some of their predecessors at the end of the Second World War. The airmen were responsible for loading military flights from Afghanistan and Oman and, over a period of time, they had succeeded in concealing some 350,000 packets of cigarettes with the authorized load. The smuggled cigarettes were then sold on in England, avoiding both import duty and VAT. Each man was estimated to have pocketed around £30,000.[9] But there was little reporting, and little assessment of the small-scale offending for which service personnel and ex-service personnel were brought before the magistrates' courts of England and Wales and the sheriff courts of Scotland. An article in the official organ of the Magistrates' Association, however, stated that these courts had dealt with 1,500 such cases in 2009 and, in the same year, another 1,500 police cautions had been issued to service personnel. It also stated the concerns of many magistrates about how best to deal with service personnel; recognizing that by keeping an offender in work was a way of reducing reoffending, did this really mean 'better employed on the streets of Kabul than unemployed on the streets of Leeds'?[10]

By the beginning of the new millennium, the Home Office was accepting that possibly between 4 and 6 per cent of the expanding prison population might have been former service personnel. In the summer of 2008, the National Association of Probation Officers was suggesting that just over 9 per cent of those in prison were former members of the armed forces—the majority from the Army. Later that year the BBC broadcast a radio programme that expressed concern about servicemen returning psychologically damaged from the wars in Iraq and Afghanistan and sliding into a life of drink, drugs, self-harm, and violent crime. Other media outlets carried similar stories.[11] In November 2009 the Howard League for Penal Reform launched an independent inquiry into former service personnel in prison and into why so many veterans appeared to get caught up in the criminal justice system.

The Howard League's inquiry published its findings in the summer of 2011. It noted that, in comparison with the overall population, there was a disproportionate number of ex-servicemen in prison for sexual or violent crimes (see Table 10.1). Yet it also found evidence to suggest that, generally, ex-servicemen were less likely to be imprisoned than others. Moreover, most ex-service personnel in prison appear to have committed their crimes many years after their discharge and they tended, in consequence, to be older than the average prisoner. While the evidence was inconclusive, and was based significantly on studies undertaken in the United States on veterans of the war in Vietnam, there was little to suggest a direct link between combat stress and criminal offending.[12] Sadly, in reporting these findings,

[9] *The Guardian*, 4 February 2011; *Middlesbrough Evening Gazette*, 5 February, 1; *Northern Echo*, 5 February, 6.

[10] Kinross, 'Heroes or Villains?' (2010), 2.

[11] Treadwell, 'Counterblast' (2010); *In Afghanistan: The Home Front*, BBC Radio 4, 'File on Four', broadcast 4 November 2008; and see, inter alia, ' "What's Your Problem?" What turns a brave soldier abroad into a violent criminal at home?' *Sunday Times Magazine*, 4 April 2010; 'Forgotten Heroes' A Panorama Special, broadcast BBC1, 10 February 2011. Interestingly the NAPO assessment of 9 per cent of the prison population being former service personnel is close to the 10 per cent of former servicemen among the inmates of Dartmoor during the 1932 riot (see above p. 34).

[12] *Report of the Inquiry into Armed Service Personnel in Prison*, London: Howard League, 2011.

Table 10.1 A Comparison of the Number of Veterans in Prison to the General Prison Population by Offence, 2010

| Offence group | Veterans Number | General Prison Population Number |
|---|---|---|
| Violence against the Person | 725 (32.9%) | 23,394 (28.6%) |
| Sexual Offences | 546 (24.7%) | 8,900 (10.9%) |
| Drug Offences | 236 (10.7%) | 12,615 (15.4%) |
| Robbery | 158 (7.2%) | 10,480 (12.8%) |
| Burglary | 87 (3.9%) | 9,370 (11.5%) |
| Theft and Handling | 52 (2.4%) | 4,313 (5.3%) |
| Fraud and Forgery | 30 (1.4%) | 2,341 (2.9%) |
| Motoring Offences | 15 (0.7%) | 1,278 (1.6%) |
| Other Offences | 198 (9.0%) | 8,059 (9.8%) |
| Offences not recorded | 160 (7.3%) | 1,081 (1.3%) |
| Total | 2,207 (100%) | 81,831 (100%) |

Source: Report of the Inquiry into Former Armed Service Personnel in Prison, London: Howard League, 2011, 17

even the supposedly liberal *Guardian* newspaper chose to concentrate on sex and violence rather than the broader, less sensational and more complex conclusions. To set the record straight, Sir John Nutting QC, the chair of the inquiry, politely, but forcefully, paraphrased the findings in a short response. He urged that, beyond individual culpability, there was one area that stood out: many recruits for the Regular Army in particular, like many young men caught up in the criminal justice system, came from socially deprived and educationally disadvantaged backgrounds. 'It may be tempting for some to find fault with the armed forces as an institution', he warned, 'or to blame controversial wars in foreign countries. But the stories of social exclusion, alcohol misuse and financial problems which we heard in interviews with ex-servicemen in prison suggest a more familiar foe. And that is *poverty*.'[13]

## HEROES TO ZEROES? HEROES TO VICTIMS?

At the end of May 1982, with odds of nearly two to one against them, British paratroops fought the first significant land battle of the Falklands campaign and captured the small settlement of Goose Green. Two weeks later the same paras, alongside other troops from the task force, seized the high ground overlooking the Falklands' capital of Port Stanley and forced the Argentinian surrender, effectively ending the war. A little over six months later one of the paras wounded in the Falklands fighting appeared before magistrates in Aldershot charged with stealing a young woman's hat, which he wanted to wear at a fancy-dress party. Alongside him stood a comrade charged with obstructing the police as they tried to arrest the first

---

[13] 'It's not true that we found a link between crime and armed service', <http://www.guardian.co.uk/commentisfree/2011/jun/30/link-crime-armed-service-forces>, accessed 1 August 2011.

para. Both soldiers pleaded guilty. One of their officers told the court that, as soldiers, their conduct was 'exemplary', though he added that the initial offender seemed 'to have an immature outlook and tend[ed] to drink to excess'. Two weeks later, at the same court, another para pleaded guilty to entering a KFC takeaway in Aldershot High Street while drunk and, while his comrades chanted 'Zulu Warrior', he had climbed on the counter and performed a striptease. He had pulled down a glass ceiling panel, which narrowly missed a woman customer, fallen off the counter and, while swinging on a metal bar, he had damaged four more glass panels. Three days later the Aldershot magistrates heard the case of another two paras, both veterans of Northern Ireland and the Falklands, who were charged with exposing themselves, through a window, to the staff at a McDonald's restaurant. The staff had told them that, since it was 11.15 p.m., the restaurant was closed; the paras claimed that they thought they were 'winding them up'.[14] Such cases were annoying, public order incidents, though one had been potentially dangerous. But soon the Aldershot press became focussed on a far nastier and far more serious case involving paras who had fought in the Falklands.

Ken Lukowiac recalled that, after one of the Falklands' battles, he and a group of his comrades gathered together to look at a photograph of a corporal's wife and baby. Immediately afterwards they switched their attention to an almost identical photograph found in the kit of a dead Argentinian soldier. A moment's compassion was followed by one of the paras describing the sexual acts that he would like to engage in with the young woman, and soon the whole group were indulging boisterously in their sexual fantasies. 'If we had been alone', Lukowiak wrote,

> I like to believe that not one of us would have passed comments of a sexual nature about the Argentine woman, but we were not alone, so we behaved in the way that we had been conditioned to behave. Conditioning that was done mostly by ourselves to ourselves.[15]

Sexual talk, boasting and fantasy were not new in the armed forces. In the civilian world, probably the number of rapes had increased since the end of the Second World War; certainly, and for a variety of reasons still the subject of argument, the statistics for such assaults reported to the police increased markedly from the late 1950s. In addition to the other causes it seems possible that, in the more permissive period extending from the 1960s, young men were more inclined to act out their fantasies, especially when fired with drink or drugs.[16] The close comradeship of the military family, in which young men took strength and encouragement from others, might also have contributed to the distasteful scene described by Lukowiac, but the tough masculinity of a 'teeth arm' of the military was probably as significant.

Technical and support units do not have the requirement for instant collective action common to infantrymen. Their skills are in demand whatever the situation

14 *Aldershot News*, 28 January 1983, 2, 8 February, 5, and 11 February, 11.
15 Lukowiac, *Soldier's Song* (1999), 88.
16 Emsley, *Crime and Society in Twentieth-Century England* (2011), 29–31.

of peace or war. In contrast infantry units particularly have few outlets for their skills in peacetime; there is training, but there is also much dead time. Such units appear to develop a super-masculine self-image; when called upon to do their job it is extremely dangerous and they counterbalance this by playing hard—brawling, collective heavy drinking, and pursuing women is what 'real men' do. John Hockey's sociological study of an infantry unit in the 1980s suggested that, in this environment, women tended to be characterized at the extremes of 'madonna' and 'whore' or 'decent' and 'dog'. Decent girls were still sex objects, but were treated and described differently. 'Dogs' were suitable for one-night stands and their only positive attribute was the granting of more or less instant sexual access.[17] Such assumptions appear also to have been behind the attitude of Lukowiac and his comrades as well as at least three multiple rapes and worse during the 1980s and 1990s.[18]

On 21 November 1981 a young para had picked up a young woman in the Globetrotter Pub in Aldershot. According to one of his mates this was 'the roughest pub in Aldershot'; another thought the girl 'a slut', since it was the pub 'where all the cows in town hang out'. The young soldier smuggled the girl into Malta Barracks. Their intentions appear to have been obvious, and he might have been telling the truth when he said that he did not know that she was only 15 years old. But whatever their intentions, matters were soon taken out of their hands when a group of drunken soldiers decided to tie the girl to a bed and to gang-rape and otherwise abuse and assault her. It is unclear how many of the men in the barracks had raped the girl; she thought there had been five or six but could not be sure. Six were identified, but the trial was held up until May 1983 because three of these had been sent to the Falklands. In the event only two men were found guilty of raping the girl, but all six were found guilty of some kind of involvement in the attack and given prison sentences of up to five years.[19] There was a surge of anger in Aldershot that was picked up by the media and portrayed particularly as a protest by the town's 'mothers'. People wanted to know how it was possible, especially during a time of threats by the IRA, for women to be smuggled into barracks and for a commotion of screams, shouts, and chants not to be investigated by NCOs or commissioned officers. There were complaints that ordinary civilians were often too frightened to go out at night and, in keeping with much of the contemporary criticism of the civilian police, there were complaints that Military Police patrols had declined significantly and were now extremely rare. It was admitted that there used to be fights and that occasionally soldiers went on a rampage but, in the view

---

[17] Hockey, *Squaddies* (1986), especially chapter 8.

[18] In addition to the offence described in the following paragraph, there was a similar offence involving a WRAC and at least 13 paratroops (see, for example, *The Guardian*, 13 November 1985, 3 and 19 December, 2; *Daily Express*, 14 November, 7 and 18 December, 8) and in 1994 two soldiers were found guilty of raping and murdering a Danish tour guide in Cyprus (see Holmes, *Soldiers* (2011), 308).

[19] *Aldershot News*, 6 May 1983, 1, 13 May, 1, 17 May, 1, 20 May, 1; and see also, *The Guardian*, 17 May, 6; *The Times*, 5 May, 3, 6 May, 3, 12 May, 12, and 17 May, 2.

of the complainants, things in the past were never as bad.[20] It is impossible to measure precisely the scale of disorder and violence in one period against that of another, partly because of the problem of the validity of crime statistics, partly because of changing degrees of tolerance, and, in the case of rape, partly because of the changing environment that engendered a growing willingness on the part of victims to report the offence. There is also the tendency for commentators and the media to view crime in the past through rose-tinted spectacles.[21] It would be difficult to prove that the paratroops who behaved so courageously in the Falklands, and so stupidly and aggressively at home were any better or any worse than their forebears.

During the 19th century the British armed services, but particularly the Army, had been recruited from the poorer sections of the working class and hence the regular repetition and mangling of the Duke of Wellington's words about 'scum'. Similar, and sometimes the same young men, with no skilled trade and little or no education, made up the majority of the individuals arrested by the police and processed by the courts. As described above, the Iron Duke's quote was echoed by generals during the First World War, even after the ranks had been filled first with patriotic volunteers and then, by conscription, with young men from all walks of life. During the interwar period when, once again, the services depended on volunteers alone, the old notions of the soldier as an unsavoury character re-emerged. In his article on the Aldershot Glasshouse published in *Picture Post* in May 1942, Macdonald Hastings reported that Army officers believed that their men were improving and that those in prison were 'the stupidest'. Particularly striking to Hastings was the number said to be illiterate and who had to have their letters home written for them.[22] Six years later Field Marshal, Lord Montgomery, the Chief of the Imperial General Staff, complained bitterly about the educational standards of recruits to the British Army; one man in ten was failing the literacy test, and this was when the service was relying heavily on national servicemen.[23]

Once the services, particularly the Army, returned to being all-volunteer institutions so, once again, recruits, especially those for the teeth units like the infantry, began noticeably to be drawn disproportionately from young men from broken homes, tough family backgrounds, and dead-end jobs They also had low educational attainments. Sir John Nutting's comments on the origins of many recruits to the Army were reported above and, at the turn of the millennium, it was reported that most infantry recruits had a reading age of less than eleven years.[24] Patrick Hennessy described his role of platoon commander, sorting out the problems of the guardsmen under his command, as resembling that of a primary school teacher. These problems included fights and assaults and often, at least potentially, the

---

[20] *Aldershot News*, 20 May 1983, 1 and 12; *Daily Express*, 23 May, 10.
[21] For an important discussion of this issue see Pearson, *Hooligan* (1983).
[22] Hastings, 'Inside the Glasshouse' (1942b), 10.
[23] *Manchester Guardian*, 14 January 1948, 3.
[24] Kinross, 'Heroes or Villains' (2010), 2; and see also French, *Military Identities* (2005), 310–11.

civilian police: 'Gdsm Y was dating a fifteen-year-old, but [he said] it was all right because her father liked him and she looked older.'[25]

These men were portrayed sympathetically, but unsentimentally, in Gregory Burke's award-winning play *Black Watch*. Basing his play, in part, on interviews with young, former soldiers who had served in Iraq, Burke portrays them as tough, working-class men, hard-drinking, always joshing, sometimes violent but proud of doing a job that they considered most could not do and that most would shy away from. Cammy, a key character and the narrator, opens the play mocking those who pity the young soldier:

> See I think people's minds are usually made up about you if you were in the Army. They are though ay? They poor fucking boys. They cannay do anything else. They cannay get a job. They get exploited by the Army. Well. I want you to know I wanted to be in the Army. I could have done other stuff. I'm not a fucking knuckle dragger. And people's minds are made up about the war that's on the now ay? They are. It's no right. It's illegal. We're just big bullies. Well, we'll need to get fucking used to it. Bullying's the fucking job. That's what you have a fucking Army for.[26]

But there had been some change in perception. By the early 21st century, when the British armed forces were engaged in small wars and difficult peace-keeping tasks, society had little or no inclination to portray the Regular soldier as a hard-drinking libertine—'the scum of the earth enlisted for drink'. British society had become much more aware of the fear and horror to which people are exposed in combat. Regardless of the complexities of debates between members of the medical profession and between academics, there was a popular awareness of post-traumatic stress and popular assumptions about its impact on antisocial and criminal activity. Moreover, when some service personnel became drunk and violent, there was a grudging recognition that other young people did much the same on the streets of towns and cities where attempts to revitalize rundown centres had resulted in an entertainments industry that, from the late 20th century, had fostered a culture of drink- and drug-fuelled binges which required an army of police and club bouncers to control and supervise, especially on Friday and Saturday nights.

Drunken, violent, and disorderly service personnel avoided much of the stigma attached to other criminal offenders, partly because they had served their country and had been in combat with the attendant potential for trauma. In April 2010 the *Sunday Times Magazine* carried a feature headlined 'From Hero to Zero' which carried interviews with three soldiers who, after distinguished service in Northern Ireland, Iraq, and Afghanistan, could not, it seemed, keep out of prison. Three months later, under the headline 'Heroes to Zeroes', the *Daily Mirror* expressed concern that 'thousands' of veterans of Iraq and Afghanistan were being arrested every month. 'Around a third are held for allegedly committing violent crimes while a quarter are suspected of drunkenness, vandalism or sexual assault.' But the tone of the article was sympathetic; the veterans needed help. 'Experts say many suffer from

---

[25] Hennessy, *Junior Officers' Reading Club* (2010), 114–16.
[26] Burke, *Black Watch* (2010), 3–4.

post-traumatic stress but are too proud to seek help.'[27] Unlike most criminal offenders the popular press portrayed these ex-service offenders as victims as much as criminals. Their crimes could be understood; the government had sent them to war and neither the government, nor the services, had provided sufficient assistance to help them to readjust to civilian life. The Howard League's inquiry explained how the services tried to help and to offer advice, but found also that the advice and help were often ignored. Three comments from veterans in prison to the inquiry's investigators were used to illustrate the problem:

> No I never had any help when I left [the Army]. I just left. I walked out of the front gate with me kit bag with all me civvy stuff in, me two medals, me book, me Army book, the red book, my personal possessions out of my room and that was it. I walked straight out of the gate, called a taxi and then went to the train station and got the train back home, that was it, done. (Julian, served nine and a half years.)
>
> They gave me some forms and stuff, some bits of paper to read and that, but I didn't bother. I just binned them. (Liam, served six years.)
>
> I wasn't interested really, I was never that bothered. I had done me time and I just wanted out really. I couldn't be arsed with all that [resettlement provision] really, just give me my compo check. (Christopher, served four and a half years.)[28]

In life, as in history, what people think and believe to have been the case, however erroneous, becomes a truth on which conclusions and actions are based.

People in the civilian world commit criminal offences for a variety of reasons ranging from anger to opportunity, from greed to exasperation. They commit their offences with cold calculation, spontaneously in anger, because temptation is offered, or because their senses are deadened by drink or drugs. Even though the pressures, opportunities, and temptations might be different, it is the same in the armed services. Service personnel who found themselves in charge of equipment or money yielded to temptation. The small 'family' of the platoon or squadron, like packs of workers on the docks for example, found opportunities for profit; and more often they fought other, similar families in different uniforms. The Regular forces, particularly the teeth arms of the Army, might recruit a higher percentage of personnel from those social backgrounds more likely to find themselves at odds with the criminal justice system, yet it would be difficult to prove that such men were responsible for more offending during the two world wars than patriotic volunteers or conscripts. Indeed, the evidence for such proof may well no longer exist. What is clear is that blaming crime on criminals is as dubious and meaningless a tautology in the armed services as it is in the civilian world.

Crime is one element of any society. If service personnel commit crimes it is essentially because they are members of a society and it would be surprising if membership of the armed forces changed them in such a manner so as not to reflect that society. This book has concentrated on the less savoury aspects of the

[27] *Sunday Times Magazine*, 10 April 2010, 14–21; *Daily Mirror*, 5 July 2010, 30.
[28] 'Leaving Forces Life: The Issue of Transition', Howard League E-bulletin, March 2011. These three passages were also quoted in Howard League, *Report of the Inquiry into Former Armed Service Personnel in Prison* (2011), 24–5.

behaviour of service personnel and, while it has not suggested that all members of the armed forces committed offences, it is, perhaps, worth concluding with two brief stories illustrating an attractive side. While some British servicemen committed rape in the field, as well as at home, Edward Watson recalled a group of unarmed British soldiers, just released from PoW camps, stepping in to prevent a German woman from being raped by armed GIs in 1945. In thanks the woman offered herself to her rescuers, asking only that her little boy be out of the room. Neither Watson, nor any of his mates, took up her offer. Similarly, while some men were shocked to find their fellow soldiers robbing civilians and behaving as they imagined enemy soldiers to behave, the mother of a German friend and fellow-academic had a very different experience of the soldiers who pursued the Wehrmacht through a village close to Osnabrück where she had taken refuge after leaving Essen. The soldiers expressed sympathy for the fact that her husband was fighting on the Eastern front; they gave food to children and let them sleep on mattresses among them; and when, after two days, they left the village, they told her where they had hidden food, chocolate, and biscuits for her and her family.[29] Technically, of course, these soldiers might have been liable to a charge of fraternization or even, in the eyes of some Dickensian pettifogger, to one of misappropriating military foodstuffs.

[29] IWM (S) 7194, Edward Lewis Watson, reel 4. My thanks to Herbert Reinke and his mother for the information about the troops near Osnabrück.

# Bibliography

Archival Sources

## 1. THE NATIONAL ARCHIVES, KEW

Admiralty: ADM 1, 156, 175, 178
Air Ministry: AIR 1, 30
Metropolitan Police: MEPO 2, 3
Ministry of Reconstruction: RECO 1
War Office: WO 32, 71, 81, 84, 93, 95, 171, 202, 204, 277

## 2. IMPERIAL WAR MUSEUM

**Documents:**
Accounts of service with ATS Provost (D. French, D. Lamb, and D. Wheatley), MISC 236
   (3354)
Brigadier E. A. Arderne, 97/7/1
A. E. Bagley, 02/04/1
A. L. Bastone, 01/32/1
M. Bendix, 98/3/1
S. G. A. Brook, 06/61/1
C. H. Butt, 02/19/1
J. Carradice, 78/71/1
J. Corbett, 96/46/1
R. L. Crimp, 96/50/1
A. E. Cross, 96/58/1
Revd C. D. H. Cullingford, 90/6/1
T. H. Flanagan, 87/19/1
J. T. Foxell, 91/24/1
T. A. Gore, 99/85/1
A. R. Graydon, 98/35/1
J. W. Hall, 01/57/1
W. Hewison, 79/32/1
W. V. Hindle, 01/36/1
F. Hollingsworth, 82/21/1
C. R. Keller, 02/55/1
Letters re. Kinmel Camp Riots, MISC 155
R. Leven, 05/59/1
Major W. V. H. Martin, 91/9/1
W. H. Mitchell, 97/7/1
Mrs L. Orde, 96/34/1
A. E. Perriman, 80/43/1
J. H. Reynolds, 99/13/1
H. E. Shelton, 06/94/1
T. A. Silver, 74/108/1

A. de Vigneral, 78/35/1
L. Waller, 87/42/1
T. W. Wood, 99/31/1

**Sound**
J. Chadwick, 10918
E. Clark, 26579
G. M. Clarkson, 679
G. Corrigan, 27718
S. Elworthy, 3187
S. P. M. Fisher, 9598
J. Gray, 20202
A. Kodin, 30403
S. Roberts, 31452
K. A. Ryland, 27312
E. L. Watson, 7194
P. White, 32399

### 3. MUSEUM AND ARCHIVE OF THE ROYAL CORPS OF MILITARY POLICE

Hatherill Report, January 1940
SIB Crime Book, Sicily, 1943
SIB Crime Book, Sicily, 1943–44
SIB Crime Book, Sicily, 1944
SIB Crime Book, Naples, 1945
SIB Crime Book, Headquarters 64 Section, 1945
SIB Crime Book, Brussels, 1946
SIB Crime Book, BAOR, 1947–48
SIB Crime Book, BAOR, 1956–57
SIB Crime Book, BAOR, 1958
SIS Ports (UK) Crime Register, 1945
SIS Ports (UK) Register of Charges, 1944–45

### 4. BROTHERTON LIBRARY, UNIVERSITY OF LEEDS, LIDDLE COLLECTION

G. B. Airton (GS)
J. W. Allen (GS)
A. B. Ashby (GS 0050)
F. D. Day (EP 015)
H. N. Edwards (GS)
A. Howes (E/PAL)
S. C. Marriott (GS)
A. J. Richardson (GS)
G. St. George Stedall (ARMY 184)
T. Tarleton (GS 1569)

## 5. OPEN UNIVERSITY LIBRARY, POLICE ARCHIVE

ACPO Bag (32) 88, Central Conference of Chief Constables, 1939–60

## 6. METROPOLITAN POLICE HISTORICAL COLLECTION

Wellington Arch Police Station, Occurrence Book 1942–48 (available at www.open.ac.uk/
Arts/history-from-police-archives)

## 7. BEDS AND LUTON RECORD OFFICE

SJC 13, (Standing Joint Committee of Police, 1915).

**Official Publications**
*Criminal Statistics, 1922*, Cmd. 2265
*Criminal Statistics, 1923*, Cmd. 2385
*Criminal Statistics, 1924*, Cmd. 2602
*Criminal Statistics, 1939–45*, Cmd. 7227
*Eightieth Annual Report of the Registrar General of Births, Deaths and Marriages in England
and Wales, 1919*, Cmd. 40
*Eighty-Second Annual Report of the Registrar General of Births, Deaths and Marriages in
England and Wales, 1920*, Cmd. 1017
*General Annual Report of the British Army for the Year Ending 30 September 1911*, Cd. 6065
*General Annual Report of the British Army for the Year Ending 30 September 1920*, Cmd. 1610
*Hansard's Parliamentary Debates*
*Manual of Military Law, 1914*
*Report of the Army and Air Force Courts-Martial Committee, 1938*, Cmd. 6200
*Report of the Army and Air Force Courts-martial Committee, 1948*, Cmd. 7608
*Report of the Commissioners of Prisons for 1920*, Cmd. 972
*Report of the Committee Constituted by the Army Council to Enquire into the Law and Rules of
Procedure Regulating Military Courts Martial, 1919*, Cmd. 428
*Report on the Criminal Judicial Statistics for Scotland for 1937*, Cmd. 5877
*Report of the Prime Minister's Committee of Enquiry into Detention Barracks, 1943*, Cmd.
6484
*Report of the War Office Committee of Enquiry into Shell-Shock, 1922*, Cmd. 174
*Return of the Number of Courts Martial Held . . . on Seamen of the Royal Navy, 1912*, Cd. 7167
*Statistics of the Military Effort of the British Empire during the Great War, 1914–20*, London:
HMSO, 1922

## NEWSPAPERS AND JOURNALS

*Aldershot News*
*Bedfordshire Times and Standard*
*The Bystander*
*The Daily Express*
*The Daily Herald*
*The Daily Mirror*
*Evening News and Southern Daily Mail (Portsmouth)*

*John Bull*
*Justice of the Peace*
*The (Manchester) Guardian*
*News of the World*
*Police Review*
*The Scotsman*
*Thompson's Weekly News*
*The Times*
*West Herts Post and Watford Advertiser*
*World's Pictorial News*

## BOOKS, BOOK CHAPTERS, AND ARTICLES

Adler, Jeffrey S. (1996), 'The Making of a Moral Panic in Nineteenth-century America: The Boston Garrotting Hysteria of 1865', *Deviant Behaviour: An Interdisciplinary Journal*, 17: 259–78.

Allport, Alan (2009), *Demobbed: Coming Home after the Second World War* (London: Yale University Press).

Arthur, Max (2010), *The Road Home: The Aftermath of the Great War Told by the Men and Women Who Survived It* (London: Phoenix).

Baynes, John (1967), *Morale: A Study of Man and Courage* (London: Cassell).

Bean, J. P. (1981), *The Sheffield Gang Wars* (Sheffield: D & D Publications).

Beattie, J. M. (1986), *Crime and the Courts in England, 1660–1800* (Oxford: Clarendon Press).

Beevor, Anthony (1990), *Inside the British Army* (London: Chatto and Windus).

Bessel, Richard (2009), *Germany 1945: From War to Peace* (London: Simon and Schuster).

Best, Geoffrey (1980), *Humanity in Warfare: The Modern History of the International Law of Armed Conflicts* (London: Weidenfeld and Nicolson).

Bidwell, Shelford (1979), *The Chindit War: The Campaign in Burma, 1944* (London: Hodder and Stoughton).

Bisset, Lt. Col. Ian (1957), *Trial at Arms: Some Famous Trials by Court Martial* (London: MacGibbon and Key).

Bohstedt, John (1983), *Riots and Community Politics in England and Wales 1790–1810* (Cambridge, MA: Harvard University Press).

Bourke, Joanna (1996), *Dismembering the Male: Men's Bodies, Britain and the Great War* (London: Reaktion Books).

—— (1998), *An Intimate History of Killing in Twentieth-Century Warfare* (London: Granta).

—— (2007), *Rape: A History from 1860 to the Present Day* (London: Virago).

Bowden, Sue (1994), 'The New Consumerism', in Paul Johnson (ed.), *Twentieth-Century Britain: Economic, Social and Cultural Change* (London: Longman).

Brown, Alyson (2011), 'Crime, Criminal Mobility and Serial Offenders in Early Twentieth-Century Britain', *Contemporary British History*, 25 (4): 551–68.

Brown, Malcolm and Meehan, Patricia (2008), *Scapa Flow: The Reminiscences of Men and Women Who Served in Scapa Flow in the Two World Wars*, 3rd edn (Stroud: Spellmount).

Burke, Gregory (2010), *Black Watch*, revised edn (London: Faber and Faber).

Carew, Anthony (1981), *The Lower Deck of the Royal Navy 1900–39* (Manchester: Manchester University Press).

Chadwick, Roger (1992), *Bureaucratic Mercy: The Home Office and the Treatment of Capital Cases in Victorian Britain* (New York: Garland).

Childs, Major. Gen. Sir Wyndham (1930), *Episodes and Reflections* (London: Cassell).

Clark, Revd Andrew (1988), *Echoes of the Great War: The Diary of the Reverend Andrew Clark, 1914–1919*, ed. James Munson (Oxford: Oxford University Press).

Cockburn, J. S. (1991), 'Patterns of Violence in English Society: Homicide in Kent 1560–1985', *Past and Present*, 130: 70–106.

Conley, Carolyn (1991), *The Unwritten Law: Criminal Justice in Victorian Kent* (Oxford: Oxford University Press).

Connelly, Mark (2002), *The Great War, Memory and Ritual: Commemoration in the City and East London, 1916–1939* (Woodbridge: Royal Historical Society/Boydell Press).

Connelly, Mark and Miller, Walter (2004), 'British Courts Martial in North Africa, 1940–43', *Twentieth-Century British History*, 15 (3): 217–42.

Cornwallis-West, George (1930), *Edwardian Hey-Days: or, Little About a Lot of Things* (London: Putnam).

Crang, Jeremy A. (2000), *The British Army and the People's War 1939–1945* (Manchester: Manchester University Press).

Crimp, Reginald Lewis (1971), *The Diary of a Desert Rat*, ed. Alex Bowlby (London: Cooper).

Crozier, Major S. F. (1951), *The History of the Corps of Royal Military Police* (Aldershot: Gale and Poden).

Damousi, Joy (2001), *Living with the Aftermath: Trauma, Nostalgia and Grief in Post-War Australia* (Cambridge: Cambridge University Press).

David, Saul (1995), *Mutiny at Salerno: An Injustice Exposed* (London: Brassey's).

Davies, Andrew (2006), 'Football and Sectarianism in Glasgow during the 1920s and 1930s', *Irish Historical Studies*, 36 (138): 200–19.

Dickie, John (2012), *Mafia Brotherhoods. Camorra, Mafia, 'Ndrangheta: The Rise of the Honoured Societies* (London: Sceptre).

Dolden, A. Stuart (1980), *Cannon Fodder: An Infantryman's Life on the Western Front, 1914–18* (Poole: Blandford Press).

Douglas, Keith (1969), *Alamein to Zem Zem* (Harmondsworth: Penguin).

Edmonds, Sir James (1987), *The Occupation of the Rhineland, 1918–1929* (London: HMSO, Imperial War Museum Facsimile edn).

Elder, Sace (2010), *Murder Scenes: Normality, Deviance and Criminal Violence in Weimar Berlin* (Ann Arbor: University of Michigan Press).

Emsley, Clive (1999), *Gendarmes and the State in Nineteenth-Century Europe* (Oxford: Oxford University Press).

——(2005), *Hard Men: Violence in England since 1750* (London: Hambledon).

——(2007), *Crime, Police, and Penal Policy: European Experiences 1750–1940* (Oxford: Oxford University Press).

——(2008), 'Violent Crime in England in 1919: Post-war Anxieties and Press Narratives', *Continuity and Change*, 22 (1): 173–95.

——(2010a), *Crime and Society in England, 1750–1900*, 4th. edn. (London: Longman/Pearson).

——(2010b), 'A Legacy of Conflict? The "Brutalised Veteran" and Violence in Europe after the Great War', in Efi Avdela, Shani D'Cruze, and Judith Rowbotham (eds.), *Problems of Crime and Violence in Europe, 1780–2000: Essays in Criminal Justice* (Lampeter: Edwin Mellen Press).

——(2011), *Crime and Society in Twentieth-Century England* (London: Longman/Pearson).

Ferguson, Niall (1998), *The Pity of War* (London: Allen Lane).

Foy, Michael and Barton, Brian (1999), *The Easter Rising* (Stroud: Sutton Publishing).

French, David (1998), 'Discipline and the Death Penalty in the British Army in the War against Germany during the Second World War', *Journal of Contemporary History*, 33 (4): 531–45.

——(2005), *Military Identities: The Regimental System, the British Army, and the British People c. 1870–2000* (Oxford: Oxford University Press).

——(2006), 'Big Wars and Small Wars between the Wars, 1919–38', in Hew Strachan (ed), *Big Wars and Small Wars: The British Army and the Lessons of War in the Twentieth Century* (London: Routledge).

——(2011), *The British Way in Counter-Insurgency, 1945–1967* (Oxford: Oxford University Press).

——(2012), *Army, Empire, and Cold War: The British Army and Military Policy, 1945–1971* (Oxford: Oxford University Press).

Fussell, Paul (1989), *Wartime: Understanding and Behaviour in the Second World War* (Oxford: Oxford University Press).

Gardiner, Juliet (2010), *The Blitz: The British under Attack* (London: Harper Press).

Gelber, Yoav (2004), *Komemiyut ve-Nakbah: Yisrael, Ha-Falestinim U-Medinot Arav, 1948* (Or Yehuda: Devir).

Gibson, K. Craig (2001), 'Sex and Soldiering in France and Flanders: The British Expeditionary Force along the Western Front, 1914–1919', *International History Review*, 23 (3): 535–79.

Gill, Douglas and Dallas, Gloden (1975), 'Mutiny at Etaples in 1917', *Past and Present*, 69: 88–112.

Glenton, Bill (1986), *Mutiny in Force X* (London: Hodder and Stoughton).

Godfrey, Barry S., Cox, David J., and Farrall, Stephen D. (2010), *Serious Offenders: A Historical Study of Habitual Criminals* (Oxford: Oxford University Press).

Graves, Robert (1960), *Goodbye to All That* (Harmondsworth: Penguin).

Gregory, Adrian (1994), *The Silence of Memory: Armistice Day 1919–1946* (Oxford and Providence, RI: Berg).

Grosman, Dave (1996), *On Killing: The Psychological Cost of Learning to Kill in War and Society* (New York: Bay Books).

Hannam-Clark, T. (1932), *Some Experiences of a Court-Martial Officer* (London: Besant and Co.).

Hastings, Macdonald (1942a), 'An Army Redcap Learns His Unpopular Job', *Picture Post* (18 April): 16–19.

——(1942b), 'Inside the Glasshouse: First Pictures Ever Taken', *Picture Post* (30 May): 5–11.

Hearn, C. V. (1961), *Foreign Assignment* (London: Robert Hale).

Hennessy, Patrick (2010), *The Junior Officers' Reading Club* (London: Penguin Books).

Hockey, John (1986), *Squaddies: Portrait of a Subculture* (Exeter: University of Exeter Press).

Hodgkinson, Colin (1957), *Best Foot Forward* (London: Odhams Press).

Holmes, Richard (2011), *Soldiers: Army Lives and Loyalties from Redcoats to Dusty Warriors* (London: Harper Press).

Holmes, Robert (1915a), *My Police Court Friends with the Colours* (Edinburgh and London: William Blackwood & Sons).

——(1915b), *Walter Greenway, Spy: and Others, Some Criminal* (Edinburgh and London: William Robertson & Sons).

Houlbrook, Matt (2003), 'Soldier Heroes and Rent Boys: Homosex, Masculinities, and Britishness in the Brigade of Guards, c. 1900–1960', *Journal of British Studies*, 42 (3): 351–88.

The Howard League (2011), *Report of the Inquiry into Armed Service Personnel in Prison* (London: The Howard League).

Hughes, Matthew (2009), 'The Banality of Brutality: British Armed Forces and the Repression of the Arab Revolt in Palestine, 1936–39', *English Historical Review*, 124 (507): 313–54.

Hurst, Major Gerard B. (1919), 'The Administration of Military Law', *Contemporary Review*, 115 (January–June): 321–7.

James, Lawrence (1987), *Mutiny in the British and Commonwealth Forces, 1797–1956* (London: Buchan and Enright).

Jeffery, Keith (2005), ' "Hut Ab", "Promenade with Kamerade for Shockolade" and the *Flying Dutchman*: British Soldiers in the Rhineland, 1918–1929', *Diplomacy and State-craft*, 16 (3): 455–73.

Johnson, B. S. (ed.) (1973), *All Bull: The National Servicemen* (London: Allison and Busby).

Jones, Edgar, Hodgins, Robert, et al. (2003), 'Flashbacks and Post-traumatic Stress Disorder: The Genesis of a Twentieth-Century Disorder', *British Journal of Psychiatry*, 182: 158–63.

Jones, Edgar and Wessely, Simon (2005a), *Shell Shock to PTSD: Military Psychiatry from 1900 to the Gulf War* (Hove: Psychology Press).

——(2005b), 'War Syndromes: The Impact of Culture on Medically Unexplained Symptoms', *Medical History*, 49: 55–78.

——(2010), 'British Prisoners-of-War: Frome Resilience to Psychological Vulnerability: Reality and Perception', *Twentieth-Century British History*, 21 (2): 163–83.

Jones, Heather (2010), *Violence against Prisoners of War in the First World War* (Cambridge: Cambridge University Press).

Junger, Sebastian (2010), *War* (London: Fourth Estate).

King, Peter (2000), *Crime, Justice, and Discretion in England, 1740–1820* (Oxford: Oxford University Press).

——(2002), 'War As a Judicial Resource. Press Gangs and Prosecution Rates, 1740–1830', in Norma Landau (ed.), *Law, Crime and English Society, 1600–1830* (Cambridge: Cambridge University Press).

Kinross, Peter (2010), 'Heroes or Villains?', *Magistrate*, 66 (10): 1–4.

Knight, Martin (2010), *'We Are Not Manslaughterers': The Epsom Riot and the Murder of Station Sergeant Thomas Green* (Blaydon: Tonto Books).

Kray, Kate (2003), *Killers: Britain's Deadliest Murderers Tell Their Stories* (London: John Blake).

Le Clercq, Geoffroy (2001), 'Sexual Violence and Social Reactions: The Survival of the Practices of Arrangement in Nineteenth-Century Rural Society', in Maria Ågren, Åsa Karlsen, and Xavier Rousseaux (eds.), *Guises of Power: Integration of Society and Legitimisation of Power in Sweden and the Southern Low Countries, c. 1500–1900* (Uppsala: Opuscula Historica Upsaliensia, 26).

Leese, Peter (2002), *Shell Shock: Traumatic Neurosis and the British Soldiers of the First World War* (Basingstoke: Palgrave).

Lilly, J. Robert (2007), *Taken by Force: Rape and American GIs in Europe during World War II* (Houndmills, Basingstoke: Palgrave Macmillan).

Lindsay, Martin (1946), *So Few Got Through* (London: Collins).

Lodge, T. S. (1956–7), 'A Comparison of criminal statistics of England and Wales with those of Scotland', *British Journal of Delinquency*, 7: 50–60.

Longden, Sean (2004), *To the Victors the Spoils. D-Day to VE Day: The Reality behind the Heroism* (Moreton-in-Marsh: Aris Books).

Lovell-Knight, A. V. (1977), *The Story of the Royal Military Police* (London: Leo Cooper).

Lukowiak, Ken (1999), *A Soldier's Song* (London: Phoenix).

Malcolmson, Patricia and Robert (eds.) (2009), *A Soldier in Bedfordshire, 1941–42: The Diary of Private Denis Argent, Royal Engineers* (Bedfordshire Historical Records Society, 88).

Mannheim, Hermann (1940), *Social Aspects of Crime in England between the Wars* (London: George Allen and Unwin).

Marlantes, Karl (2012), *What It Is Like to Go to War* (London: Corvus).

Marshall, S. L. A. (1947), *Men against Fire: The Problem of Battle Command in Future Wars* (New York: William Morrow).

Mchugh, John (1999), 'The Labour Party and the Campaign to Abolish the Military Death Penalty, 1919–1930', *Historical Journal*, 42 (1): 233–49.

Mckee, Christopher (2002), *Sober Men and True: Sailor Lives in the Royal Navy 1900–1945* (Cambridge, MA: Harvard University Press).

Miller, Stephen M. (2010), 'Duty or Crime? Defining Acceptable Behavior in the British Army in South Africa, 1899–1902', *Journal of British Studies*, 49 (2): 311–31.

Morton, James (2000), *East End Gangland* (London: Little, Brown and Company).

Mosley, Nicholas (2006), *Time at War* (London: Weidenfeld and Nicolson).

Mottram, R. H. (1979), *The Spanish Farm Trilogy 1914–1918* (Harmondsworth: Penguin).

Myers, C. S. (1915), 'A Contribution to the Study of Shell-Shock', *The Lancet*, 1 (13 February): 316–20.

Newark, Tim (2011), *Lucky Luciano: Mafia Murderer and Secret Agent* (Edinburgh and London: Mainstream Press).

Noakes, Lucy (2006), *Women in the British Army: War and the Gentle Sex, 1907–1948* (London: Routledge).

Oram, Gerard (1998a), *Death Sentences passed by Military Courts of the British Army 1914–1924* (London: Francis Boutle).

——(1998b), *Worthless Men: Race, Eugenics and the Death Penalty in the British Army during the First World War* (London: Francis Boutle).

——(2003), *Military Executions during World War I* (Houndmills, Basingstoke: Palgrave).

——(2011), 'Armee, Staat, Bürger und Wehrpflicht: Die britische Militärjustiz bis nach dem Zweiten Wetkrieg', in Peter Pirker and Florian Wenninger (eds.), *Wehrmachtsjustiz: Kontext, Praxis, Nachwirkungen* (Vienna: Braunmüller).

Page, Martin (ed.) (1975), *Kiss Me Goodnight Sergeant Major: The Bawdy Songs and Ballads of World War II* (London: Granada).

Pearson, Geoffrey (1983), *Hooligan: A History of Respectable Fears* (London: Macmillan).

Peaty, John (2002), 'The Desertion Crisis in Italy, 1944', *RUSI Bulletin*, 147 (3): 76–83.

Prysor, Glyn (2011), *Citizen Sailors: The Royal Navy in the Second World War* (London: Viking).

Putkowski, Julian (1989), *The Kinmel Park Camp Riots 1919* (Llawarden: Flintshire Historical Society).

——(1998), *British Army Mutineers, 1914–1922* (London: Francis Boutle).

Putkowski, Julian and Sykes, Julian (1992), *Shot at Dawn*, revised edn (London: Leo Cooper).

Pym, Revd T. W. and Gordon, Revd Geoffrey (1917), *Papers from Picardy by Two Chaplains* (London: Constable).

Reid, Fiona (2007), 'Distinguishing between Shell-shocked Veterans and Pauper Lunatics: The Ex-Services Welfare Society and Mentally Wounded Veterans after the Great War', *War in History*, 14 (1): 347–71.

——(2010), *Broken Men: Shell Shock, Treatment and Recovery in Britain, 1914–1930* (London: Continuum).

Renwick, Aly (1999), *Hidden Wounds: The Problems of Northern Ireland Veterans in Civvy Street* (London: Barbed Wire).

Roodhouse, Mark (2003), 'The "Ghost Squad": Undercover Policing in London 1945–49', in Gerard Oram (ed.), *Conflict and Legality: Policing Mid-Twentieth-Century Europe* (London: Francis Boutle).

Rothstein, Andrew (1980), *The Soldiers' Strikes of 1919* (London: Macmillan).

Rowntree, Griselda and Carrier, Norman H. (1958), 'The Resort to Divorce in England and Wales, 1858–1957', *Population Studies*, 11 (3): 188–233.

Royle, Trevor (1997), *The Best Years of Their Lives: The National Service Experience, 1945–1963* (London: John Murray).

Rubin, Gerry R. (1992), *Durban 1942: A British Troopship Revolt* (London: Hambledon).

——(1994), 'The Status of the Judge Advocate General of the Forces in the United Kingdom since the 1930s', *Military Law and Law of War Review*, 33: 243–71.

——(1997), 'Parliament, Prerogative and Military Law: Who Had Legal Authority over the Army in the Later Nineteenth Century', *Journal of Legal History*, 18 (1): 45–84.

——(2005), *Murder, Mutiny and the Military: British Court Martial Cases, 1940–1966* (London: Francis Boutle).

Samuel, Raphael (1981), *East End Underworld: Chapters in the Life of Arthur Harding* (London: Routledge and Kegan Paul).

Schrijvers, Peter (2009), *Liberators: The Allies and Belgian Society 1944–45* (Cambridge: Cambridge University Press).

Sears, Jason (1991), 'Discipline in the Royal Navy, 1913–1946', *War and Society*, 9 (2): 39–60.

Sellers, Leonard (1995), *For God's Sake Shoot Straight: The Story of the Court Martial and Execution of Temporary Sub-Lieutenant Edwin Leopold Arthur Dyett* (London: Leo Cooper).

Sheehan, William (2011), *A Hard Local War: The British Army and the Guerrilla War in Cork 1919–1921* (Stroud: The History Press).

Sheffield, Gary (1981), *A History of the Royal Military Police and Its Antecedents from the Middle Ages to the Gulf War* (London: Brassey's).

——(2000), *Leadership in the Trenches: Officer–Man Relations, Morale and Discipline in the British Army in the Era of the First World War* (Basingstoke: Macmillan).

Shils, Edward A. and Janowitz, Morris (1948), 'Cohesion and Disintegration in the Wehrmacht in World War II', *Public Opinion Quarterly*, 12 (2): 280–315.

Shore, Heather (2011), 'Criminality and Englishness in the Aftermath: The Racecourse Wars of the 1920s', *Twentieth-Century British History*, 22 (4): 474–97.

Skelley, Alan Ramsay (1977), *The Victorian Army at Home* (London: Croom Helm).

Skirth, Ronald (2010), *The Reluctant Tommy: An Extraordinary Memoir of the First World War*, ed. Duncan Barrett (London: Macmillan).

Small, Bernard (1983), *The Reluctant Gunner* (Aberdeen: Aberdeen University Press).

Smith, J. Stuart (1969), 'Military Law: Its History, Administration and Practice', *Law Quarterly Review*, 85: 478–504.

Smithies, Edward (1982), *Crime in Wartime: A Social History of Crime in World War II* (London: George Allen & Unwin).

Snape, Michael (2005), *The Redcoat and Religion: The Forgotten History of the British Soldier from the Age of Marlborough to the Eve of the First World War* (London: Routledge).

Spencer, John C. (1954), *Crime and the Services* (London: Routledge and Kegan Paul).

Spicer, Andrew (2001), *Typical Men: The Representation of Masculinity in Popular British Cinema* (London: I. B. Tauris).

Spiller, Roger J. (1988), 'S. L. A. Marshall and the Ratio of Fire', *RUSI Bulletin*, 133: 63–71.

Spraggs, Gillian (2001), *Outlaws and Highwaymen: The Cult of the Robber in England from the Middle Ages to the Nineteenth Century* (London: Pimlico).

Stanley, Peter (2010), *Bad Characters: Sex, Crime, Mutiny, Murder and the Australian Imperial Force* (Millers Point, NSW: Murdoch Books).

Starke, Wilhelm (1884), *Verbrechen und Verbrecher in Preussen, 1854–1878* (Berlin: Enslin).

Summers, Julie (2008), *Stranger in the House: Women's Stories of Men Returning from the Second World War* (London: Simon and Schuster).

Swank, R. L. and Marchand, W. E. (1946), 'Combat Neuroses: Development of Combat Exhaustion', *Archives of Neurology and Psychology*, 55: 236–47.

Thomas, Donald (2003), *An Underworld at War: Spivs, Deserters, Racketeers and Civilians in the Second World War* (London: John Murray).

Thompson, E. P. (1991), 'The Moral Economy of the English Crowd in the Eighteenth Century', in E. P. Thompson, *Customs in Common* (London: Merlin Press).

Thomson, Basil (1922), *Queer People* (London: Hodder and Stoughton).

——(1939), *The Scene Changes* (London: Collins).

Treadwell, James (2010), 'Counterblast: More Than Casualties of War? Ex-Military Personnel in the Criminal Justice System', *The Howard Journal*, 49 (1): 73–7.

Trenaman, Joseph (1952), *Out of Step: A Study of Young Delinquent Soldiers in Wartime; Their Offences, Their Background and Their Treatment under an Army Experiment* (London: Methuen).

Trow, M. J. (1994), *The Wigwam Murder* (London: Constable).

Tullett, Tom (1956), *Portrait of a Bad Man* (London: Evans Brothers).

Turnbull, Jack and Hamblett, John (1994), *The Pegasus Patrol* (Privately Printed, Jack Turnbull).

Van Walleghem, Achiel (1964–7), *De oorlog te Dickebusch en omstreken 1914–1918*, ed. Jozef Geldhof, 3 vols. (Bruges: Genootschap voor Geschiedenis).

Vickers, Emma (2009), '"The Good Fellow": Negotiation, Remembrance and Recollection—Homosexuality in the British Armed Forces 1939–1945', in Dagmar Herzog (ed.), *Brutality and Desire: War and Sexuality in Europe's Twentieth Century* (London: Palgrave).

Vincent, David (1998), *The Culture of Secrecy: Britain 1832–1998* (Oxford: Oxford University Press).

Waddy, H. T. (1925), *The Police Court and Its Work* (London: Butterworth).

White, Peter (2001), *With the Jocks: A Soldier's Struggle for Europe 1944–45* (Stroud: Sutton Publishing).

Wiener, Martin J. (2004), *Men of Blood: Violence, Manliness and Criminal Justice in Victorian England* (Cambridge: Cambridge University Press).

——(2009), *An Empire on Trial: Race, Murder, and Justice under British Rule, 1870–1935* (Cambridge: Cambridge University Press).

Williams, Isobel (forthcoming 2013), *Crime and Disorder: Allies and Italians under Occupation. Sicily and Southern Italy 1943–45* (London: Palgrave).

Williams, Neville (1959), *Contraband Cargoes: Seven Centuries of Smuggling* (London: Longman).

Wood, John Carter (2004), *Violence and Crime in Nineteenth-Century England: The Shadow of Our Refinement* (London: Routledge).

Wyeth, Romy (2007), *Swords and Ploughshares: Codford during the Twentieth Century* (Warminster: Gemini).

Ziegler, Philip (2010), *Edward Heath: The Authorised Biography* (London: Harper).

# Index